Understanding Evil: My Soul Contract

Zora Zustimmung

Written in Western Washington

2015- 2019

Copyright © 2019 by Zora Zustimmung

All rights reserved. No part of this publication may be reproduced, distributed or transmitted in any form or by any means, including photocopying, recording, or other electronic or mechanical methods, without the prior written permission of the publisher, except in the case of brief quotations embodied in critical reviews and certain other noncommercial uses permitted by copyright law. For permission requests, write to the publisher, addressed "Attention: Permissions Coordinator," at the address below.

Printed in the United States of America

Village Books Publishing. 1200 11th St, Bellingham Wa, 98225

Publisher's Note: While all the stories in this book are true, the names, locations, and identifying details have been changed to protect the privacy of the people involved.

Book Layout ©2019 Sheridan Ealey

Cover Design ©2019 Emma Fitzpatrick

Ordering Information:
Quantity sales. Special discounts are available on quantity purchases by corporations, associations, and others. For details, contact the "Special Sales Department" at the address above.

Understanding Evil: My Soul Contract/ Zora Zustimmung. -- 1st ed.
ISBN 9780578482385

Table of Contents

Preface..5-11

Introduction..13-24

Abstracts..25-26

Cast of Characters................................27-29

Timeline...31-32

Come to Me...33-56

Serve Only Me.....................................57-76

Trust Me..77-106

Promise Me...107-156

Join Us...157-186

Believe Me...187-228

Say My Name......................................229-264

Wield My Sword..................................265-304

Post Script...305-311

Understanding Evil: My Soul Contract

Preface

The provenance of these essays is a record of fits and starts. The first version of them, I wrote in graduate school. I had planned them as a creative project that was to be the equivalent of a thesis; however, I could never get it off the ground. A review of similar literature would have been necessary, but I had no way of producing one of those. Searching for non-fiction anecdotal essays about encounters with demons and evil occultists proved impossible way back then. (more than three decades ago now) Cross-referencing even remotely related topics in the university library provided me with nothing. The occult was not a typical or popular topic for study, I guess. At that time, there was no Internet yet either.

Professors on my committee, albeit fascinated by my stories, had no advice to offer about a context into which to put them for the sake of an academic project. No one among them had experiences like mine from which to make any suggestions. So, instead, I took up the standard literature reading lists, and after eight months, took my comprehensive exams and finished my master's degree in English.

The essays, however, still existed, and I could not let them go. There were seven then, with a completely different thematic organization, but but they still lived. I thought of trying to publish them, but didn't have a clue how to do that either. I mentioned my wish to an on-again-off-again lover, who meant a great deal more to me than I meant to him, as I was to discover many years later. He said he knew someone who knew something, and took them away to the unnamed expert. Who this "expert" was, I never found out.

A couple of weeks later, he brought the essays back, and unceremoniously dropped them on the floor of my apartment, telling me his expert had said they were nothing more than teenage whining. The expert had said there was nothing worthwhile in them to contribute to the field. For years, I couldn't look at my essays without feeling sickening shame.

In spite of that, my experiences with the occult continued to accumulate, and some seemed worthy enough for two more essays. The body of work, though, didn't seem to have real purpose yet, still, no focus, no thesis. Then someone said such stories might make lots of money as fiction and from a third person point of view. So I rewrote five of the nine. The process was tedious, and I ended up hating them. So they sat. My life went on.

A few more years passed, and I joined a writer's group. It was made up of colleagues (other teachers), most with master's degrees, two with PhDs. I condensed the old version of the essay about my trauma at the Old Hospital (it's always the first one, the one I broach the topic with) a little bit and brought it in. I read it aloud. Then came the questions. The exasperating muggle questions. I would have thought that people who taught and read literature would have had more imagination, would have traveled the depths and breadths of knowledge a bit more, engaged with a few more archetypes, maybe looked into a couple of alternative philosophies or metaphysics, or, for Pete's sake, watched a few more movies, but apparently not. It was not the first time, nor the last, that my paradigm didn't have much in common with others'. I can never quite get used to that – to the limitations the disparity poses. It's hard to communicate when there is no shared vocabulary, when realities are

Preface

based on different truths.

Every detail that was even the slightest bit metaphysical caused consternation. How? What? Why? I don't think I've ever felt so exhausted by a writing workshop. I just couldn't get any traction. If I were to add all the explanations and definitions my fellows suggested, the essay would have stretched to two hundred pages of occult primer in which my intentions would have been completely lost. Clearly, a general audience was not for whom my essay was intended.

Also, some of the group made suggestions that might have applied had I been trying to write moving, poetic literature. But I wasn't. My goal was to present anecdotes plus analyses confined to a thematic framework. I was not shooting for beauty. After the debacle of the writer's group, the essays sat dormant again.

Then later, when I was fifty, I found myself facing a surgery, which I might or might not survive. My lower jaw was for some reason receding, blocking off my air passage. I needed the surgery to save my life, but it would take a complete rearrangement of my face. In the year preparing for it, I disposed of more than four dozen fat 3-ring binders (which I kept as proof that I was telling the truth when my mother falsely accused me of things) of notes, receipts, journals, correspondence, memorabilia, and, of course, the essays. I went so far as to burn every paper copy I could find and to delete every electronic copy. My failures were not going to remain behind for anyone to find were I to die. That was it. So I thought.

Forward a couple of years. I survived the surgery, but I was no longer the same person afterward. The event and recovery, punctuated by one loss after another, simply took the life out of me. Before everything slid into oblivion, I gave up everything – home, job, friends – and moved 1400 miles away, only to get into a massive car accident five weeks later. It took nearly a year for me to become even more or less functional again, but in that time, the specter of my long dead essays came around to haunt me again.

I was never going to get away from the stories. They ceaselessly circled my other thoughts; everything in a synchronistic sense related to them – books, movies, conversations. Even before my move, I realized something strange had begun to happen with my friends. The stories had become part of *their* mythologies, their understanding of the world. The stories became teaching tools. My young friends found in them illuminating confirmations or explanations of their own experiences. They referred to them in relationship to their own experiences or understanding. They, my friends and others like them, I realized, were my audience; I had found my purpose. I began to write the stories completely anew, with brand new themes and theses. The compulsion turned into a mission and finally produced what was destined after all.

By destined, I am referring to a most extraordinary vision I had. From my late twenties to late forties, most every Samhain (Halloween to the muggle world), I made it a practice to create a wreath for the coming year. I would buy a plain ring at a craft shop, sew a fabric backing to it, and attach small amulets or tiny sculptures I made out of clay. They symbolized goals I had for the year. That year, (I was thirty three) as I was creating a representation of the book about demons I intended to write, something incredible happened.

An enormous hologram appeared before me; it filled room floor to ceiling. It was in the shape of solar cross (like a plus sign), and it was made of golden flame. It hovered and burned for a few seconds. Then, a gigantic blue eye appeared in the center, then spots of color like gems manifested on the arms of the cross, two red, one to the north and one to the west, four purple, three to the east and one to the south. Then the vision cracked diagonally from the top (northeast to the southwest), and a thin stream of blood misted in through the golden flame. At the eye, the crack turned south and split the purple spot at the bottom of the cross.

The entire time the vision was manifesting, a voice sounded all around me, repeating three times: "*April, Aryan (or Arian – as in "of Ares"), Four, Element of Air, Love Connection to the Soul, and Place of Light.*" Three times. That supernatural solar cross graphic and the ambiguous poetic script symbolized, I guess, what my book would contain, what I would need to research or discover empirically before it could be written.

I asked around at that time what it meant. Two of my colleagues who did have some knowledge of the occult said it was an alchemical symbol, but neither could tell me anything more. There were no answers in reference books. The library still didn't stock the right ones. Imagine that! Also, there was still a lot of drama and learning ahead of me. It took a long time before the time was right.

Do I know now what all the details of the vision meant? Most of them. Maybe. Am I sure that all the implied predictions have come to pass whether I know what they meant or not? Yes. For once I began writing the essays this time, they caused changes in my soul; they put things into perspective. This is my book about evil, evil people and evil demons. This is the book I was intended to write. Each essay has brought a piece of my broken soul back to me, at least enough for me to feel almost whole again.

However, once again, crazy stuff happened this time, as it did every single time I worked on the essays, regardless of which version. Strange household mishaps. Computer anomalies. Illnesses. Injuries. Items in the house vanishing and returning. Tappings. Voices. Things moving around on their own. Cold Spots. Shadow figures. Insect invasions. Plumbing incidents. Appliance malfunctions. Strange encounters with even stranger people. Disturbances that could come right out of a demonologist's handbook. For example, this time, after the first full draft of the essay "Say My Name" was finished, something got in behind the closed glass door of my shower and urinated in the corner. How lovely.

But, in addition to these shenanigans, with this version of the essays, came a confounding aphasia. Not only would I forget what I was about to write, so would my friends to whom I would divulge the details beforehand for the specific purpose of having them help me remember. I would write lists, and they would disappear never to be seen again. So I sent myself emails. That finally helped. Still, I wonder where all those slips of paper went . . . .

This project is for those who already know the world is not what we are told it is. Hence, I do not weigh my stories down with endless, tedious documentation and evidence. Sceptics would remain sceptics, no matter what. Either way, I am aware that I claim some pretty fantastic things, even for those who already believe. No apologies. There is also an element of "shouting from the rooftop" to these stories, my chance to finally and completely state my case to the world, no matter how bizarre or complicated or personal. It is at as much a purging as an explication, a self-portrait as much as a reference.

While I changed all the names, including mine as author, the narratives are all true and unenhanced. On the contrary, I have reduced them whenever possible. I've left out many characters and events in order to focus my themes. Of course, I also left out stories that were not mine directly. My brother's stories, my friends' stories are not here. And while they helped me come to the conclusions I did, they weren't mine to tell.

I pray that all the pseudonyms and obfuscations do their job – of assuring anonymity for all involved and preventing anyone from contacting me with requests or proposals. I pray that no one uses anything I've written to harm anyone else – or sees anything I say as an invitation

Preface

to fly off to Neverland.

In the writing of these essays, I have chosen to refrain from using second person. The old-school grammarian in me balks at the sound of "you this" and "you that" to the point of livid fury. But the choice also had a magickal component to it. I am not talking to the reader directly. I am telling stories. Talking to the reader implies an inclusiveness that I do not wish to acknowledge or promote. Also, imperative sentences are commands, are impositions of will, are, in other words, spells. I will do no such thing here.

The essays should, ideally, be read in the order presented, but they also can be read in isolation. They are not chronological; they track back over the same territory for different purposes, links in a parabola perhaps. I provide parenthetical cross-references to related essays. Each essay focuses on a theme, and, therefore, briefly repeats just enough information from related essays to be complete in and of itself. The themes circle back through one another because that it is the nature of anyone's biography.

The introduction outlines my thoughts and theories about evil. The narratives are autobiographical. The time line and cast of characters should help keep the details straight. I have also provided abstracts of the essays in order to make the loops of the storytelling spiral easier to follow. The post script comments on how the supernatural is depicted in the media presently. More than anything, I am relieved this project is finally completed after more than thirty difficult years in the making. May it serve the purpose I intended.

Understanding Evil: My Soul Contract

Introduction

I was born aware of evil. From long before I had language to define it or describe it, I could feel it as a presence that flowed about like air, not in the air, but in addition to the air. I wouldn't see it as a cloud or mist, for it had no color or substance, but experienced it as a vibration and a vacuum, always a vacuum, that pulls light and hope into it.

In one of my photo albums, there is a photo of me at three years old in a pale blue gingham dress sitting on the front cement step of my family's townhouse feeling an almost unbearable sorrow. My mother caught the moment on film. When she and I more than four decades later assembled sets of albums for me and my brother, she asked me if I remember that day and wanted to know why I was so sad. I told her it was then, at that moment, that I knew I would never get away from evil in my life. I felt its shadow on me. My mother had not been unable to comfort me then, nor understand me when I told so many years later.

People say that no one remembers their lives from babyhood. But I do. I can still recall the floorplan of the apartment my parents and I lived in before I could crawl, details of the stairs leading up to it, and of the ruffled curtains in the kitchen. I remember lying in a basket, in the hallway in my grandmother's house, presumably packed up and ready to be carted off somewhere. As I lay there waiting for an adult to pick me up, I became aware of beings closing in on me, with all sorts of strange visages looming over my helpless form. How interested they all were in me! My screams did not chase them off.

The beings stayed with me. Some were terrifying and terrible, but others were beautiful and playful. It was the latter that I first wanted to talk about, they that befriended me. In second grade, I got myself in trouble at show-and-tell by bringing in a little piece of embroidery I finished. When I also talked about the amazing elemental beings that sat with me as I sewed, I found myself suddenly silenced and barred from bringing in any more such items and or any more of my "lies." The horrified school marm didn't know what to do with me. Wow. I was seven and devastated.

But I never learned *not* to talk about the beings I saw. As children, my brother and I told the neighborhood kids all about them. It was "The Mystery (capital M)" that we shared with our friends. They sat enraptured as I told them about seeing a glowing, grinning, dramatically costumed spirit standing over my brother's bed one night, levitating his sleeping form, blankets and all, several feet above the mattress. Or about not being able to find our cat and dog one night, but discovering them locked in the family car in the garage. Or about the ghost of my dead grandfather warning me of my father's car accident two days before it occurred. Or the cuckoo clock that leaped off the wall and flew across the room. Or the time all the Jacks from our Bicycle playing card decks vanished, only to turn up laid out neatly in a row on the cement pad under the furnace in the crawlspace. Or any of the other incredible things that happened around us. The neighborhood kids were fascinated.

As we got older, the beings became more malevolent, and while my brother chose to stick with a mainstream public face and keep quiet (except when talking to me) about our other-worldly contacts, I did not. People reacted in all kinds of different ways, some with incredulity, some with hostility, some with pity for what they considered lunacy, and some, unfortunately, with predatory motivations to "save" me or, incredibly, to "recruit" me.

Introduction

Still, I talked and talked. I wanted to warn people. I wanted to enlist them in a battle. I wanted them to help me figure out what was going on. I wanted someone on my side. Most people just fled. Others, however, turned out to be as evil as the entities. Clearly, the entities did not have exclusive proprietorship over evil. It turns out humans have their share of it too. It took me a long to time to reconcile myself with this truth.

I have chosen to refer to these entities as demons, not because I think of them in the traditional sense as agents of Satan. I don't believe in an all-powerful head-honcho Devil any more than I believe in an all-powerful one-and-only God. I use the term demon for those entities that cause harm because it is a useful word, and I've always used it. It has enough history and ambiguity to suffice. It has been suggested to me that I should use the word djinn, which might in one case at least be more accurate, but I'm going to stick with demon. It is more culturally accessible and has the right flavor of connotation. It also excludes dark elementals, vengeful ghosts, ET's, thoughtforms, poltergeists, vampires, and many others. It refers only and directly to that sort of entity whose primary purpose is annihilation and the destruction of hope or psychic terrorism and enslavement.

I tried to make it my mission to convince people that demons existed. So few people could see what I could see. It was infuriating. No one listened. No one believed me. Some believed that *I* believed it, but it was easier to assume I was projecting blame, or that I was delusional, or that I had developed my mythology as a way to provide a context for the outrages I experienced. Ironically, more than a few people have tried to force me to accept *their* mythology as a way to provide context for the outrages I experienced. But I wouldn't give in. Generally, people tolerated my chatter about ghosts or were fascinated by it, but my talk of demons chased most others away.

Yet, here I am bringing up the subject of demons once again. The difference between then and now is that I don't care anymore about convincing people to believe that demons exist. These narratives are for those who already believe they do. My stories here are for those among the next generations of souls who might encounter what I encountered. People need to know that they are not alone in their perceptions or convictions. It can be a lonely place.

The demons I've encountered in my life are not like those I've seen described in reprints of ancient grimoires. They're not the kind that requires a specific sigil, a name from liturgical literature. They don't need some dramatic evocation. I encounter them as I would encounter people passing on the sidewalk, fellow shoppers at the grocery store. They just are. Mostly, I just observe (or they observe me), and we move on. But certain ones had an agenda specifically with me. Now, it is not my intention to theorize about the origins of demons or their hierarchies or categories. None of that really matters anyway, for I'm not trying to establish a cosmology or bestiary here. I just want to describe what I have been dealing with my entire life.

I can still recall the day I realized there was more one demon affecting my destiny. I was sitting with a spiral notebook, listing the things that I thought I could attribute to demons, trying to find a pattern, a purpose. As I filled the page and moved things from one list to another, it suddenly dawned on me that there was more than one purpose/pattern. I think I actually blacked out for a moment. More than one. And I was right.

The demons themselves, I do not, will not, name, not here, not in conversation. I do know the names of two of them. What I've chosen to do, instead, is refer to them by the color light (green, blue, red, black)

Introduction

I saw them emit from their own eyes or through the eyes of those they possessed. The blue-eyed demon is also the DBB (the demon in the book in the box). These colors are really the colors I saw, not just symbolic.

The way my clairvoyance, my mediumship vision, works is fairly simple. When I open myself up to seeing beyond this world, it is, for me, like watching two films simultaneously on the same screen. They are usually similar, but not exactly the same. The one in the foreground is more opaque; it is the physical world. The translucent one contains additional information about the past (like ghosts or astral records), present (elementals, for instance, or secret information about people), and future (especially when I read cards), and that which is outside this plane, in which time is indecipherable. It's like a series of double exposures, triple exposures. Holograms superimposed over holograms.

This is how things have always looked to me, especially when I "turn up the volume" on my clairvoyance. When the evil is supernatural, I literally see it. I see the entities operate autonomously or see how they affect humans through suggestion, possession, or peripheral recruitment (affecting those in the vicinity). I have seen entities of evil enter people, use them as vessels. I have seen the entities of evil peering from the depths of the human hosts' eyes. I have seen entities lurking about as partially manifested shadows or holograms, leering and hovering, whispering into people's minds. However, when the evil is human in origin, I sometimes don't see it until it has substantially harmed me.

From all the research I have done, all the reading, all the consulting, all the experiments, all the just plain living, I think I learned a few things. Evil requires an agent or agents, supernatural, human, or both – or other (I've chosen not to explain that here). Evil can be extravagant, dramatic, horrific, outrageous, all of that. Sometimes, it is. But it can also be petty, pedestrian, tedious, banal, and ridiculous. Human evil can operate by itself or in combination with demonic. My experiences bear that out.

People who engage the occult are especially open to evil, for all kinds of reasons and in all kinds of ways. Not because they're in league with some sort of arch-fiend, or because their occult practices actually give them power (the instances where that happens are rarer than one might think), but because they use the tools, the rhetoric, the mystery, the promise of the occult to dupe and otherwise prey on their victims. Regardless of what various neo-pagans say, there aren't *really* any rules – only, as the pirates in the movies suggest, guidelines; there is no supervision. Demons are real, as are ghosts, as are a number of other types of entities. But the occult is also open territory for fraud and tyranny – by human agents.

Human evil in general is often the result of an overwhelming and tragic failure at self-awareness, which includes, among other things, the mindless repetition of one's families' or cultures' behaviors, keeping up traditions because those who came before upheld them, including the tenets of organized religions. It comes from tribalism and following orders without question. It comes from colonizing, entitlement, and denial. And while it is easy to identify the evil caused by power mongers and narcissists, it's harder to identify evil that is less flashy.

But something I learned about evil is that it is as much a result of ignorance as arrogance. Stupidity is its own form of evil and a door to greater evil. People take action without knowing what they are doing or take on more than they are ready for. Inevitably, destruction results. My stories are living proof. I blundered into more than I should have survived.

But, in the reality of evil, there is always happenstance. People don't always cause misery or call up the demons or evil on purpose. They might stumble upon it unwittingly or cause it to happen accidentally through some foolish non-supernatural act. Alternatively, it is possible

Introduction

that evil (or an evil being) simply finds certain human beings by chance or by designs that are no fault of the victims and latches on. It can be as random as that.

In graduate school, I wrote a paper contrasting how two different cultures viewed evil. I chose fairy tales told from a Germanic point of view and the identical fairy tales told from an Eastern European point of view. I chose these two worldviews to contrast because my cultural heritage is split between the two – Germanic and Eastern European. My findings were amusing and oddly comforting at that time, but not until many years later, would I be able to apply my little academic thesis to my life. It isn't all-encompassing, but offers an interesting contribution to the big picture.

The Germanic worldview, as depicted in the folktales, places the culpability of evil on the person who encounters it. Regardless of what brought the evil in, the mark is still responsible. The evil either already existed in the person or found him/her a suitable host or was deliberately evoked by him/her. Once the interaction takes place, the person's soul is permanently changed or damaged, and because, in this worldview, the soul answers to a higher power of some sort, it will also never be forgiven. Judgement will be passed, and the punishment is forever.

In the Eastern European version of the tales I read, the evil exists in the environment. The person accidentally comes upon the evil or is duped by it into acting out some particular deed. Once the person becomes aware of the truth, he/she can separate himself/herself from the evil, let it go back to wherever it came from, and be free. The outward damage may remain, and there may be fallout, but the soul is intact and clean. The process has nothing to do with forgiveness from some omniscient, omnipotent deity. It is the soul's transaction with itself, with its own sovereignty.

The Eastern European worldview seemed to me truly pagan and quite preferable. It certainly made more sense to me when I applied it to my experiences with demons. My demons came to me on their own or at someone else's behest. I did not bring them into my life (not this life anyway). As for my own transgressions, they did not originate in me. They (most) were reactive, necessary, unavoidable, instinctive, but not intrinsic, immutable, or illustrative of my soul's character. They did not evolve in a vacuum.

As much as that mythology project or this autobiographical project sounds simply like a psychological breakthrough (it is, of course), it cannot be dismissed as merely that. I still insist, as I have my entire life, that we are not alone on this planet, and that the other entities do interact with us. Finally, I have the skills, the expertise, to determine both in retrospect and in the present whether the perpetrators of crimes against me were human or demonic in nature or both. I can also determine what's what in real time. Finally.

The narratives where demons play a role, I reveal what it was that I observed that told me such an entity was present. The indicators. The patterns. The sensations. The specifics might not apply to all demons, but the generalizations will. Demonic evil is different from human evil. It reaches deeper, feels colder, transcends time, separates one from one's sense of self, tears its way through all the soul's bodies. But it is a force that is separate from the soul.

The narratives in which humans are the central villains, I include detailed descriptions of those people and the problems they caused to illuminate the absurd environment in which I lived, day to day, without reprieve. The accounts are not merely litanies of complaint (maybe a little bit) even though sometimes they focus on the most ordinary, most non-metaphysical concerns. The descriptions are, instead, testimonials to my constant misunderstanding of how the mundane world operates, how its inhabitants operate, how the mind-boggling predicaments and violations I suffered could possibly have occurred. My grief and trauma resulted often from my simply not be willing to believe that what was happening was really happening, that people were really doing what they were doing, that no one was going to help me. I have included lengthy accounts here to demonstrate just how far people will go if unchecked, how, without mercy or reason, they will persist if no glimmer of self-awareness breaks through, how the demons had/have an endless supply of fallow ground.

I have read thousands of books in my life, listened to hundreds of lectures, questioned everyone I possibly could, experimented with all sorts of ideas. I have been both victim and witness, and sometimes perpetrator. The resulting advice or insight I offer in these narratives is based on what I accept as knowledge, what I hope is common sense, what I admit is cynicism, and what I'm sure seems at times paranoid. I have tried to reveal the "reality checks" that provided me some closure (by definition or absolution) for my experiences. Each narrative became an exercise in soul retrieval for me. I found I could take back what the experience or event had stolen from me by telling the story.

Survival and recovery are complicated. I've presented myself in these narratives as honestly as possible, deliberately revealing my own psychological issues right along with my supernatural ones. It's not as if I could hide my problems from an astute reader anyway. I have to say, though, that my psychological issues didn't affect my *perception* of the events and characters or my recall of details as much as one might think. They did, however, affect my *interpretations* and certainly my *reactions* at the time.

Time has provided me the luxury of objectivity. In review, I could reevaluate what I remembered. The result is that I can truthfully say that my memory is accurate. I saw what I saw; I heard what I heard; I felt what I felt. The evil was the evil, demonic or human, exactly as I perceived it. What I did in response, however, was, in almost every instance, not what I should have done, and not what I would have done had I known better. And that is the point.

If I had had other people's stories to read right about the time that demons started coming for me, I might not have had such a difficult time of it. In my case, the doors to the other worlds were opened for me before I ever had a chance to choose. But I could have just as easily blown them open myself, as I've seen many young people do. The doors don't just close again. There is no reset button. The demons are waiting. Mostly, though, evil humans are waiting.

I don't have answers for all of the situations I've written about. I specifically don't offer magickal solutions to demonic evil. I don't think there are any, only temporary patches, or fixes that are quite costly. The real changes must come from within, and I do not mean positive thinking or surrounding oneself with light and incense or other such superficial nonsense. I mean profound alteration of one's core.

Therefore, no one should think of this as a "how-to-defend-yourself-against-demons" text. In it are examples of what *not* to do – in both the mundane world and the metaphysical world – in the form of mistakes I either made or barely avoided. But it is not a manual. It is simply my testament about the evil I have encountered, its methods and minions, its effects on me and my reactions.

My victory, if I can call it that, is that I am awake now, in many ways broken, but awake. I hope to save someone from the same rough passage, if people who read these essays recognize their own souls' sovereignty and act accordingly to both evolve it and preserve it. Understanding the players and the territory is essential to the process. I've been there. My

Introduction

anecdotes are intended to provide vicarious instruction to spare at least one reader the same trauma.

This is my clean-up incarnation, my chance to sever silver cords, disassociate from the entities of my family's associations with various occult groups, and balance out the books of karma. I hope it's my last round on this plane. It seems that it really might be. Two years ago, just after my arrival in the Northwest, a car accident nearly crippled me. Unable to work, I began trying to find some social connections. I began looking for a community. So, I joined a local metaphysical group. Members took turns leading sessions.

The woman who led one particular session claimed to channel one of the archangels. This archangel, it seems, was very concerned with humans' nutrition and self-esteem and need to rest and have fun (yes, I am rolling my eyes as I am typing this). But either way, this session included a loosely guided visualization. These always work for me; I can slide off this plane and go to another instantaneously if prompted correctly. The timing was right.

> In this particular visualization, I met one of my own guides. He was waiting for me in a room with windows all around open to night sky. He, an alien being (that I'm not going to describe here out of respect for him), was seated at a table opening a scroll of bluish silver gossamer, through which shone lights. There were holes in the fabric – cuneiform wedges, rectangles, a mathematical pattern. I approached the being with my own scroll, made of brown parchment material and unrolled it as well. When I laid it down on top of the silver scroll, the holes in mine lined up with his. He nodded his approval. I had done it. I had done it right

this time. The scroll was a record of my life, my "report card" for the astral records. I was so relieved that tears began streaming down my face in real time as well as astral time. I nearly melted into the floor with relief. I passed (I hope) whatever test this life had been.

When I opened my eyes, I was facing the woman who channeled angels, but it was not she who was looking back at me, and certainly not her angel. It was the black-eyed demon, who had pursued me into this incarnation with the intention to destroy me. I went cold, but still said to him/it, "Oh, I know you." He/It whispered, "It's OK to live." We stared at each other for a while, and after a few moments, the woman turned her attention away from me, and the demon was gone, this time, I assume, forever. I guess I am done.

In my life, I have only gone on a few "astral journeys," never indulging in them more often than occasionally. I feel certain of the significance of this one. Momentarily, I experienced the sensation of time spiraling around me, of millennia of effort and trauma and senseless battles falling away. It felt as if my soul were shedding the bonds I had carried incarnation after incarnation. This liberation is what I have worked for.

Even though implied in these essays is a warning against involvement in the occult, it is not the occult that is at issue. The warning is against *foolish* involvement or *corrupt* involvement. I am not saying that the Veil should not be breached. In fact, I think it should be. I believe that the sooner and the more thoroughly a soul learns that this physical plane is not all there is, the more productive a life can be here. It's not all evil. There is also so much beauty, ecstasy too, both here and "there." This plane, this place, is a laboratory of cause and effect to be mastered, enjoyed, and then outgrown. It is full of philosophies and philosophers. But it is also full of lies and liars. It is best to make the journey well-informed.

Abstracts

"Come to Me" is about an incident at an abandoned Old Hospital, when I was eighteen, and attempted to "move on" the spirits who were trapped there. It's about the black-eyed demon, a soul-eater, and the sociopath who housed it, a fellow student at the community college. It is about how demonic evil enlists human agents. The caution I urge in it is against taking on more than one is ready for. It is also intended to begin the discussion of how to recognize that a demon is present.

"Serve Only Me" is about my relationship with my family demon, the green-eyed demon, and the muddy-eyed one, its servant. I reveal how my grandmother presented me to/with her demon and how I became sexually involved with it. The themes are magickal enslavement, jealousy, obsession. I include a warning against seeking any sort of psychiatric help if a demon is present.

"Trust Me" presents my relationship with Karen, the psychic who attached herself to my family. I reveal my difficulty dealing with the contradictions between her words and actions. The themes are dependency, mental illness, coercion. The advice is to stay away from self-appointed mentors.

"Promise Me" tells the tale of my second marriage. I detail what it's like to live with an abuser. The villain in the story is a colonizer, my former father-in-law, and the red-eyed demon in his family. The themes are abusers and abuse. The admonitions are about gaslighting and objectivizing. I also outline the terrible history of my medical trust fund.

"Join Us" is about a neo-pagan couple who tried to take control of my life. I explain how dangerous and deceptive recruiters can be. I tell the story of how this couple tried to bring me into their coven. The themes are fanaticism, evangelism, and self-righteousness. The warning is about brainwashing and cult behavior.

"Believe Me" warns the reader about occultists like me, necromancers, dollmakers. I talk about my powers and my vulnerabilities. I present a caution against allowing the unworthy into one's realm. The essay also reveals the ends of friendships. The themes are trespassing, entitlement, sacrilege, loss, and retribution. The message is about listening to warnings.

"Say My Name" is the story of my young companion and the demon that nearly destroyed us. The villain is DBB (the demon in the book in the box), the blue-eyed demon. I recount the story of attracting and then having to battle a demon, and how much a demon can affect in one's life. The themes are self-sacrifice, loyalty, and ramifications of both. The caution is against hubris and martyrdom.

"Wield My Sword" describes my relationship with my mother and with the Goddess. It includes the story of my first marriage. It traces the progression of significant Beltanes in my life. There is no entity villain, necessarily, just the fool (me) who had unrealistic expectations. The themes are betrayal and despotism. The caveat is about believing in forever, making contracts with deities, and trusting questionable partnerships.

Cast of Characters

The Humans

Bjorn – my beloved artist friend

Daisy – Riley's college roommate

Daniel – Robin's father

Darren – the male half of the neo-pagan couple that took an interest in me in my forties

David – my first real magickal partner

Dorothy – my department chair (my supervisor) at the college where I taught

Francis – a fellow grad student with whom I had occult connection

Fredrico – a brujo who took an interest in me in my thirties

Gavin – my first husband

Greg – Gavin's younger cousin

Jack – my dragon friend

Janet – Robin's mother

Justin – Riley's temporary boyfriend

Karen – the psychic who attached herself to my family when I was in high school

Marge – my former friend in my late twenties, early thirties

Mark – an on-again-off-again lover for nearly two decades

Marla – the female half of the neo-pagan couple

Riley – my young gay companion

Robin – my second husband

Rudyard – my younger brother

Sherrie – my colleague who wanted to be a witch like me

Terry – the sociopathic teenager from the high school where I taught

Winston – the sociopath that housed the black-eyed demon and orchestrated the Old Hospital incident

The Demons

The black-eyed demon that followed me into this life, a soul-eater

The green-eyed demon that my grandmother promised me to

The muddy-eyed demon – the green-eyed demon's servant; animal form

The red-eyed demon that came to me through Robin's family

The blue-eyed demon – the DBB – the demon in the book in the box that invaded the Beltane ritual

The Cats

Luca – my tuxedo cat who died of pulmonary edema during my marriage to Robin

Silver – my gray and black tabby who died of kidney failure after my surgery

Trixie – my tuxedo cat who survived kidney failure and moved to the Northwest with me

The Non-Humans

Death Angel, the – a spirit that warns me when a death will occur

Emmanuel – my ghost/spirit lover when I was in my teens

Mars – the Roman god of war who came to speak to me

Watcher, my – an entity that both guards me and spies on me

The Dolls

Kylie – my doll that my grandmother took from me

Lazlo – the doll that housed my grandmother's son's soul

Understanding Evil: My Soul Contract

Time Line

Ages 0-9 (City on the East Coast)

Ages 9-14 (City on the Plains)

Ages 14-29 (Town on the Plains)

Age 18	Karen enters my Life
Age 18	Events of the Old Hospital
Age 19	First Marriage to Gavin
Age 21	Witch Grandmother's Death
Age 21	First Divorce from Gavin
Age 22	Graduation with Bachelor's
Age 22	Second Marriage to Gavin
Age 26	Graduation with Master's

Ages 29-30 (Desert Southwest)

Age 29	Encounter with Vampire
Age 30	Decision to fully embrace Witchcraft

Ages 30-32 (Town on the Plains)

    Ages 29-32   Work as an Art Model

    Age 30   Second Divorce from Gavin

    Age 31   Relationship with David

    Age 32   End of Friendship with Marge

Ages 32-41 (City on the Plains)

    Age 32   Relationship with Robin begins

    Age 36   End of Relationship with Karen

    Age 37   Father's Death

    Age 39   Relationship with Neo-pagan Couple

Ages 41-52 (Town on the Plains)

    Age 41   Divorce from Robin

    Age 45   Relationship with Riley begins

    Age 47   The Beltane out on the Plains

    Age 50   Orthognathic Surgery

Ages 52-56 (Pacific Northwest)

    Age 52   Rollover Car Accident

    Age 56   Mother's Death

Come to Me

When someone wants to hear my story, and people do, *really* do, I always begin with the Old Hospital. Always. It is a good starting point because it acts as a hub around which the other tales can fan out like spokes. So I'll begin with it here, of course. It opens the conversation as much as it describes the opening of the doors. It is the single most monumental event of my entire life, for it altered my fate completely.

As with all my stories, it involves both human and supernatural agents. This one is about a type of demon I think of as a soul-eater and about a sociopathic person. The soul-eater's singular purpose is to destroy. When present in a sociopath, it is at once a demon and its host. Where one leaves off and the other begins is, for all practical purposes, indiscernible and probably irrelevant. When the soul-eater sets its sights on someone, there is almost no defense anyway. There was none for me. I was so very vulnerable. Eighteen years old and caught among conflicting paradigms, I was an easy target. The soul-eater didn't even need to search for me; I came to him.

My family lived in a town at the edge of the Great Plains. We lived in a small motel that we had owned for four years. It was both our home and our place of business. We had no employees. We, mostly my mother, did the work. My father still had a job at that time. My brother, Rudyard, and I worked weekends too. Rudyard had finished high school a year early and was working part time at a restaurant. I was heading into college.

I hadn't really meant to go to college in the first place, as my fiancé, Gavin, at that time had no intention of going, and I feared that a rift would form between us if one of us were to become educated and the other not. I might not have gone at all except for pressure from an older woman, Karen, (See essay "Trust Me") who had by then quite soundly established herself as my family's psychic advisor. So, since I had missed the application deadline to the university on purpose, the local community college was the only workable alternative. It was also much less expensive.

At that time, I already knew my future would have a substantial supernatural component. I was reading cards, talking to ghosts, having prophetic visions and dreams, and quite naturally doing small spells. Karen found me when I was just seventeen, took one look at me and claimed me. She made her way into my family. Her plan was for me to fill her shoes someday, to be a psychic advisor like she was. She didn't really ask, just assumed I would fall in line because, of course, it was my destiny. I was supposed to learn astrology, palmistry, "white magic," and other undertakings.

My very first quarter, I enrolled in a course called Occult Sciences at the community college. What a great opportunity that such a course was offered! I would learn so much, I thought, about what Karen wanted me to learn. So, off to the college, with a not exactly realistic plan for my future, I went. And I most certainly learned a lot . . .

There, I met Winston, the host for the black-eyed demon, the physical vehicle for my contact. On the first day of class, he/it stood in the doorway, waiting for me. "I've been waiting for you," he/it crooned. Before me, in the form of Winston, a fellow student, a handsome young man, was my doom. Winston was tall, with pitch black hair and eyes and skin so very pale – a combination I would later refer to as the irresistible androgynous vampire look. I recognized the demon from two previous encounters. The first was a dream, which I believe was a past life memory or representation of if that my soul retrieved from the depth of the past to warn me.

    The setting of the dream was set somewhere in Europe (dreams are not that specific) more than two centuries ago: horses, farming, stone wells; rough wooden and straw dwellings; heavy, ugly peasant clothing. I was walking along a dirt road, my skirts brushing up dust. Beside the road was a ditch. In it was a man. He had been staked, and yet he was blinking at me. The long stake, more an instrument of impalement, went diagonally through the side of the head, down through the torso, and out the other side of the abdomen. "Oh, no," I thought, "they didn't succeed in killing him. He's still alive!" I turned around, ran back into the village to get someone, to warn someone. Some of the people followed me back to the ditch. But the man was gone. I stood there looking at where he had lain, stunned, while the villagers went back about their business, quite angry at me for leading them on a fool's errand. But I knew that from that moment on, I was locked into some sort of complicity with the man (demon), that he/it and I were permanently bound together. I would never escape. Our association was to be forever.

The second encounter was an actual visitation. He appeared as an apparition, substantial enough to cast a shadow across my doorway. "When you see me the next time, I will bring bad tidings," he said cryptically, and then vanished. And just as he prophesized, his reappearance darkened my young life before it had even had a chance to begin. "Let's go inside," Winston spoke for both himself and the demon, and situated me in a desk he had preselected for me. Really, honestly, what drama! As if hypnotized, I did as he asked. And so began a four and a half month journey into a labyrinth that still holds part of my soul prisoner.

Winston and I instantly became a couple. We spent hours and hours together on the campus and off. He lived in a trailer park on the other side of town and worked as a DJ at a radio station in one of the nearby little towns. He was maybe two years older than I. My addiction to Winston was absolute. To say I cheated on my fiancé, Gavin, is to minimize the crime as, for a while, Gavin didn't even exist to me. Between hormones and what really must have seemed to anyone observing the situation from the outside then or hearing about it now, a death wish, I was out of my mind. I'm not sure it *was* a death wish, not then. When it was *over*, though, the death wish truly came, and, to be honest, never left. At that time, however, I was utterly enthralled, for the glamour, the image he projected, was all encompassing as Winston and the black-eyed demon were inseparable and indistinguishable.

The sexual relationship with Winston was not what I expected. In so many ways, I was naïve. Obvious reasons existed for his inadequacies. Winston smoked a lot of pot and so was high a lot. I did not know then how the drug might affect sexual interest or performance. His distraction simply baffled and frustrated me. I suspect, also, that Winston hadn't yet entirely decided on his sexual orientation. He wanted me; he didn't want me. When he did, the demon in him made him greater than he was. When he didn't, the demon in him made him cold and diminished. I know now it was the demon, not Winston, whom I couldn't resist, with a preternatural compulsion, a mania, and a sense of emptiness looming.

Oddly enough, Karen voiced her approval of Winston. I still

wonder why she was unware of the demon. I think it had a way of blinding people to its presence. But she was supposed to be the expert! It still floors me how exuberantly she pointed out how stylishly Winston dressed and how well-groomed he was (in contrast to Gavin, who was a mechanic and never cared about fashion or even hygiene sometimes). I assumed I was doing the right thing.

The college course itself was also not what I expected. I had assumed it would cover concepts of magick in depth, all organized into a comprehensive whole, everything subject to one overarching theory. I had assumed we would learn how to manage our relationship to the occult. I wanted theories, esoteric insight, demonstrations of ritual, arcane grimoires. Instead, our textbook was one of those popular encyclopedias of the supernatural. There were no lectures really, just discussion about the chapters in the "textbook," or guest speakers, or popular movies. I wasn't learning anything. Any questions I asked went unanswered.

It was not the first time, nor would it be the last time that the paradigm in my head did not quite correspond with the paradigm in which I found myself. It was the one time I wish most of all I could have understood the discrepancy in real time, not just in retrospect. But I was so young, with no reliable mentors, and hadn't even begun to hone my cynicism yet. I kept thinking maybe the instructor was starting at a primary level and would build up to something advanced. No luck. Karen was no help either. She, also, was under the impression that a college course was a college course, and without a doubt would be respectable. Times had changed from when she had been a student. Clearly.

The course requirements included an original project, which Winston and I decided to complete together. We pondered one topic after another. The instructor had no suggestions. The assignment was "open to interpretation." Then Winston suggested we go visit a place he had "stumbled into" by accident and to which he had returned several times already. Even though I had lived in the town so many years, it was the first time I ever stepped onto the grounds of the Old Hospital.

And as much as I am tempted to indulge in poetic description of the afternoon, the building, the season all around us, I won't, except to say that the advent of autumn always brings with it a vague sense of hopelessness that my mind links directly to this one. When light is yellow and filled with the sound and scent of drying corn, I would be transported back in time to the location of the event that turned everything upside down.

The building was enormous and in terrible condition – and full of ghosts and other spirits. Its having been an Old Hospital accounted for the number of disincarnates, and its having been abandoned and overgrown for over two decades accounted for the physical wreckage. The place was packed full of sorrow, terror, shadows, psychic noise – and rodents, bats, garbage, and broken furniture. It was a location typical of so many of those reality TV ghost investigations these days, but this was the very early 1980s, before any such show was on the air. There were none at that time for me, for us, to emulate. Perhaps, *we* gave those future ghost shows the idea of stomping around old buildings disturbing the Dead.

One of the clues I might have paid attention to had I been better prepared was that Winston admitted that he had been followed by "something dark" every time he entered the hospital grounds. When someone says something like that, one should pay attention, maybe be a little suspicious. But I just ignored it. Winston could feel it behind him, he said, sometimes really close, as if curious. It must be, he concluded, the ghost of his friend Tom, who had died in a car wreck just months before. For whatever reason, Winston had a piece of the bumper of the death car in his trunk, and he thought maybe the artifact attracted the ghost. I accepted the explanation foolishly. In retrospect, I realize that if there had really been a ghost with him, I should have been able to see it – because I always do. But I saw nothing.

The place was intriguing, tragic, and full of supernatural screams and moans. I felt empathy for the suffering of its entities. What Winston felt, I'm not really certain. But we agreed to focus our attention on the beings that dwelt in that abandoned monument. For our project, we decided to help usher the spirits of the Dead into the afterlife, to do an exorcism of mercy; that is what I *thought* we were going to do. My brother, Rudyard, and his best friend at that time were to go with us. Afterward, Winston and I were going to write about it.

Sometime, in the middle of October, we went set about our task, arriving after sunset, armed with a Tibetan chant and a Catholic banishment (provided by Karen from a book by a then famous British witch), some incense, some salt, and our good intentions. We parked, went into the dark open hallways, and tried to find the center of the place in order to begin our ritual. What happened, instead, was that on the night we chose for our ritual, we were not alone.

Completely unprepared for the encounter, we walked right in on a Satanic worship session. As we entered, equally unexpected by those already in the hospital, and literally and figuratively, all hell broke loose. Satanists scattered in all directions, not wanting to be caught. They left behind smoke in the air from whatever they'd been burning and blood from their sacrifice (a large crow) splattered onto the charcoal symbols drawn on the decrepit floor. The abused, dead bird had been pinned to the wall.

In the tumult, Winston shouted that an entity Rudyard and I had told him about from out childhood experiences had appeared, that it was pointing at Rudyard with the intent to kill him, and that he stopped it, but now it was inside him. (since he was an open door for one entity, he was easily taken over by another.) We ended up using the salt, incense, and words of exorcism on Winston, having dragged him back to his trailer for the task. He was, true to form, suddenly endowed with preternatural strength and threw Rudyard and his friend around as if they weighed nothing. It took more than hour of crashing and shouting. Finally, silence.

I am pretty sure it was not the supernatural being from our childhood that caused all the trouble that night. The one from our childhood never intended any real harm to Rudyard or me; he just created mischief, mostly. I think what possessed Winston was something else, not the black-eyed demon, but something that originated at the Old Hospital, a passenger picked up in the chaos of the ritual, a disruptive entity that wanted to come along for the ride. Winston, I realized later, truly enjoyed the temporary symbiosis, for there was a repeat performance.

Two nights later, when Winston, nonchalantly came to the motel, to the rooms (two separate sleeping areas with a bathroom in between) in the back that my brother and I shared, he, as he admitted when it was over, "let the demon emerge" again, and so the shouting and throwing of salt ensued once more, causing an alarm throughout the entire motel and getting us in terrible trouble with our parents. Karen, over the telephone, in the middle of entire episode, told us to have Winston say the Lord's Prayer as proof that he wasn't really possessed, but was only faking it. He managed to say it, and so, as far as she was concerned, he had passed the test. I hadn't learned yet (though Karen really should have!) that "the Devil can quote scripture" for his own purposes well enough if need be. It's also possible that Winston staged this second possession, either inviting the entity in or putting on a show for the attention it earned him. We did not initiate the chaos, but were held responsible.

Unfortunately, the uproar resulted in a full-sweep clean-up by our parents of anything that could lead us into further ventures. We were forced to get rid of all incense, amulets, and other paraphernalia, including a Ouija board. We burned it at my brother's friend's house in the fireplace. A couple of days later, his mother swept up the ashes to put them in the trash, but that night, called us to say that her garage had nearly burned down. The ashes had re-ignited again. She was lucky to have noticed in time to use a fire extinguisher.

I'm not sure what we contacted through the Ouija board. It was certainly no Captain Howdy or Zozo, but when we did use it, we received answers to our questions. One time, however, our activity attracted a swarm of flying bugs, little brown beetles, so many they blocked all the light coming in the windows, as they covered the glass from the outside. The bugs stayed a while, spreading throughout the motel and becoming a nuisance for quite some time. The Ouija board was a quite a novelty. At the time, Karen didn't see anything wrong with it, even when I told her that I could her that the planchette would move for me when I worked the board by myself. Anyway, at the conclusion of the event, the Ouija had to go.

My father went beyond of all of this, though. "Your witchcraft or your family." Such an ultimatum was typical of my family's way of coercing me. Ironically, what he really meant was *his mother's* witchcraft. The family legacy is an old one, tracing back to Eastern Europe, and with its own place in history. I was part of it and was beginning to feel it guiding me. Yet my father assumed he could just pound his fist on the table and dismiss my destiny. Right. Because that always works. Truthfully, there was really not that much witchcraft going on at that time, just playing around, but the prohibition also would mean no Winston as well. The thought of that made me insane. My parents had all my life separated me from any friends I had tried to make, and had already taken the one relationship I might ever in this life consider a soul match (a classmate of mine, Bjorn, an artist) from me. Later, they would take Gavin too, but now, it was Winston's turn.

In the end, my choices weren't about him anyway, for he vanished shortly after the Old Hospital incident. The trailer was empty when I tried to find him. He didn't come to class or his job anymore. Just gone. But my father with his demand had crossed a line with me. My sovereignty was at stake, whatever sovereignty was actually mine with parents such as I had. Also, there was something else to my motivation. I had had a taste of the extraordinary and would never give it up. My witchcraft was not a negotiable commodity.

In reaction to my father's demand, I moved out, to an apartment I had secretly, with Gavin's help, rented a few blocks away. He had purchased a waterbed for me (yes, it was the time when those were popular). I moved out late one night after another terrible argument with my family. My father took away my keys to everything, home and car. I was now without transportation, just the bus. A complete persona non-grata.

My exile must have caused perceptible vibrations all the way to the East Coast, to my grandmother, my father's mother, the witch whose legacy was to be mine. Or she had demonic "eyes on me," but either way, she made the one and only call she would ever make to us way out west. She wanted to know if I was living at home still. My parents lied and said that, yes, I was. The next day, they commanded me to come to their home and call her while they listened in on the other phone extensions. I did. I asked my grandmother why I was being pursued by these terrible entities. They were chasing me down, leaping on me, growling. She said, in her German dialect, that I was homesick and should come see her.

Then, of all things, she asked what I was doing in the crematorium (a word she had to say in English as there was no equivalent in her language that she would have known). She was nearly 1,800 miles away, but she knew where I had been. No one had told her. No one had told anyone who might have told her. The Satanic ritual had taken place in the section of the Old Hospital known as the crematorium. Our family's demon was indeed watching me, but I did not know that *then*. It knew I had moved out of my parents' home.

Because I couldn't afford the rent by myself (only a part-time job), I enlisted a girl I knew from high school to be my roommate. I couldn't have made a worse choice. What I didn't know was that the roommate was a client of the same psychic who had come to the Occult Sciences class as a guest speaker. My mother, whom I had told about this woman, made appointment after appointment with her after she had come to speak to our class. The purpose was to get as much information (dirt) on me as possible to assert some control over me. Well, the roommate obliged, making up false stories about my behavior (imaginary "pot parties" with Gavin, for instance), which the psychic then passed to my mother as "clairvoyant insight." It took me a long time to figure out where the false accusations originated.

Why did the roommate do that? The only answer I have for that is demonic instigation, for there was no other reason for such malicious meddling. She and I weren't enemies. Whatever it was, the result was my mother's daily brutal, lengthy, outrageous phone calls, my banishment from the motel property entirely, my brother being denied permission to come see me. I gave Rudyard a key to my place anyway.

On top of everything, there was still the quarter to finish at the community college. For the Occult Sciences course, I wrote a paper on Theosophy. Karen was a card-carrying member of the Theosophical

Society, and was laying the groundwork for me to follow in her footsteps, so she was honored. The instructor, who passed himself off as a shaman to the class, with his long black hair, dark skin, gleaming dark eyes, gave the paper an A. He just wanted me gone, for when I had come to him to tell him what had happened at the Old Hospital, he literally ran out of his office. He kept starting sentences without finishing them, claiming that he had no idea what I was talking about, and then fled, closing his office door behind him, leaving me standing in the hallway to deal with my situation on my own. I couldn't understand why until years later.

The weeks went by, and the storm seemed to be over. There was no more sign of Winston; I had kicked my roommate out of the apartment; Karen talked my family into associating with me again; and Gavin and I were officially settling into our engagement. I had promised my fidelity to him, and we were making plans for a wedding. My mother was busy trying to find ways to prevent it, trying to figure out what she could withhold from me if I persisted. So, everything was back to normal.

My mother also found another psychic to sic on me, a big, loud, woman, who barely spoke enough English for me to understand her. That woman told my mother that there was something "dark" in my apartment, and my brother was sent to dutifully retrieve it – "it" being a small stuffed black panther toy from my collection of stuffed animals. He figured out which of my stuffed animals housed the most powerful entity (an important aspect of my magick) (See essay "Believe Me"), and so took it away. The woman herself, after the offending entity was removed, came to see me as well, banging on my apartment door like a cop. She launched herself at my bookshelf, pulling all the "evil" books down.

Choosing LaVey's *Satanic Bible* and setting a *King James Bible* next to it, she told me to close my eyes and held my hands over the two books so I could "feel the power of the Good Book" as she pushed my right hand down to the Bible with such force that my palm smacked right down on it. "See," she screamed hysterically. "See how the Lord's word has so much more power." I tried to tell her the books were all just to fill an academic curiosity, that I had no interest in being a Satanist, that I just wanted to find out what I had walked into at the Old Hospital, but she wouldn't listen. And she wouldn't leave until I promised her (lied) I would get rid of the books. Holy Roller Crap! Finally, thankfully, she went away too. I kept my books.

Then, one afternoon, Winston came to my door, or should I say, Winston's body did. Winston wasn't in it; it was the black-eyed demon. I have no idea how he/it found me. I had never had a chance to tell him where I moved before he disappeared. Yet somehow, he knew which street, which building, which apartment. I was stunned.

I was alone in my apartment when the demon stood in my doorway. The whole episode of the Old Hospital had isolated me from my family in the previous months. Because of my family in general, I had no friends. I didn't know any of my neighbors. Gavin was at work. Rudyard was with his martial arts guru (who came into his life at the same time Karen came into mine). No one dropped by to see me. My roommate had been sent packing, needless to say. I didn't even have my cat with me – she was at my mother's. So, for the most part, when I was home, I was entirely by myself.

Winston/demon came in, closed and locked the door, and after addressing my collection of stuffed animals (all of which housed entities that were friendly to me) with "So nice to see you all gathered by the fire," said to me, "So, we're off to bed," and led me to the bedroom. He had to pull me along, nearly toppling me from my feet, for my soul had gone cold. I had no will left, no strength. I couldn't move, let alone talk. I remember saying, "No," or did I just think it? *No.* Not of my own accord.

No. No. He removed his clothes and then pulled off my clothes, laid me down on the bed. I remember thinking his skin was very strange, very blueish. There was no sign of his old impotence. When he finished with me, he redressed, left me lying there in shock, then departed. I never saw Winston again.

Winston/demon took with him my wholeness, my light, and he left behind a shell of wreckage. I, whatever "I" means, had been corrupted, defiled (to use the old word). When we became engaged, Gavin forgave me my tryst with Winston, but now it looked like I had betrayed Gavin again. I couldn't forgive myself, but there was more. The guilt, albeit heavy, was just on the surface. Beneath it, I had been laid to waste, utterly desecrated. In the very deepest levels of my soul, I had been touched by something loathsome. I was unclean. It had left a shadow mark, a void, a tear in the fabric of my identity. The wound never healed, not even to this day. Its effect permeated everything, my five senses, my perception and dreams. I had been so deeply violated that I didn't want to breathe any more. I wanted nothing but to die.

When Gavin came over that evening, I was in the bathroom, my body an entirely alien and inadequate vessel for the soul agony coursing through me. I had been contemplating the knife in my hands for a couple of hours. I spoke through the closed door, unwilling to let Gavin even look at me. He again believed I had betrayed him, but was willing again to forgive me. Eventually, he pleaded me out of it, made me promise to live, if not for myself, but for him. I somehow felt a sense of obligation to Gavin for being so generous. By the close of that day, a part of me had been packaged, sealed up, stored away. I was ruined and numb.

Within a few months, our wedding took place. There was no joy in it, though, not in envisioning it, nor planning it, certainly not in the execution of it. I was helpless. My mother, irreparably and intentionally, on my wedding day, destroyed any hopes for the marriage's success. Her evil, tangential to the entire chronology of my life, is an evil of a different sort. (See essay "Wield My Sword") Let me just suffice to say that my marriage was doomed in so many ways right from the start. Another demon lay in wait anyway.

Shortly after the wedding, my family sent me to a hypnotist who specialized in regression. The goal was to get an understanding of my grandmother's witchcraft. I went through two incredibly terrifying, exhausting sessions that took me into my early childhood, the horror show that a good portion of it had been, and beyond that time, beyond this incarnation. A third session had been planned, but I refused to go.

Everyone claimed a stake in the outcome, the anticipated revelations. My mother had wanted me to name names of the people in the ceremonies, to identify who had damaged her daughter. It was my price for "readmission in the family"; I had to snitch, to rat out figures from my memory. Karen had wanted information she could use to persuade me into her philosophical "camp." She was going to use what she could learn from the sessions to "help me." I felt like a puppet being pulled this way and that way simultaneously. All I wanted was the truth. What was going on? Was this my fault? Why did I have certain images in my memory?

My session did reveal the activities of my family's coven (See "Serve Only Me"). I say coven with caution because I do not know the structure really of their association. The memories were of ritual, some small bloodletting, my grandmother's basement, the faces of people I knew and some I didn't, candle light, and my first encounter with my family's demon. To it, I was bound as a consequence of my legacy. Knowing about the binding helped explain other events later in my life. My relationship with it, however, was yet to develop.

Understanding Evil: My Soul Contract

The hypnosis was stupefying, but at last, the sources of the images from my dreams and visions were revealed. These were not the cliché images and scripts of ritual abuse that children at that time and in the decades that followed produced under hypnosis. The hypnotist did not "plant" ideas in my head. The sessions were taped, and I listened to them over and over afterward to make certain. No, all the information came from me, *my* words, *my* recollections.

No one planned on taking the regression to where it ended up. At some point in first session, I moved into the interim between lives, between my past incarnation and this one. In that interim, I saw it/him – the black-eyed demon. He was floating after me. I saw his eyes and knew him, then, and now, in other lives and in this one. "He's followed me," I said, in my state of deep hypnosis. "There's so much evil." I was hysterical. "They're all dead." "He's followed me. He's followed me. They're all dead. There's so much evil." "It's so cold . . . so cold." The hypnotist pulled me back into the present, made sure I was calm enough to go home, but provided me no means to deal with what I had seen.

In the second session, the hypnotist focused on my memory of having been promised to the demon by my grandmother. She had me "revisit" the event under hypnosis. The intention was to reconstruct it. She had me, as the child I was them, get up from the bed and face the demon and invoke Jesus's name and declare myself free of it. As if changing my memory would do away with the demon! As if altering a photograph of an object from the past would change the object in the present! She was the first in a long line of meddlers that never understood the nature of demons at all! How the demon must have been laughing!

I refused to go back for the third session that was planned for me. I had had enough. As it was, for weeks afterward, I experienced a sensory dissonance and delay. When I walked, my feet would engage in the motion normally, automatically, but my awareness of the sensation of walking would only register about a second later. I ran into things. My hands would reach for a coffee cup, grasp it, but a moment would pass before I became aware that I was holding something. I dropped things. Sometimes I felt as if I were floating just outside my body, as if someone had drawn me as a cartoon character, just slightly outside the lines. I half expected my shadow to be blurred around the edges. Maybe it was.

Most of all, I was overwhelmed by my discoveries. Under hypnosis, I had made the connection between this life and the last, this world and the other world. Of all the components to my new understanding, the most profound ones were that I/my soul had been aware, had been conscious, while it moved through the interim between lives. It was awake. It was not blank.

I also had proof that the entities of evil can move between planes and times and lives and bodies. They are aware of me. Evil is sentient. It's not that I didn't know these truths, for I did, vaguely in dreams, in moments of clairvoyance, but now I knew with my rational brain as well. The black-eyed demon was real and had an agenda.

When it came for me, I had no protection. My grandmother was far, far away; my mother stood between me and my grandmother anyway. My father, who probably could have done something for me (he had grown up with his mother's magick), was more interested in preserving his peace with my mother. Karen, also, for all her "I-know-more-than-you-mere-mortals" attitude had no idea what was happening to me. Even if she had, she would have had no way of dealing with it anyway. Not much of a "defense-against-the-dark-arts" instructor in her! I'm not sure she was even remotely aware of how much of a fraud she was. Thus, the black-eyed demon was my own problem whenever he/it chose to appear.

I would see the black-eyed demon several more times in the future, whenever he/it found it convenient to move me as a figure on a chessboard so he could set me up for whatever the new script was. But in the next few years, he didn't do much more. He didn't need to. My next round of danger didn't issue from him/it; it was from my family demon, who came to me after my grandmother's death, and who would lead me the rest of the way down the rabbit hole.

It's interesting, though, that destiny, a quarter of a century later, allowed me to confront the teacher of the Occult Sciences course. He still taught part-time at the community college. Of all departments he could choose, he chose the one in which I worked. Evenings, the instructors would often go out for drinks. He accompanied us, and I reminded him of the Occult Sciences course. Over the next months, he cracked jokes; he snuck up behind me in the hallways and said cryptic things; he sat in my classroom on Halloween to "see what I was wearing" for the special day. He was such an ass, a bully, and found this topic a great way to make fun of me.

He also didn't seem to have any beliefs in anything spiritual. He didn't remember what happened! When I asked my colleagues why he taught the Occult Sciences course way back then, the answer nearly made me lose my marbles. It seems the college wanted to attract students any way possible and so encouraged faculty to INVENT INTERESTING COURSES! It was a scam perpetrated by a charlatan instigated by what I thought was a valid institution of higher learning. The course should have been legitimate. Instead, the situation provided fertile ground for a travesty.

It would have been preferable to find that there had been some insidious conspiracy instead of a truth so utterly banal, so insipid. Still, the instructor kept making his jokes. So, I sent him a lengthy email in which I let him know the depth and breadth of the damage he'd caused.

Come to Me

I let him know how the circumstances of the class allowed Winston to find me. I told him that the circumstances of the class had allowed that psychic, carrion feeder that she was, to have access to me, and thus, my mother, and how the subsequent exchanges between my mother and that psychic resulted in "proof" my family needed to justify their trying to "put an end" to my participation in this "nonsense." There would be no recovery from this fiasco.

Most of all, the circumstances of the class brought me into unprotected contact with the Satanists and all the entities involved in that Old Hospital. Every now and then, in the decades that followed, I would trip over one of them. I would sense he/she knew me, but since I never saw any of their faces, I couldn't be sure, but I would feel a particular and familiar malevolence. If it turned out that said person was a banker or a doctor or a lawyer or an employer, I might, for instance, find myself at the mercy of whatever otherwise unjustified bureaucratic sabotage he/she could inflict. Mostly, the circumstances of the class allowed harm to reach me on a soul level. I would never fully recover from contact with the demon.

The instructor had exploited people's prurient interest in taboo subjects. In his paradigm, the occult was perfect fodder for entertainment. To him, as to many, the subject WASN'T REAL. It could, therefore, from his perspective, be treated any way he wished. In my paradigm, the supernatural was very real. Our two worldviews were *never* going to overlap. I was too young at the time of the Old Hospital to know that, and until I pointed it out to this irreverent, egotistical joker in my email nearly thirty years later, the thought hadn't occurred to him either. I wrote him a several page email.

I entitled my indictment of him, "Welcome to my world." The grievances I laid out against him must have hit home, for I was asked later by a mutual acquaintance, "What did you say to him?" He sent me a short apology, and started to avoid the FAC's. A few weeks later, he had a heart attack, not fatal, just fateful. If there were such a mitigating force as justice, if the universe had mercy or were interested in balance, then maybe ... but I don't believe in such nonsense anymore. I'm more sure of the demons.

As for Winston, there is every good chance that a thorough psychological analysis would have revealed his sociopathic nature, as well as other, supplementary diagnoses. These would have been notable with or without the demonic presence. They probably acted as invitations to the demonic presence. Winston displayed many characteristics indicative of assorted personality disorders. There was a coldness, a detachment, to his actions. He acted without consideration of consequences, no worries about his effects on other people around him. He began projects, made commitments, but didn't follow through. He concerned himself with image, with theatrics. He used people around him for his own entertainment.

Winston didn't express, and presumably didn't feel, true affection. His initially charming manner eventually became unsustainable. His reneging on his bills caused him to lose his home time and again. A verifiable sociopath. He/she may look human, but cannot be expected to behave like a human. The mechanism is alien. The core is hollow. Psychology offers no cures for the sociopath.

What happened to me was rape, yes, and the effect even without the supernatural element was utterly and completely annihilating. The sense of violation was absolute and still lingers, for all that that implies. But there was more to it than the ordinary scope of psychology can accommodate. Some psychologists would be tempted to write all the drama off as the myth a victim builds around the horror of a rape: the guilt, the justifications, the suicidal thoughts, the sense of uncleanness, the fear of the super villain, and so on. All of that is true, but in this case, the event was not just of the mundane world.

But for me, this was not the first rape. I had been molested as a toddler by a family member. Nor was it the last I experienced in this life. As my life spiraled wildly from then on, I attracted like to like, as though a precedent had been set. I can say for certain, from my perspective more than three decades later that the soul-eater cut me far beyond, far deeper, and more profoundly than any other similar experience. It/He was amplified by the demon. This particular demon's only purpose was annihilation.

What Winston provided most of all was a perfect host body for the black-eyed demon. A sociopath is the ideal vehicle for such a passenger. That's not to say that all sociopaths are vehicles for demons, or that rape is always in the tool kit of the destruction, or that demons only use sociopaths to commit rapes, or that all sociopathic behavior is due to demon possession, or that rapes by sociopaths are somehow more horrific than rapes by other monsters, or that all sociopaths are rapists, or that all rapists are sociopaths, or that any other such overgeneralizations are true or provable. It's to say that sometimes the right sets of circumstances converge, and that while a mundane explanation might be valid, an occult explanation might be valid AS WELL. Not instead, but as well. As above, so below.

The vileness of rape is undeniable. Any rapist is despicable. The damage to the victim is thorough and long term. It is impossible to feel clean, to find relief from that nauseating, festering spot on the psyche, to not feel like one's very breath is polluted. To recall the event is like sinking in quicksand. All of this is true when the rapist is a human.

When the rapist is enhanced by a demon, the effect is magnified. The demon lets the abyss into one's soul. The entrance, the acquisition, is accompanied by a loud chaotic roaring, a whirling vacuum, and the sense of falling, falling, falling, and darkness thick as mud. I understand now the full scope of what happened to me. To enter the memory is like entering a grave, the claustrophobic confinement of one. All I have to do is recall the little paralysis the demon caused, its capacity to freeze one in one's place, and I feel the terror rising, the helplessness, and the despair.

Long after the events of the Old Hospital, the black-eyed demon made use of other bodies. He/It didn't just limit himself/itself to using Winston for his agenda with me. As far as I'm concerned, that alone proves that something out of the ordinary had occurred, that I had been raped by something BOTH inhuman and unhuman. There were witnesses to this demon's taking possession of other bodies. Also, more than once, when he's appeared in a form of his own, he was visible to others in my vicinity, not just to me. These incidents took place far apart in time and geography and involved different people. A *folie a deux* doesn't happen *that* often.

So, Winston himself, his form and personality aside, was not the key factor in whether the black-eyed demon was present or not. The demon indicated his/its authentic presence by its/his particular idiolect – the tone and rhythm of his/its voice, the way he/it phrased things, the vocabulary it/he used – and the look in the eyes of the "possessed." Whenever, wherever, at other times he/it showed up, he/it would indicate his true identity. It would be consistent from one body jump to another, from one materialization to another (yea . . . just like in that movie . . .). The expression, the sound, the syntax, the presence. The presence. That specific unearthly presence. It is unique to this demon, to my relationship with it/him.

To a sociopath, other people are toys, objects, tools, resources. Sociopaths are bereft of empathy. They may or may not have a system of logic to their actions. They may not even enjoy the suffering their cruelty inflicts. They may feel nothing. They are, however, destructive. Add to that the demon, the soul-eater, and the extent of the ruin is immeasurable. If a demon chooses to make use of a sociopath, the sociopath may or may not be aware of the demon, and could arguably be considered a victim. But it is more likely that the sociopath, who may feel nothing else at all, will become enamored of the soul-eater anyway. The sociopath could easily develop an addiction to the "symbiosis." It's an incredibly enticing power trip. It's a compatibility. The suit fits, in other words.

It is also important to note that a soul-eater demon can have an entire entourage of minions. A whole collection of minor villains (mostly humans) will deliberately or just by chance come along for the ride. With their stupidity or greed or power lust, they just compound the devastation coincidentally. In my experience at the Old Hospital, the entourage included the instructor of the class, the assorted psychics, the Satanists, Karen, the roommate, and others. All the pieces were characters and had a role in the game. It's as if the statistical possibilities and the most destructive personalities all came together as though orchestrated. They were. The connections were intricate and many-layered, like a spider's web in which I found myself inextricably captured.

The black-eyed, soul-eating demon was never dependent upon just the one sociopath. If it hadn't been Winston, it would have been someone else. Strong evil wrangles lesser evil as a matter of course. It can feel like a convergence, many small things coming together for a single purpose. What *seems* like a conspiracy is *probably* a conspiracy, with the other-worldly being as orchestrator. It is as though entities of all types will be compelled to bow to a common purpose. Identifying the purpose means identifying the demon.

How would someone know that such an entity is present and

about to act? Sometimes, there is no way to know. But generally, the body knows before the mind knows. There might be a momentary flash of vertigo, a sudden chill, a few seconds when one is unable to speak, a tiny sensation of freeze-frame. Something. If someone has any sensitivity or sense of self-preservation, there will be a warning bell. It might even be the sound of a bell – a faint ringing sounding from the astral plane that advises, "Run!" If in the initial encounter with someone, something feels wrong, it probably is! One should trust one's body. The reptilian reaction of the autonomic nervous system is wiser than the thinking brain sometimes.

The problem is that if someone has even the slightest death wish, the sensation might sound like an invitation. But even *that* is a warning that something unnatural is present and that contact is imminent. I should have heeded the signs. If I had known what I know now, I would have. Secret death wish or no, I could have kept my entire life from derailing.

Serve Only Me

Practitioners of the occult, especially those who pass on family legacies again and again, will likely form some sort of partnership with a being or beings from another plane or dimension. At least, I assume that to be inevitable. It is not hard to imagine that as part of such a lineage, a system of "arranged marriages" were to become established between the human practitioners (the witches) and the non-human partners (usually demons). Or it's a sort of slavery passed down generation after generation, a slavery kept in the family. Is the witch the slave or is the demon? Either way, they are bound, one to the other.

My grandmother (my father's mother) was one of those witches although her exact relationship with the green-eyed demon is uncertain. I believe that she herself had a relationship with this demon and intended to pass on the connection to me, or she had a relationship with another demon and just chose this one for me. Of course, I might have been the price for something the demon had done or would do for her. Or it could have been something else. I'll never know. It doesn't really matter.

I do know that I didn't choose. Before I was even old enough to speak, the roles had been decided for me, the effect on me malignant or beneficial depending on the situation. When I finally, deliberately, engaged with the demon, my own complicity opened a permanent wound, raw and humiliating. From the demon's perspective, I was property, a slave. Yet the demon was also to serve me although I never learned how to make it do that, not exactly.

The bonding happened, though. I recalled the details of the

dedication ritual under hypnosis when I was nineteen. But I had had an idea of the framework, the essence of it, all along. I always knew that there were "extras," an entourage, with me. Under hypnosis, I learned how they came to me, at least the green-eyed demon. The ceremony during which I was bound to the entity took place when I was a toddler, just barely walking. In it, I was in my grandmother's bedroom, in my little plaid jumper and patent leather Mary Janes, my arms and legs pinned to the bed by her dolls, which had become animated and acted on her command. My grandmother was levitating, her long hair out of its braid, flying fee as she spun in the air. She was chanting. Something was burning in the room.

In the corner by the door stood a man, a relative, most likely my grandfather. I don't know the larger context of the situation, why he would have been there. It is possible my grandmother and her local coven were in the service of a larger, more international society, and the demon belonged to them, but it is impossible to prove that. There are indications in old family stories to that my grandfather was associated with one of those larger organizations.

However, the night before he died, Samhain no less, my grandfather tried to walk to our house to tell my father "the truth" about something. But he collapsed on the street. He tried to make his way despite his Parkinson's because no one would call my father to come see him. He never had the chance to say what he wanted to, for he died the next day. Whatever he meant to say would probably explain why he had participated in this ritual as well as many other practices. Otherwise, his presence in the ceremony is hard to justify.

In the other corner, beside the dresser, stood a figure composed of ether, in the form of a man as well, but not the remnants of a living being; it had never been a living being. It/He was tall, pale, in white clothing, with longish hair and a brimmed hat, and a greenish glow in his eyes. Before him squatted a beast on a leash, an enormous disgusting thing, a gruesome mix of rhinoceros, toad, and who knows what – something with long tufts of fur, a wolverine? It was a concocted being, more than a thought form, but not autonomous. It had mud-colored eyes.

I think this is where I got confused. I remember my grandmother saying I was being given to one of the two beings. My child's mind was more afraid of the beast, and so assumed *it* was to be my keeper. Looking back on the event as an adult, I know that I had been given to the green-eyed figure, and that the beast was *his/its* servant. Throughout my life, the servant, muddy-eyed creature, would spy on me, and perhaps, ironically, protect me from other beings, but the one I bonded with was the master, the green-eyed demon.

Clearly, my grandmother had had a plan for me, some intention, a duty handed down to me, but one that I never fulfilled. Not that the green-eyed demon or his servant didn't try to bring me to heel. But no one ever explained the rules to me. At the age of nine, I was separated from my grandmother by a move of 1,800 miles. In that day and age, it might as well have been 3,600 miles. My mother prevented phone calls and letters. Eventually my use of German faded, and so communication with my grandmother became almost impossible anyway. She never learned English.

My grandmother did fly out once to visit. She stayed with us about two weeks. That was the last time I would ever see her. That still makes me sad, and so very lonely. I was twelve. During one of those days, when I was playing in the basement, she came down to sit with me. I didn't know then what was happening, but knowing what I know now, I am sure that the strange "poetry" she recited was an evocation. For, in response to it, I saw something approach from the far wall, eyes gleaming with green light; then, it was hard to breathe. Then, there was nothing.

I woke up on the floor. My grandmother was gone. The lights were out. Hours had passed. Every molecule in my body was cold. From that time on, I felt as if I carried something in my body, as if in addition to my own soul flitting around in that great inner space, I had acquired a connection to something outside of myself. Something had been planted in me, a psychic microchip of sorts, or a paranormal transmitter – I was marked. The relationship between me and the green-eyed demon had been consummated. My biochemistry had been altered. No one but I knew what had happened, so life just bumbled along.

My family moved again, from the city to a town near the Great Plains. My parents bought a small motel and ran it themselves, with my brother's and my occasional help. How I survived my mother these years, I do not know. She drove away any friends I tried to make, and for all practical purposes, drove away my soulmate as well. Social or even athletic activities were impossible for me.

Around the age of 90, my mother was finally diagnosed with a borderline personality disorder, complete with its complements of narcissism and sociopathy, when the personnel in the nursing home became the target of her abuse and manipulation. She had managed to escape detection until then. But finally, age and infirmity at last lessened her lethal force, and the juggernaut of destruction she had been her entire life finally lost its most of its power. But all through my teenage years, I lived on the edge of suicide every day, carried a death wish that attracted all kinds of curious spirits.

Between the ages 14 and 18, I formed crushes on various boys, as any teenage girl would. I tended to choose boys who were distant, unresponsive, troubled. Often the boys who chose me inevitably horrified me. They were so ordinary, sometimes pathetic, unappetizing, blundering idiots. They wanted to hold my hand, hang out at the mall. Ugh! I didn't care if they were kind or funny. All the niceties and protocols were boring! I wanted them to devour me. I wanted to devour them. I wanted something more. And I got it, in the form of my ghost lovers.

Emmanuel was the one with whom I interacted consensually, who became nearly corporeal when our bodies met, and the "other," who would pretend to be Emmanuel, and suddenly reveal himself. I would then throw him off horrified. The "other" was the green-eyed demon, but I didn't recognize him yet because the hypnosis session where I officially "met" him was still in the future. It was the green-eyed demon, though, for he had a green glow to his eyes, a pale green cold light.

The light would start deep in the being of the manifestation of Emmanuel as a flicker, then emerge, the entire shape of Emmanuel transmuting into the shape of the "other," as though Emmanuel were being obliterated from the inside. I, at that time, found the green-eyed demon horrible. I learned to be careful, to ask beforehand for the entity to tell me his/its name. The "other" would, of course, lie, and claim to be Emmanuel, but he couldn't disguise his voice. Then, the "other" would laugh and laugh and dematerialize.

Later, at my 30-year high school reunion, the green-eyed demon would remind me of those times. One of the boys I had had a terrible crush on in high school, but who never noticed me then, no matter how I tried to get his attention, spoke to me. But it was not really him. He thanked me for the "wonderful times" he had had with me at my home. In fact, he practically gloated over how nice it was for me to make him so "welcome" then. He winked at Riley, the young man who accompanied me to the reunion. *He winked! That boy had never been to my home!* But clearly the demon had, and 30 years later, he let me know.

Schoolwork during high school was nothing for me. I was in

the Honors Society and had finished all my credits half a year early, so, instead of or therefore or because it was more important than schoolwork, something else developed in me. In the last year of high school, I began having visions of the Death Angel in places where suicides had occurred or before classmates died. I communicated with ghosts in some of the older neighborhoods, read cards (I finally learned to use tarot cards, not just a poker deck), and kept company with entities that lived in my room with me.

I was also being attacked by invisible animals. When I was outside, walking anywhere, I would hear claws scratching the floor, hear growls or screeches, and then feel sudden pressure on my back and shoulders as though something had pounced on me (the muddy-eyed servant to my grandmother's demon, most likely, and the minions who worked with him). People watching me would wonder what was wrong as I flailed about or ducked to avoid unseen forces.

In my "real world" life, my boyfriend, Gavin, proposed to me. High school ended. The next year and a half, however, was among the worst times of my entire life. As a consequence of my enrollment in an Occult Sciences course at the community college, I attempted a hands-on supernatural project at a local historical landmark – an old abandoned hospital (long before the ghost shows made such a venture popular!). (See essay "Come to Me") It didn't turn out very well, but changed the course of my life forever.

During this time came the first real evidence that the muddy-eyed demon appeared on occasion to see what I was doing and report back to my grandmother. I would see a shadow out of the corner of my eye, a squat, bulky lumbering form, with a leering presence. Shortly thereafter, she seemed to know of my activities without actually having ordinary means of doing so. It made noises and left an odor behind. In those days, it was very present, but I didn't know what to make of it. It was just something disgusting that I chose to ignore.

Finally, when the trauma of the Old Hospital event settled, Gavin and I were married. Karen (the psychic who came to stay at my parents' motel) had inextricably woven herself into my family. My brother, Rudyard, was entrenched in the martial arts cult which would control his thoughts and actions for 25 years. I began classes at the university this time and was hopelessly and pointlessly trying to begin a normal married life, to build a normal home.

My grandmother, when I was twenty, developed a lethal cancer. She sent me money to come see her, but I did not go, a choice I will always regret. I sent the money back, with a note I feel sick over now, full of the family "party line" of blame and retribution. To a degree, I think I even believed it. I had to. My mother had made it clear that if I went to see my grandmother, she would no longer pay my tuition (the money had come from her mother, my other grandmother). Most of all, if I had tried to make any connection with my grandmother, I would no longer be part of the family.

It's hard to imagine someone doing that in a family, but my mother had forced my father to separate from his brother permanently, and so I knew she *would* throw me out of her life and bar the gate. I *would* lose my parents and brother and any sense of belonging I might ever have felt – imagined or real. She *was* capable of following through on any and all terms of her extortions.

I never saw my grandmother again. A year later, she died. My parents and brother went to the funeral while I had to remain at home. They were not going to risk my being tempted or kidnapped or brainwashed or inducted into the coven, they said. So, I stayed behind. And exactly during the hour of my grandmother's funeral, Gavin's (now my husband) younger cousin, Greg, came to my home. He was the first physical vehicle for the green-eyed demon. For the first time, and absolutely clearly, the true sexual nature of the bond between me and the green-eyed demon came to light.

The visit was not entirely out of the blue. For whatever reason, Gavin decided that maybe I should initiate Greg into sex. He suggested, in a perverse foreshadowing of circumstances to come years and years down the road, that I "give" myself to Greg as his teacher, that I share my expertise with him. I agreed. Why? I was young. I had hurt Gavin with Winston (during the episode during the occult sciences class), and felt I owed him. I was starving for something, and would try anything. They talked about it, but Greg didn't seem interested. *Until that very hour of the funeral.* After that, he and I began an affair that could have laid the groundwork for a drama that could have easily ended in murder, and I'm still surprised it didn't.

Greg came over to the house every few days. Gavin was quite comfortable with it. A few times, as obscene as it sounds, the three of us were together. Those times, I'm certain it was just Greg who was with us, no demon passenger. He was, after all, a very young man, in fact, just past the age of consent. At that age, sex is second only to breathing.

But mostly my sexual relationship with him/the green-eyed demon was not normal, not healthy, not joyful. Its focus was a struggle to deprive me of my sense of self, to force my total submission, not just a role-play submission, as it was disguised. It was a struggle for power, dominance. The reason the demon didn't ultimately win was that a part of me always remained outside his/its sphere of influence, was simply out of its/his reach, perhaps out of my own reach too. The surrender could never be complete, no matter how much he wanted to break me.

In the process, in the bizarre tango we danced together, Greg, with the green-eyed demon in him, was extremely inventive, seductive, and terrible, an old pro, calculating and callus, a bit suave, a bit mythological. I should make it clear that this behavior was completely out of character for Greg himself. Even today, Greg is lethargic, passive, perhaps on the autism spectrum, without passion or theatrics, a nerd, and sometimes completely irresponsible.

And yet, the moments I came closest to having all psychic barriers breached occurred in the violent interactions when Greg and I were alone, and the green light of the demon shone in his eyes. In those times, his grip on me was stronger, his intent to control me more intense. His voice was deeper, angrier. I carried on two simultaneous conversations, one with Greg, and one with the demon. They overlapped only superficially. Greg's use of language would change, and I would instantly know a different speaker was present. The way he said "you" when he addressed me came from an entirely different paradigm.

Once, Greg let himself in the back door of the townhouse in the middle of the night. I heard him downstairs and met him in the living room. He pinned me against the bookshelves, with an incredible strength, and in purely the green-eyed demon's voice, the green gleam terrifying in his eyes, he demanded of me, "Do you think you and Karen can defeat me?" I was terribly confused. Karen and I had no such plans. She and I had been talking about a demon, yes, but the wrong demon (the black-eyed one), as an anonymous entity that was harassing me, and as something distant, in the past, the one from the Old Hospital. Neither Karen nor I had the story straight. But certainly, we were not discussing the entity in Greg as its own demon.

As for Greg himself, Karen had no problem with him or with his and my being together. I had told her all about the relationship, and she thought the situation was quite amusing. She had no idea that the green-eyed demon was right in the middle of it, and I didn't know enough to know it myself in order to tell her. Besides, the green-eyed demon had little to fear from those who might hunt him (as in Karen). He was the one doing the hunting. Plus, he had his servant. Sometimes the muddy-eyed servant lurked outside the fence or in the alley, listening, I guess. We would see him. The lackey was clearly spying on me. I think Karen mistook the servant for the master and never realized the truth. Her advice or suggestions for helping me navigate the impossible road ahead of me were woefully inadequate.

At the core of my turmoil was that I was not doing/being what my grandmother had set out for me when I was a child. I have no idea what that was. Since I never took my grandmother's place in the coven, I assume I did not continue whatever relationship with the green-eyed demon I was supposed to have, not exactly anyway. As the interaction was sexual, and I became adept at sexual magick as an adult, I can only speculate about what it was supposed to be. Still the green-eyed demon was determined to collect on the debt, the promise, even with my grandmother dead, even without my knowing what was going on. He/It was going to get his due, and if not, he would destroy me.

Also, there was my having been already plundered by the black-eyed demon; I was damaged goods. For, in spite of the promises from my grandmother and all the others, in spite of my acquiescence to the green-eyed demon/Greg on a basic, if not almost thorough, level, there was an aspect of me, of my being, that remained untouchable. It wasn't even mine anymore. It belonged to black-eyed monster that had violated my soul. But the green-eyed demon wanted even that lost part of me, and he would destroy me to get it. No matter that it was no longer in my possession.

Again, at the time I did not know anything but that the green-eyed demon wanted something I couldn't give. I had a hollow in my soul where it had been, but was no longer present. I wonder if my grandmother had known the black-eyed demon had taken it, if it had disrupted her plan for me, if the black-eyed and the green-eyed demons had been in competition for my soul, and the green-eyed demon had already lost. The green-eyed demon would keep trying, though. The whole soap opera tension to it was (and still is) a bit tiresome.

Paradoxically, too, is the other side of the interaction. It is still disconcerting to describe (impossible to deny) the extent to which the green-eyed demon evoked a hunger as dark as a death wish in me that only he could fill. From the moment of my grandmother's visit when I was twelve and woke up on the floor of the basement, it had lain dormant. Then, it raged, starving and furious. When it unseated Emmanuel, I found it unappealing, but the universe had shifted. Just one taste of the green-eyed demon in Greg, and I became a mad thing. It was (at least from what I'd heard) like certain drugs, how after one try, all control is forfeited, all sense gone out the window. If Greg skipped visiting me for a few days, I became hysterical. I would ambush him in places I knew he frequented. I stalked him, completely unable to not do so.

When Greg began to see a girl his own age, I threatened him, threatened her. He was mine. I was absolutely, utterly insane. When he didn't come around anymore, I nearly drank myself into a coma a number of times, had fits of violence (once, I kicked the back door into splinters, for instance) or crying fits that went on for more than an entire day. I paced the street up and down in the middle of the night for hours, with a drink in hand. Was the demon finished with me? Maybe. Did he/it accomplish what was intended? Maybe. I was changed.

What the green-eyed demon had done was set a precedent. I would for the rest of my life try to find the same intensity, the same ecstatic annihilation, the out-of-body exhilaration. I would seek out lovers who, if they couldn't house him might emulate the green-eyed demon. The failures were to me infuriating, disappointing, disgusting, exhausting, appalling, anything but satisfying. Only a demon would suffice. Human lovers were tragically unsatisfactory. I wanted my demon back, but he never came back, not in a body I could touch. Something in me still howls at the sense of loss. That is not to say that the green-eyed demon didn't make appearances now and then, but only to express his jealousy, do outrageous things, but never again to feed my hunger.

That green-eyed demon never took possession of a body again, except to deliver assorted taunting little "sound bites." My need did not, however, diminish. Not ever in my life. So, I kept hunting. My marriage to Gavin, needless to say, did not make it after the Greg drama concluded. There were, predictably as well, a stream of failed relationships, some phenomenally spectacular after that. My sights having been set so high (supernatural) worked remarkably as a bench mark, an assessment, for all those who didn't measure up.

Then I met Robin, my second husband. He was not the green-eyed demon, not even a vessel for the green-eyed demon, but he was, as close as possible, of the same *nature* as the green-eyed demon, and not yet inhabited. We managed, when we were together, to transcend the mundane. Robin was never benign, was, in fact, not exactly human, but one of those other type entities that do incarnate into human bodies. He could, therefore, emulate the vibration of the green-eyed demon, another non-human being. He was the perfect substitute. How I love(d) my demons! But, my relationship with Robin, needless to say, ended cataclysmically. In so many ways, the demon won. It always won. How audacious I was to ever think otherwise.

As for the muddy-eyed demon, the servant to the green-eyed demon (as Renfield to Dracula), it caused mischief here and there when someone tried to use me or my power for his/her own benefit. He would sabotage vehicles or livelihoods of or cause accidents for people who had the nerve to assert some authority over me they didn't deserve. When a recruiter for a not-so-savory neo-pagan coven tried to trap me, according to the recruiter himself, "something" pushed his car into a curb, and "someone" stole his tools and "someone or something" pulled up plants outside his house, caused the dogs to go crazy, broke a window, and so on. Although his espionage at crucial moments had at times cost me dearly, the muddy-eyed demon acted on my behalf at other times. None of it was predictable, and all of it was out of my control. Entities helped me or hurt me according to their own arbitrary motives.

In the years between my grandmother's death and my meeting Robin, I found myself teetering right on the edge of sanity. There were days I was terrified I would lose control. Between my mother's effect on me and the demons' effect on me, sometimes I could barely function – or I nearly drank myself into oblivion. Coping was impossible. Progress in my state of mind was impossible.

Something had to help me! I wanted to understand. I wanted to stop hurting. I wanted to function with some sort of dignity. I wanted to end my hunger and soothe my humiliation. I wanted an explanation, guidance. Karen offered me only her Christianity, which I tried on for a while, but ultimately could not buy into. So, I did what one does in the modern world. I went to see a counselor, then another, then another. That was a bad decision. I do not recommend that anyone having experiences with a demonic entity go that route. Psychological counseling is not meant for those of us who travel in unconventional territory. Not only is it not going to help, but it will make everything worse.

Psychologists operate in the mundane world. They look for mundane explanations. They work from a mundane playbook. I was foolish enough to try to insist they understood me, to try to convince them of the reality of my experiences, of the entities. *I* knew what I was experiencing was not only in my head. But the psychologist's job is to maintain a certain worldview that says it is. But the demons were real, *are real*. They were not going to go away because someone said they don't exist. That's not how this works.

Parents who say there's no such thing as ghosts are lying! I remember once hearing a woman in a department store telling her little daughter that there is no such thing as witches! I wondered if I said that about Christians if they would all just disappear! It's insulting and infuriating when someone else says that something isn't real because it defies textbook explanations. Doing so creates a cycle of re-victimization. If it walks like a duck, talks like a duck ... IT'S A DUCK!

My sojourn into the psychiatric realm resulted in a whole long list of "this-world" diagnoses. Most, although quite fascinating, were just distractions from the real issue, and often contradictory. Sometimes, they were nothing other than whatever the therapist specialized in or whatever was in vogue. Most importantly, every time I talked to a professional, I put myself in grave danger of being locked up. Hospitalization is extremely expensive – and inconvenient. And the call for it is often arbitrary. I am lucky I escaped incarceration.

Also, the other favorite weapon of the psychiatrist, the prescription, stays on record permanently and can influence employment, insurance, security clearance. The drugs can permanently alter the brain. THEY DON'T, HOWEVER, DISSUADE THE DEMONS! What's worse is that the drugs allow demons better access. One cannot resist demonic influence while under the influence of mind-altering medication, as I learned through testimonials from those who had been tricked into taking it. I am happy to say I evaded all attempts to medicate me.

Turning oneself over to a psychiatric professional means surrendering one's power; it is no different from surrendering to a demon. It means to capitulate. To give up one's truth is to violate oneself further. But that doesn't mean that there is nothing to be learned. I took seriously the list of "diagnoses"; it gave me something to work on. Having a vocabulary for the effects of my experiences provided at once a means for self-analysis (so I could work on some of these issues on my own) and self-defense (to protect myself against those who might try to "help me see the light"). I learned to deal with my own problems without having to convince someone else that what caused them was real.

So, knowledge of psychology is helpful only to the degree that it helps define and remediate the *effects* of traumatic experience (which the supernatural can certainly deliver), but does nothing to help with the *causes*. The causes (the demons) are supernatural; they require a whole different expertise. The psychiatric community does not recognize pursuit *of* or *by* a demon as a valid cause. In fact, the traditional protocol is to treat such a cause as if it were the *effect* of an illness, as a *symptom*. The job of the shrink is to treat the illness, in other words, to reframe the truth into something that fits a "normal" paradigm. Not helpful here.

I also naively sought help from one of those "survivor" groups. What a shock I had there as well. First of all, the members were "victims" of Satanic cults. That was way out of my terrain (I don't believe in a Satan any more than I do a God), but I didn't bolt right away. I figured maybe they could offer me some way to ward off the entities that were pursuing me. Ha! To belong to the organization, I would have had to sign a contract promising that I would refrain from any and all occult practices. Was that going to deter the demons from interacting with me? No! Besides, I wasn't going to give up my tarot reading, my talking to the Dead, my association with elementals. Why would I? So I ran from them too.

There is no conventional treatment for damage caused by demons, only the development of wisdom. Understanding the entities necessitates a metaphysical paradigm. It requires a framework that accepts the fact that the demonic interaction defies time and place. In such a paradigm, it must be accepted that a demon's trespass in someone's life is not confined to one person, one incident, one time period, or even one life, but is, instead, an on-going whack-a-mole. The perspective must acknowledge the intensity of demonic presence. The worldview should not question the uncanny coincidences, the synchronicities. It should accept that logic does not offer much comfort. It must define wisdom as not second guessing oneself.

For me, the demons' attraction to me was preset by my family, but that doesn't mean that demons don't seek out relationships on their own. They do. I think a certain approach to magick attracts them. The minute someone engages in these magickal ventures, he/she could attract all sorts of visitors. Once an intimacy is established, the practitioner/the witch might find himself/herself in a predicament similar to mine, a life changed, his/her will and focus completely unhinged.

There's also another peculiarity worth mentioning. It's about the glamour a demon can cast over the bodies it inhabits, who would otherwise not be appealing. It's ironic. But I have had conversations with other witches about this phenomenon, and more than one has confessed to being entirely embarrassed by relationships they've found themselves in. For, once the demon vacates, and it *will* vacate, the witch is left with the vessel, who is often a completely nonfunctional and/or repulsive person. A bait and switch. It's the demon who's charming, not the human. It's like a wolf in sheep's clothing story, only backwards.

The discrepancy can make one feel so stupid! It's more than just the psychological tendency to endow a partner with qualities he/she doesn't have only to find out one has fooled oneself. It's as if the partner becomes an entirely different person. That is actually what happens. The demon and the human smell different from one another. They move differently. They sound different from one another. They have different habits. The human, one could resist; the demon, not so much. The difference between the demon's effect and the psychological parallel is that in the former, other people witness the "enhancement," whereas in the latter, only the partner suffers the illusion.

So what does one do? What did I do? Read. And read some more. I gained as much information as possible and learned to recognize when a demon is present immediately, and then make an informed decision about what to do. Becoming knowledgeable returned some of my power to me. In addition to all the literature on the various related psychological diagnoses which I read in order to be my own shrink, I also read volumes and volumes on entity possession, soul-retrieval, demons, elementals, sex magick, and so on. Archeology as well. Any and all of the assorted religions. The literature is boundless. From all the sources of knowledge, some insight might emerge, an understanding might evolve, a synthesis of all the research. Maybe a solution will present itself, maybe not. But it's better than the alternative of blundering around in ignorance.

Other than destroying a demon, which really can't be done, I found a number of other options, and not all of them are combative. Over the decades of my life, I learned that, in addition to intensive study, there are two powerful tools for dealing with demon. One is viability in the real world, the ability to keep a home and pay one's bills, being a responsible citizen and working at something valuable. It helps prevent weak spots or openings.

    The other tool for me has been trust in my own perception. It's the ability to detect the presence instantly and say, "I see you," not as a challenge, but as a statement announcing and confirming that I know what I am dealing with. A perverted *Namaste*, yes, but it has proven itself quite useful. The acknowledgment removes any doubt about what is going on, and urges that everything must be carefully analyzed and assessed.

    There are others out there who have, like me, fallen into a demon web. We have all probably tried to convince those close to us that what we have experienced is exactly what we say it is, only to horrify them or find ourselves ridiculed. We'll have to content ourselves by accepting that what we know is what we know, and it does not depend on anyone else's believing us. It's convenient when proof manifests before the doubters' eyes, but we can't count on that; we can just hope. Occasionally, it will. Objects will move, doors open. Noises. Smells. Apparitions. Belongings will disappear and reappear in strange places. The usual.

    Coping with a demon, however one might have acquired it, means trusting in our perception of it, believing in what we see, and hear, and feel. It means recognizing the pattern(s) by keeping track of all the details, finding repetitions, sorting what's vital from what's not vital, identifying the one or two specific indicators that serve as proof (for me, the green glow in the eyes, the tone of voice, and way language is phrased). When everything seemed the most absurd, I know that just being able to put my finger on something undeniable helped me. I have an incredible memory, and so when I sat and reviewed details of my autobiography, I was able to find the small pieces of information that confirmed that what I thought/think was/is true was/is really true. I was not hallucinating, never was. That alone affirmed my sense of self and my right to be here. That alone let me hold on to my power.

Outside help is available too. True and competently trained shamans exist in most every city these days. Many (though not all) have legitimate methods and belief systems that include the acceptance of otherworldly entities. They can work not only on the effects but on the true causes of supernatural encounters and addictions. Most importantly, they can help the patient empower himself/herself without extorting a worldview from him/her first.

My grandmother acted as slaver, promising me to a particular demon. She gave me to it (and it to me) in a strange arranged marriage. Whether she meant to help me or harm me, I will never know. But that the demon to which my grandmother promised me was real is not something I ever questioned. The times it/he appeared, I knew from the sensory clues that I wasn't dealing with just a human. I knew because of the initial compulsion to throw myself at the vessel with all my might, the lure to annihilate myself. I knew/know because I knew/know.

Just as recently as a few weeks ago, the green-eyed demon flashed a glimpse at me, and I almost fell for the challenge, but then I remembered. I finally know better than to fall into the old patterns, despite the almost automatic response to the siren call. I dismissed the body in which he appeared (a participant in an open poetry reading I attended) and walked away. I think maybe the compulsion has ended. That's the best victory I'm going to have.

Understanding Evil: My Soul Contract

Trust Me

Among the various personalities who engage in occult or metaphysical pursuits, there will be self-ascribed mentors in search of protégés, followers. I've had several such types choose me, but one exerted so much influence over me the effects are still incalculable. She selected me, and I fell into the role she prepared for me before I ever had a chance to understand what was happening to me. It took me more than fifteen years to pull myself free. A true Svengali. And maybe Mephistopheles as well.

Karen entered my life when I was seventeen. I was about to start my last year of high school and was living with my parents and brother, Rudyard, in the small motel our family owned in a town at the edge of the Great Plains. Our motel had small kitchenettes and was generally very quiet. We had some regular long-term tenants. Karen came to stay with us for the summers, then, at least for a few years, wintered in Hawaii. Eventually, she moved into an apartment in a nearby town, and no longer traveled seasonally.

When she entered the office the very first time and set her eyes on me, she said, "Ah, now I know why I stopped at this motel. God sent me to you." With that, the dye was cast. Ownership of my destiny from then on for a decade and a half was divided between her and my mother, no matter who else came into my life. Who was going to argue with God? Right.

Karen was old enough to have been my grandmother, but unlike anyone in my family, she had always been in the company of educated people. Her husband, who was with her at the motel, had been a professor of economics, and she herself associated with (at least I was under the impression she had) various social elite. She had done work as a journalist in her younger days, but most of her career was as a psychic advisor and astrologer. So, one of the first things Karen did was lure me, actually all of us, into her ring of devotees. She didn't charge for her readings anymore (not unless, she said, the purpose of the reading was to make money), but she sure knew how to make her clients dependent on them, on her.

The timing of Karen's arrival couldn't possibly have been more significant. I was in my last year of public school; I had a steady boyfriend, but had no plans for my future; and most of all, my relationship with my mother was extremely volatile. All I wanted was to escape. Then, as if in answer to my wish for something, for anything outside of my terrible confinement in my family's madness, I began experiencing supernatural phenomena regularly. What better time for an experienced manipulator to come on to the scene! And so we began.

Karen read palms and astrological charts. She sent away for charts of all of us: me, my brother, my mother, and my father. A year later, when Gavin, my boyfriend, and I became serious, she sent away for his too. We all individually and collectively spent hours and hours with her, going over all the mystical details of houses, signs, planets, life lines, heart lines, fate lines, head lines, Atlantis, Mu, guardian spirits, past lives, and the lingering Dead. It was the first time we as a family had an outsider with whom to talk about ghosts and family tragedies. Karen wormed her way into every aspect and corner of our biographies.

It was I, however, who spent the most time with her. It was she who guided, molded, sometimes forcefully, my thoughts and beliefs about anything and everything: new age books, the soul, the Bible, psychic abilities, hauntings, marriage, college, reincarnation, my family dynamics, alcohol, food, magick, clothing, and on and on infinitely. Karen claimed to have been my mother in a previous life (a classic "capturing" mechanism – establishing an a priori intimacy). She had come to find me again, she assured me, because she still wanted to take care of me, to make sure I succeeded on my sacred path. I have to say, though, that while I might have taken her word as gospel on so many other topics, for some reason, this assertion, I did not accept. I should have used my incredulity as a preliminary measure of all that followed.

The ideas Karen espoused included an assortment of Christian and Hindu tenets. Of course, they were, as she was a card-carrying member of the Theosophical Society. The list of the various truths that she attempted to impart to me was fairly standard Christian with a twist. To these, it seems, Karen added several adaptations that pertained just to me. I was not exactly a willing audience at first. When I walked out of the Lutheran Church at the age of twelve, refusing to be confirmed, I dismissed the associated belief system entirely and utterly. The approach of the pastor back then wasn't very subtle, though. Karen's was.

The following list of precepts is not comprehensive, but serves to portray the general worldview Karen wanted me to adopt. To begin with, she taught me the purpose of the soul's journey through reincarnation is to evolve until all karma is paid off and an appropriate level of awareness is reached. An evolved soul is evident from the person's loving behavior and call to service. Guides and ascended masters help the soul in its progress. Some people are more evolved than others (race, intelligence, physical attributes, paranormal abilities, correct breeding, among other measures, were indicators). It is the responsibility of those who are more evolved to help the less evolved. What racist, elitist ideology! I was very uncomfortable with it.

I was, Karen assured me, well on my way to being evolved. She, who was, of course, (there should be a font for sarcasm!) fully evolved and karma-free, would teach me how to use my gifts to help others. Finally, as I progressed, in other words, proved myself worthy bit by bit, the secrets of the universe would be revealed to me. When I was ready, when *she* determined when I was ready, I would find the answers to all my questions.

    I thoroughly bought into her truths, at least most of them, that is, for about a decade. But until then, as unreasonable as it seemed to me, I tried to rely (lest I disappoint Karen) on the idea that belief in God – as well as God himself – provides protection against evil. As long as one committed oneself to God and to Light, evil would be rendered powerless. I tried for years to become "evolved," in order to live up to the expectations Karen had of me. I couldn't please my real mother, so I did the best I could to please my substitute mother. Dutifully, I allowed my thinking to be revised and edited. Karen's praise and affection filled my empty heart. What Karen provided me with was someone to listen to my grievances, fantasies, and achievements, hopes, and everything I could never share with my mother. I needed to share my life with someone! I wanted family I could trust.

    Karen was a participant in all of the highlights of my life during those years. First was my graduation from high school. Second was my beginning college and the terrible events of the Old Hospital. (See essay: "Come to Me") Then came my marriage to Gavin, my first divorce from Gavin, the completion of my bachelor's degree, my remarriage to Gavin, the completion of my master's degree, my brief move to the desert, and my second divorce from Gavin, my years of working as an art model, my first full time teaching job, the assorted and numerous significant and insignificant relationships I had in spite of my mother, the beginning of my marriage to my second husband as well as several car wrecks and other episodes (for instance, one home I lived in was destroyed by a giant cottonwood tree felled by the wind). Each and every one of the important events of my life had her input imprinted on it.

I did nothing without consulting Karen. It never even occurred to me to make my own choices. My mother never let me, and honestly, Karen didn't either. Their approaches were just different. My mother's method was extortion. Karen's method was brainwashing. Both, as I can see now in retrospect, were arbitrary. Luckily, once I was no longer living with my parents, I had a little freedom, at least in small things, at least some of them. The larger life choices, however, were never purely my own. Never.

As my mentor, Karen thought nothing of trying to interpret or direct my actions or my point of view to match what she thought was right. Being unaccustomed to trusting myself, I allowed her to do so without resistance until shortly before I broke ties with her. Most of Karen's advice fit her agenda of preparing me to live a life as she lived, or imagined she lived. In the end (and still to this day), instead of learning to protect or assert myself when someone hurt me, I learned a whole host of alternative reactions.

I learned to forgive the sometimes unforgivable, to always look for the explanation behind others' behavior, or to accept that there must be a karmic or divine plan behind everything. Whatever happened to me, I believed, was the result of actions I had taken in another life or was a requirement of the service evolved souls had to perform to demonstrate their devotion. I came away with the belief that in order for my own soul to become lighter, I would have to sacrifice on a continual basis.

For reasons that I'm not sure were altruistic, Karen took it upon herself to fight against my grandmother. The more we uncovered of my grandmother's legacy through long, exhausting treks through our memories and through my visits to a hypnotist who regressed me to early childhood and beyond, the more determined Karen became. It was clear that my grandmother's plan for me was for me to take her place in her coven (I use the term loosely, as I suspect it was more of a cabal). Well, I couldn't do that and be Karen's protégé simultaneously. My grandmother lived nearly two thousand miles away and died three years after I met Karen. The dedication to my family's legacy of witchcraft that my grandmother had begun with me when I was very young and long before we moved away was never finished. I was stranded, incomplete. Karen took full advantage of my situation.

Karen made all sorts of promises, telling me that *she* would teach me magick instead, the right kind of magick, white magick. But she never did teach me, even after a lengthy process of trying to convince me that that was what I wanted. It wasn't. I wanted a way to deal with the demons, and I wanted to learn the big Why's. It is interesting that she approached Rudyard as well, but offering him the ability to wield power over others, which he declined. Around the same time, my brother's martial arts Svengali made him the same offer, which he accepted.

Karen may or may not have tried to banish the ghost of my grandmother, who did stay around me after her death. I don't know. I do know that my grandmother's contact with me met with interference. It might have come from Karen, who still had most of her faculties in order then. It could also have come from another source: Karen had allies. During those winter visits to Hawaii, in the 1970s and early 1980s, she met with a circle of famous psychics, an established group, whom I'll refrain from naming, for I have no wish to cause myself any more trouble than I already have had. She told me they strongly urged her to intercede "on my behalf" and prevent me from becoming something monstrous, that my soul was in danger if she didn't. They would help her help me anyway they could. To me, anyone's unbidden interference in another's destiny is an outrage. How dare they!

This is another reason I do not trust groups. I have more than once heard that neo-pagan covens will cast spells to bind a member or an outsider if they think the person is harming himself or herself or presents a danger. But what counts as harming oneself or presenting a danger is determined arbitrarily. What they do is no different from methods of the Inquisition. They adhere to some dogma, endow themselves with a moral superiority, and exercise a stewardship over what isn't theirs – no matter what the intentions. I wonder how many have tried to bind me. I know some have, for there have been times in my life when I felt myself struggling against invisible shackles.

My brother, Rudyard, was the focus of such a group's intentions. The former girlfriend of his martial arts guru wanted to get her revenge on said guru. She contacted me to come join her in "saving" my brother from the guru. The implication was that she would cast a spell on the whole martial arts group, that they would wreck their motorcycles, for instance, when out riding together, but that my brother, the guru's first hand man, could be spared if I joined her. They could use my contribution. I told her I'd think about it and left her, hoping that nothing more would come of this preposterous proposal. I never called her back.

Over the next weeks, something very strange and unnerving happened. My apartment became absolutely inundated with spiders. They were everywhere – in my shoes, in the kitchen cupboards, in my shoes, on the toilet paper roll, crawling across my computer screen, dangling from every doorway, scurrying across the shag carpet, on the bed – hundreds, it seemed. I bought and emptied can after can of insecticide, nearly poisoning myself, but not having any effect on the spiders. They persisted.

Then, I finally realized this was a supernatural event, and that I had better figure out what was going on. So I listened to them, to the spiders, yes. What they were trying to get me to hear was that the girlfriend of the guru was really going to do harm and that I had to tell my brother about her and her plan. Immediately, I called him. We were at odds with one another at that time, but he took my call. We met at his house, and I told him what I had been offered. When I got home, there were no more spiders, not even any carcasses. And then, I made a doll of the woman, which I gave to Rudyard the next day to do with what he wanted. My brother was safe. For her, however, began a series of unfortunate events that brought her misery. Ever since that spider invasion, when spiders come at me in particularly frequent and freaky manner, I know there is something I should be doing that I'm not.

Warning Rudyard and making that doll are not what Karen would have done. I managed on my own. However, my grandmother's path would have provided me with more calculated power, yes, power – the means to determine my *own* destiny. I make no apologies. She had promised me to her demon (and it to me), and would have taught me how to make that supernatural symbiosis work. I would have learned spells the way she cast them. She would have perfected my innate ability as a dollmaker, a proficiency I would have to master on my own. By dollmaking, I do not mean only those poppets used for sympathetic magick, but the greater task of imparting life to them, animating them, and of asserting control over all kinds of entities as a necromancer. (See essay "Believe Me") I will always wonder what else I might have become had my original destiny not been interrupted by distance and interference.

Certainly, had I had proper guidance, I would not have done some of the stupid things I did. For instance, during the tumultuous time of Greg and my grandmother's demon, another entity pestered me relentlessly. Every time I went to the laundry facilities in the apartment complex, it would manifest. It was a crippled child, a boy with polio crutches. He was about eight years old, pale and thin, both pathetic and menacing. He would block my way in and then block my way out, and I'd have to dodge to the side.

"What do you want?" I shouted at him finally, after months of this. "Ten years," he answered. "All right, dammit, you have them!" I answered. He immediately disappeared. What had I done? I never saw him again, not in that form, but I'm certain he collected his due in the decades that followed, even if incrementally, in other forms (which I could enumerate, but there's no point). Ten years of what? Of performing a duty he seemed to think I owed him or to which he considered himself entitled? Of being trapped or disabled myself? Ten years cut off of something? Sure, maybe, who knows?

When the entity first appeared, I told Karen about it. She didn't see any danger in it, wanted me to be sympathetic, suggested that I offer it prayer. None of that worked. Karen did not respect my intuition that told me whatever the thing was, it was evil. Its presence informed me so, and so did the vacuum it left in its wake when it vanished. Instead, Karen condescendingly lectured me that spirits will be attracted to me because of my psychic abilities, and I should learn to help them. My grandmother, at least in my imagination, would have told me the right way to deal with it, which, for sure, wouldn't have included promising it a damn thing. When I told Karen what happened, she said, "Maybe that's what it wanted to hear." Of course, it did!

What Karen knew of my grandmother's craft is questionable. Most of it, she "gathered from the astral." She kept a lot of information from me, always telling me that the time wasn't right or she wasn't prepared to tell me yet or I wasn't prepared to hear it yet. So many questions I asked were answered with an evasion or were addressed sideways. She skewed her responses in such a way that they upheld at least one of the principles Karen wanted me to follow. If I dared to come up with my own conclusions, I found myself contradicted, my viewpoint revised. Eventually, because of all Karen didn't say, and certainly because of all she *did* say, I began to doubt my instincts and ability to reason and to feel guilty or anxious if I defended them – as if the core of my being were unreliable. The cumulative effect of Karen's efforts was total.

The mind-twisting occurred in a setting and by a means that seemed on the surface so benign, so congenial. A typical evening would involve my arriving at her apartment late afternoon or early evening. Karen would just be finishing up feeding her husband and cleaning up the kitchen. Dinner for them was ALWAYS canned soup and a sandwich on whole wheat bread. Then jasmine tea, steeped just exactly so. Then we would sit at her counter, for hours (until one or two in the morning most times), and smoke cigarettes and drink terrible, cheap, pink wine from brandy glasses, no less. But from the moment I entered the apartment, however, something in me was put into suspension.

How absurd it seems now, the ritual of it, the wrongness of the glassware and setting. But I repeated the visits countless times, leaving Gavin at home, not even thinking of him until one day, he sadly asked me if I was going to leave him alone again. I never even asked him what he did to amuse himself when I was gone. Karen had that kind of pull on me, so intense, I'm not sure I thought of anything else. It defied logic. I left my home and cats and husband at least once a week to spend hours with this proselytizer. She had me spellbound, perhaps literally so.

As soon as I came in the door, Karen would present me with a question or a topic to consider. Sometimes, it would be an anecdote from a book or someone else's biography. Sometimes, she would ask me what's on my mind, and then press me with "That's not really all you want to know ...", and weave the evening from there. Sometime after midnight, I would feel a little out of body, and not even sure of what the moral of the evening's story had been. How I made it home those 25 miles on the highway in the dark so many times, I don't know. Once, I did wreck, in winter, flying off the road because of black ice, right into a ditch, concluding the life of one car. It was all absurd. I ignored my housework and homework and even my own safety for these "lessons." And so, her worldview became mine.

We also met in restaurants, where, without fail, Karen would change tables sometimes more than once because of the light or the temperature or something. I pitied the poor server who had to deal with us. A small pot of coffee AND a small pot of hot water – and there had better not be an extra charge! The amount of salad dressing had to be exactly right, with the lettuce properly drained of water. Spoons had better not be bent. Honestly!

But oddly enough, Karen found a way to enchant a few of the wait staff. She would ask for their birthdates and offer astrological advice. Or she would grab their hands and do an impromptu reading of their palms. Sometimes, she would turn on them with a certain look of mischief and "predict" a love affair or some small life success, and full of gratitude, they would bring her anything she wanted. But then, they were always young and/or mostly uneducated, often broken in some way or another. She has a sense for the weakness. She knew how to mesmerize, mesmerize me too, clearly.

Meeting in restaurants was always uncomfortable, due to Karen's shenanigans and due to my own problems. Gavin and I didn't have money for me to go out to eat, but Karen insisted I meet her at the restaurant (not come later), and then, of course, pay my way. I also didn't like restaurant food, especially at the inexpensive places we patronized, and was not happy with the effects on my body, but I was a captive, a prisoner. How foolish I feel now. On top of that, there were some evenings when the voyage to the restaurant was preceded by errands, impossibly awkward or tedious errands.

Once, the errand was to take her husband to get a haircut, during which she told me to wait in the car. AND I DID! For over two hours, because, well, who knows what conversation she started with the barber? I even went into a nearby bar and had a couple of shots and still had to wait a long while after getting back into the car. She showed no sign of recognizing my fury when she returned.

Now and then, though, things occurred that just made no sense at all, but I was helpless in the face of them. In retrospect, an awful lot seems inexplicable, both from the perspective of her asking as from mine of cooperating. The more Karen aged, the stranger and more frustrating things became. I was not equipped to comprehend or cope. I barely even allowed myself to question her. When Karen's behaviors contradicted either common sense or the worldview she counseled, I didn't know what to do. Denial or compliance seemed the best options, so those were the ones I chose. There were times, however, when I had to fight back or come up with some sort of compromise.

Most of the troubling circumstances (I can recall dozens and dozens!) were simply ridiculous, and sometimes, I had to put my foot down. Sometimes, the concerns were simply inane, and sometimes, Karen was downright psychotic. Eventually, I believe, something inside of her turned against her, and the turn-around caused the bizarre behaviors to intensify. They all, however, began when she no longer went to Hawaii for the winters. Something happened to her on her last trip into the Pacific, but I'll never know what.

Among the ridiculous issues was a white brocade sofa. She had purchased it cheaply and had it delivered to my and Gavin's house. We put it in the basement. The storage was supposed to be temporary, just until Karen could find another apartment. Two years later, it was still in the basement, in our way, and causing fights between me and Gavin. Weekend after weekend, Karen would say we could deliver it to this place or that place, but then call at the last minute (usually after we had secured a truck to haul it in) to cancel the delivery. Finally, I had to threaten to give it to the Salvation Army, telling her it was already on the truck. That afternoon, she selected a young couple at a restaurant and somehow sweet-talked them into storing it for her. She got these complete strangers to take it! Every now and then, I wonder what ever became of that damned thing, for Karen never did find a new apartment.

Karen also expected *me* to talk strangers into doing favors for me. When I divorced Gavin the first time and had to move all my books out of his house. I was a student at the university at that time, and so Karen's solution to the dilemma was for me to convince a janitor at the school to find a location to store them for me. Surely, he would be interested in doing something charitable to earn some good karma. It would certainly make him feel good to help me, so I would be doing *him* a favor by allowing him to help me. I'm still not sure in what universe such a plan might have worked. Karen was furious with me for rejecting her suggestion, but in this case, making her angry was less taxing than trying to implement her idea. Refusing to comply with Karen always made fear there would be some terrible repercussions even when I knew I was right.

So, many times, I just did what she said. That included several times talking Gavin into taking time off work to drive her car from one town to the next (and once, she changed her mind, after we arrived at her doorstep to do the chauffeuring, costing Gavin the entire day's wages for nothing). Without any regard for his responsibility to his job or the pay he was losing, she told him to come back the next day instead, as if her were her servant or slave. She was stunned when he said he could not do it.

Once, when I planned a day with a new friend, and made the mistake of telling her about it, Karen called my home and convinced Gavin to tell her where I was and called the phone number I had left him to say she was having a heart attack. I told her to call an ambulance, but no, only I could save her. So I had to leave the woman with whom I was trying to become friends. (I never had a chance to reconnect)

When I got to Karen's apartment, she was calmly making a sandwich. She did not let me leave the apartment for nearly twelve hours. Each time I tried to go, she began panicking, acting short of breath. Once I finally was allowed to leave, it was four in the morning. I missed work the next day and became extremely ill for two weeks. When I asked her for an explanation, she said nothing, acting instead as if she didn't understand what I was talking about.

As the years went by, Karen really started unraveling, more and more, and then came some monumentally incredible episodes. One time when I went to visit her, she was agitated about her dinner choices. She demanded I take her can of tomato soup back to the store to exchange it for chicken noodle because she changed her mind about what she wanted for dinner. She gave me the can and the receipt and ushered me out the door. Well, I simply went and bought the chicken soup with my own money and left the tomato soup in my car. I was not going to explain the exchange to the customer service at the grocery store.

When she fumed that she hated my new eyeglasses, and I told her I couldn't afford to just replace them again, she said I would just have to find a way to convince the eyeglass place to take back the glasses and make me some new ones. She wouldn't let it go. Opticians had no satisfaction guaranteed policy back then, and the company didn't care much about karma, so to avoid any more discussion about the glasses, I had to wear my old out-of-prescription pair around her. She wouldn't let up otherwise. My wonderful soft gray wool pants somehow offended her as well – so I never wore them again. There was nothing I could do, however, when she bemoaned the fact that my facial features looked so very Eastern European. Why couldn't I look more American? I had no answer.

Some of the things Karen did were more than petty or mean, bordering on cruel. For instance, during my short stint in the Southwest, for instance, I made two purchases that ruffled her feathers for some reason. They were a couple of small bottles of amber oil (to wear as perfume) and a string of amethyst beads. I had purchased the amber oil at a small shop whose name I couldn't recall, run by a West African woman whose name I never knew. Karen insisted I find a way for her to buy some of the same oil. This was long before the internet, websites, Google, anything. I told her it was impossible, but she wouldn't let up, so I gave her my two bottles. I know for a fact she never used the oil herself. The bottles just sat on her dresser until, I guess, she was moved out of that apartment.

My amethyst beads, she wanted to buy off me, for the price I'd paid at a gem fair because she said that I was in no position financially to own a luxury like those beads, and since I needed the money to live, she would be doing me a favor by buying them. When I was better situated in the world, I could buy new ones. I absolutely refused. I was so hurt. What she was essentially saying was that I wasn't worthy of those beads, that I hadn't earned the right to wear something so beautiful. I loved those beads. The fifty dollars they had cost me would have made no difference in my finances. I did not let her have them. My solution was to pack them away, hide them, never wear them, except for during one spell. She was entitled to them, she thought, and in her opinion, I was not.

Understanding Evil: My Soul Contract

I was also supposed to split up my beloved three Siamese cats. Why should I be so selfish to keep all three of them? Wouldn't I want someone else to enjoy them too? I should keep one and share the joy of the two remaining cats with other people. My gut still wrenches at the thought that to please her, Karen was asking me to experience the most terrible grief and loss, for no reason but to "build my character." These three cats were also so attached to each other that to separate them would be a cruelty beyond measure. I remember how I cried and cried, begging her not to push the issue. I would keep my cats: I loved my cats. Well, then, apparently I was not ready to be an advanced soul yet. So be it.

This was her theme: I was just not perfected enough to be let in on the secrets of the universe. More evidence of my primitiveness, according to Karen, was that I insisted on sleeping under a heavy blanket. An evolved soul should just sleep under a light sheet (and turn the heat up!) as she so informed me one night when she talked me into staying with her. I never once realized that she was mentally ill until long after I separated from her. I just let the dramas take their toll on me, one after another.

One summer night, when she insisted I come stay with her (at the time, I was living more than sixty miles away), I had something come up and tried to call her to say I couldn't make it. She didn't answer the phone. I tried for three hours. Finally, I cancelled everything and drove up to her apartment anyway. Traffic was horrendous, for a major football game just let out. There were no cellphones yet. I was pretty late when I knocked on her door. In those days, I wore a lot of black. Nothing too Goth, but black. When Karen opened the door that evening, she took one look at me and said, "You look like a witch. You can't stay here." AND SHE CLOSED THE DOOR! I had no choice but to drive the sixty miles back home, exhausted and hungry and quite honestly devastated.

The next day she called to ask me if I were perhaps possessed by some strange entity.

One birthday, she promised to call to tell me with a time to meet her at a local restaurant. I waited and waited. Again, when I called her, there was no answer. Other people invited me here and there, but I told them, no, I was waiting for her to call. Finally, I reached her. Oh, she said, she was going to have to reschedule. It was late afternoon by then, and I ended up alone on my birthday. So I drove out to the abandoned old wheat farm where I conducted my outdoor rituals, and received an interesting sort of gift from the land. Bones. Bleached white bones – probably from a horse – that had somehow appeared in the two weeks since I had been out there last. I bunched up my skirt to make a makeshift sack and filled it with bones! I kept them for several years before returning them to the field. Karen never apologized.

The incidents fester in my memory still. So many. So outrageous. When my phone was turned off (when the tree fell through my house and I had to move) because I couldn't pay (these were pre cell phone days) the accumulated long distance calls – all of which were to her – I asked for a loan. She said no because she thought I needed to learn to live more frugally. When I made a little medicine bag just for the novelty of it, I included a small unopened pinecone as a symbol of ideas not yet manifested. Karen saw the bag, grabbed it, felt the pinecone inside, and said, with a nasty condescending tone, "I hope his penis is bigger than that." I was absolutely speechless. I am still speechless.

These out-of-the-blue blows to my psyche punctuated the generally benign interactions I had with Karen. We had had such wonderful, literary, philosophical talks. They meant so much to me. I needed the love she professed to have for me. I needed her. So when these events occurred, I was devastated. After a while, I became wary, anxious, confused. I was torn between wanting to please her, to be worthy of further learning and starting to distrust her and myself. A few times, though, I did some extreme things to appease her.

In the very first few years of her time with me, shortly after my grandmother's death, Karen made me give up my stuffed animals (some years before trying to get me to give up my cats). That, on the surface, doesn't sound like much, but in my world, it was extremely significant. The stuffed animals were shells for entities I had befriended and who were staying with me as allies, as guests, as familiars, as I'm-not-sure-what-else to call them. I loved them. In my loneliness and pain, they were my companions. But Karen insisted that in order to become a higher being, I couldn't engage in that kind of low magick. She couldn't teach me anything if I persisted in associating with entities of that sort.

So, I packed them in plastic bags and gave them away, every last one of them, as I couldn't be made to decide which one to keep – couldn't make that decision. They were like children. I could not live with keeping one or two and losing the rest, so they all had to go. The mind crunch would have been too much for me. Then, with them all gone, I was suddenly plunged into a psychic silence. But I had a dream that first night.

In the dream, I was under an open night sky, a magnificent dark blue. I was walking between two rows of tall, white-haired people in blue robes. When I reached the end, one of them stepped forward and placed something in my hand, saying I had finally passed the test. I clutched it tightly, and when I awoke, I found my hand clasping the gold/diamond chip cross I was wearing (a gift from my mother).

Karen was so proud of me. She said the people were the Ascended Masters (how that still creeps me out!), and I had earned their approval by taking the steps I had. But I felt something was very wrong. I had been persuaded to do something against my nature, to give up what amounted to my family, in a way, for the sake of a promise of truth, of light. These beings were ready for me to join them, but I didn't know them. How could I be sure they were benign? I don't like the idea of auditioning for a secret audience.

Later, when I was in graduate school, she tried to make me give up Francis. (See essay "Believe Me") Francis was a fellow graduate student at the university, a poet philosopher, a self-proclaimed mystic. Mostly, he was the, I mean THE, catalyst for the greatest transformations of my identity and destiny. I met him in literature class, connected to him through poetry, remembered him from a past life (when he was the Aztec priest who cut my heart out on the stone altar), and was absolutely entranced. And afraid, afraid of … it's complicated. But I voiced my fear to Karen, and she offered to help; in fact, she insisted on doing a spell to make sure I could resist him, to make sure that he had no hold on me anymore. I didn't even have a chance to think about it.

What happened next happened so fast I couldn't imprint it fully in my memory. In a flurry, she collected a few things from here and there in her house, and told me to go into the bathroom with her "special" scissors to clip a lock of my pubic hair to use in the spell. I was stunned, hesitant, yet unable to resist her sudden enthusiasm and urgency. So, with the parcel of items assembled, she shooed me out of the house so she could do her spell – by herself, not with me. I left, suddenly pitched out the door.

A few days later, I couldn't help feeling uneasy. What did she do? So, I called Karen and tried to talk about my disquiet. I wanted to know exactly what the spell was designed to accomplish. She wouldn't tell me. If I didn't trust her, then it didn't matter, she said, and she was just too hurt to talk about it further. She became agitated, insulted, defensive. Well, if that's how I felt, then on my next visit, she would give me everything she used in the spell. That next encounter was very uncomfortable, and I did skip a couple of visits with her after that. Did she give me all the materials? I don't know. She would not tell me that either.

Did she have an effect on Francis? Or was the spell designed to have an effect on me? I believe the answers are yes and yes, but the particulars aren't exactly clear. Francis did complete his "cosmic purpose" in my life, however, much later, and perhaps the totality of that purpose was equally benign and malignant. Without him, though, I might never have given the proverbial Wheel of Destiny a spin when I did. My remarriage to Gavin, as much as we tried to patch it up after all our troubles, ended absolutely because of Francis. Not because of the physical reality of the one afternoon I spent in bed with Francis (Gavin never learned of it), but because of the alchemical metamorphosis that occurred in me as a result of it. A transformation began at a soul level; something was activated; and the trappings of this plane, this incarnation, started to fall away. And a few years later, during the few months I was in the desert Southwest, it was Francis who confirmed the fateful choice I made there.

My temporary move to the desert Southwest provided me circumstances that ended my continuance on the path Karen had set for me. After fifteen years, after all of her promises that her way would protect me from my grandmother's demon and lead me to enlightenment, after all the hours and hours of indoctrination, all it took was one small event to bring it all down. In the first place, she did not let me move to the desert when I was ready to go, in the middle of the summer when I would still be able to find a part-time teaching job. She made me wait till November, or at least by then, I had finally had enough of being in limbo, and stopped listening to the "something's going to happen" if I go now warnings, and left.

My mother also went with me to make sure I ended up in a place she approved of – and without roommates who would "take advantage of me." The result was a lease I had to break almost immediately because I was never going to be able to afford the place, not to mention all the issues I found with it. The extra move cost me all the money I had set aside. Getting a job was imperative.

Unable to find work as a teacher, I took work as an art model (the best decision of my life at that time), which didn't pay a lot, but at least kept me from going completely under. But it also left me a lot of time and put me in places that allowed assorted dangerous people to find me. There in the Southwest, I met a beautiful young vampire. Even knowing how dangerous he was, and perhaps *because* of how dangerous he was, I couldn't stay away. True to his nature, he drained my life energy to such an extent that I was forced to take it back from him by the same means (which I'm not going to explain here, as I do not want to promote any misconceptions about vampirism). He had simultaneously murdered and awakened something in me. When I took back from the vampire what he took from me, I was simply reactivating an expertise I had had in another life.

That night, oddly enough (the night of my retrieving my energy), Karen called me (she actually sprang for the long distance call!) to say I was in danger and not to do whatever it was I was doing. It was already done, though, and I told her so. "Oh, no," she kept saying, "Oh, no." Then I hung up. It would be weeks before I talked to her again. But I had learned something significant, something powerful about my own being, the boundaries of my body and my identity and my force of will. It was that knowledge, I believe, that she didn't want me to have. It was one bite of the forbidden fruit.

Understanding Evil: My Soul Contract

The event that triggered the entire overthrow of my beliefs happened a few weeks afterward. In the short time I was in that desert city, I found myself pursued by predators of all kinds. My solution (and in fact the main reason I was compelled to move there to begin with) was the old Spanish mission about fourteen miles from my apartment. In another life, I had been there. My soul's attachment to it was profound. Twice a week, I would drive down to it, go in and sit in the alcove devoted to Mary. Karen claimed to know the mission and was so very happy that I was being called by the wonderful energy there.

Once, after a terrible episode with one of the men I had attracted and an unshakable feeling of being pursued, I went to seek my usual refuge at the mission. Up at the front altar, before the large central crucifix, I stood there pleading with the divinities that are supposed to reside in such a place or that could be reached from such a place, to help me. Nothing. Nothing spoke to me. Nothing answered me. But when I turned around, I saw the green-eyed demon, my grandmother's demon, coming for me, with the green glow in its eyes bright and cold. It floated in over the pews till it hung in the air right before me, its face close to mine.

My entire body went cold. I looked around to see if anyone else could see it. None of the people lighting candles or praying paid any attention to me. I looked at the sculptures of Jesus, Mary, the saint of that particular mission. Nothing. No more light. No more love. Not a one of them, not one prayer of mine, not any of this was going to help me. Ever. I turned back to the demon and told it I was done with this charade. No more trying to be what I wasn't and couldn't be. No more compulsory piety to please Karen. The entire paradigm was useless. It was over. And that was it. Whatever Christianity Karen had tried to brainwash me with dissolved like the demon hovering before my eyes, who winked and vanished.

After a few more catastrophes, I couldn't stay in that beautiful desert any longer and had to move back to where I'd begun. But first, I had to make sure I wasn't alone until my departure, so I picked up a young man who by chance was on the hunt for new recruits to some distant coven and quizzed him for all he knew. I decided to learn witchcraft to fight witchcraft. The terms for things. The customary practices. All of that. I decided to learn to work *with* demons and other entities in order to defeat demons and other entities. The night I made the decision, I received a phone call from Francis. How he got my phone number, I do not know. I had not sent it to him. Still, he called me. The conversation was very brief. I told him about my intentions, and he said, "Welcome home" and hung up. A new journey had begun for me.

My first meeting with Karen after I returned was awkward. I was no longer the same little acolyte who had left months earlier. Over the next few years, she didn't stop, however, trying to re-establish my dependency on her. We argued vehemently over issues both small and large. Her sanity was becoming more and more questionable. She became jealous, envious, petty, and mean. When I took up with Robin, who would become my second husband, she came entirely unglued. He terrified her. She refused to be in the same room with him. The irony!

What the final transgression was, I do not remember, but I broke the connection once and for all with a spell. In it, I smashed into pieces a small ceramic candy dish inscribed with the Lord's Prayer that she had sent me during the first year of my first marriage, right around the time of my disposing of my stuffed animals. The night before it arrived, I had woken up saying that prayer in my sleep. The next day, the dish arrived in the mail. Clearly, it had been charged with her intentions. In a very forceful separation spell, I shattered it into smithereens.

On the way home from the field where I conducted the separation spell, some wild and angry entity chased me in my car for a good long while. During the spell, I wore that string of amethysts as protection for myself, and they did their job, but their dark purple clarity absorbed the counterattack. They turned milky. It has taken more than two decades for the white spots to mostly clear up. Not all of them, but most.

Four days later, Karen fell, breaking her hip. She never came out of the nursing home again, and she refused to speak to me when I called. Despite the love she purported all those years to feel for me, because the puppet strings wouldn't make me dance anymore, she first became hostile, then ended all communication. And that was that. Except for the lingering effects of the Francis spell she did and the effects of the years and years of brainwashing. Except for those matters.

I realize now that Karen had truly mesmerized me. I didn't have a chance to assert myself. Upon each entry into her apartment, something happened to me – a trigger? If there was one, it was activated perhaps over two hundred times. Even now, I can recall the smell of her apartment, the way either the end of daylight or streetlight shone in the kitchen window, the sound of the parking lot traffic below. I still feel my entrance into a world that didn't feel like mine, didn't feel like a place I belonged. I would give anything to go back to retrieve all those hours, but I can't. I gave them to her foolishly.

Karen never gave me what I needed most. A way to deal with my mother. An effective way to deal with the demons. A way to understand the real nature of my power. No, what she did instead was distract me for years and years from a path I should have been on. She compounded the psychological damage my mother caused me. But where my mother made me terrified to say yes to ventures, people, interests (because she would destroy them), Karen made me terrified to say no to requests that were made of me, no matter how absurd or troublesome to me. My duty as a servant to the divine, she had me convinced, demanded that I accommodate others' needs. If I said no, I was being selfish, self-centered, uncharitable, and I was dismissing an opportunity for soul development. It was through this mechanism that Karen controlled me.

A good number of my neuroses can be traced right back to Karen's influence, deliberate or not. Crazy begets crazy. How does one distinguish crazy from uncanny, insane from powerful? Sometimes, they go hand in hand. Sometimes, one is the price for the other. Karen was probably in her late sixties when I met her (she never told me exactly), but hardly suffering any diminished capacity then. Slowly, however, age and the cumulative effect of her way of living caught up with her. The fact that she reached a tipping point during the years she was in my life was a lucky break. Good timing. If she had been fully functioning, I might not have been able to break her hold on me.

There are others like her out there, ready to snap up the unwitting. Around the time I met Robin, another of her type showed up in my life, Fredrico, a brujo actually, one also with an agenda for turning me into a protégé of his, with the promise that I could lead others even though I said I was not interested. Karen and Fredrico met face to face, once, each trying his/her tricks of dominance on the other. At the time, I was a bit oblivious, but in retrospect, I have to say, it was pretty amusing. As if I were a prize they were battling over. In the end, neither won.

Some years later, Fredrico and I would battle each other. He would break into my house, leave tiny magickally charged spell items that manifested little goblin type beings in my home. Fredrico, too, it is worth noting, informed me that he and I had known one another in the other world. Why do they always do that? It's a universal pickup line for psychics, I guess.

Karen truly believed she was engaging in a sacred duty, at least

Understanding Evil: My Soul Contract

I think she did, at least that's what she convinced herself she was doing, or that was simply the propaganda she chose to disseminate. From her point of view, she was engaging in a sacred duty – to bring me around to a particular way of thinking. People who proselytize are willing to abandon reason and loyalty for their faith, and certainly, they do not respect other people's boundaries.

Karen took control of my life. She took to her grave a portion of my potential that I will never regain. And as much as I would like to blame a demon for this enormous scar on my soul, I cannot. The evil was human, assembled out of lunacy and power lust, the ultimate colonization of souls. Nearly twenty years after her death, I am still realizing my liberation from her.

When I finally had my own home with an enormous and private backyard, I created a sacred space in its center, a circle for ritual. One Samhain, I invited the Dead I had known into the circle, to live with me for a year and speak their peace. Spirits from both sides of my family showed up plus a couple of extras, but the place I had "set" for Karen remained untouched. All of the others partook of the offerings I laid out for them, but she wouldn't face me, wouldn't grace me with her presence. If her belief system were correct, she had to have been aware of what she had done, as once out of the body, the soul is allowed a much more enlightened perspective from which to review one's life. She didn't want to show herself. If I concentrate on the world beyond this one, I can sense her anger with me, or maybe I am still recycling Karen's programming in my mind. No. She is still furious with me.

It makes me sad that Karen died alone in the nursing home. Her husband preceded her in death by four years, but his mind had vacated long before then. She never had children of her own due to an early hysterectomy, and no one in her family came out from the Midwest to be with her. I would have been happy to visit her, but she didn't want me anymore. I didn't turn out to be what she thought I should be. I am certain that if she and I were in contact at the close of her life, I would have been shanghaied into servitude as her nursemaid, caretaker, servant. Her vampire soul would have drained mine of all light. How blatantly, unforgivably ironic!

She decided, in the end, that *I* was irredeemably evil and scary. I just wouldn't conform. My insistence on my sovereignty made me unforgivable in her estimation. She died disappointed in me, feeling I betrayed her, thinking of me as a dangerous being. Never once did she trust that my character was and remains incorruptible – my sense of honor and fairness and mercy were not ever negotiable elements. I did not/do not need to be subjugated to keep me from being a danger to innocent people. But she lived by the same madness that many evangelicals do – the belief that those who do not "buy in" are damned and that associating with the damned risks one's own soul. She was incapable of seeing me in any way other than through her "saved" or "not saved" lens.

How I wish someone would have warned me when I was very young about the Mephistophelian type of person. The inevitable bargain one makes with him/her is for the benefit of Mephistopheles only; the price is immeasurably high; and the results are false or never manifest at all. The pursuit wastes time and focus, money and energy, and relationships with other people. When people immediately claim to have had a past life connection or divine mission, the temptation begins. When they make promises of wisdom or reward, but keep putting off on the delivery until another time, until one has proven oneself (aka jumped through hoops), the spin begins. Sometimes, they have no wisdom to offer. Most of the time.

The guru type will insist that there is only one way to enlightenment:

his/her way. That path, also, may not remain consistent. One time, it's this one, the next, another. He/she may recite truths from ancient texts or rituals or philosophies. Many of these will turn up as general knowledge to a person well-read in the field. He/she will claim connection to organizations or great personages. There may or may not be proof, though, of those associations. The guru type will always make sure the novice knows he/she still has a long way to progress and must, therefore, keep returning and returning for more. Karen was no better than that preacher who screamed at me for two hours about how I was going to Hell if I didn't believe in Jesus. She was just more subtle.

What I know now is there is no *one* path. There may not be a path at all. Hunting for the truth is a lone endeavor. Those who place themselves in between the seeker and the prize (whatever it is) do a great disservice to the seeker. It would have been better for me to have spent all the hours I spent with Karen reading instead. Reading anything and everything about all those topics we discussed would have given me all the necessary data from which I could have assembled my own theories.

The information wouldn't have cost me anything and I could have analyzed it, evaluated it, and then synthesized it in countless ways if one or another theory didn't work out. No one author could possibly provide THE ANSWER. But many authors might provide an *idea*. That's as good as it gets. I wish I had chosen to educate myself then, not just later. What terrible heartache I might have spared myself.

I don't know why I attract people who want to take me apart and remake me. There was yet another woman in my life who had a similar effect on my self-image, deep and profound and as unconsciously inflicted as Karen's. In my tenured teaching job, which I began in my mid-forties, my department chair shared a lot of Karen's behaviors. She was only ten years my senior, instead of forty. I came into Dorothy's life exactly as her daughter was leaving for college. I'm not sure she ever realized that transferring the controls she assumed over her daughter to me was not appropriate, any more than Karen ever realized that stepping into my spiritual development was not her right or business.

Dorothy would regularly put me into unbelievable predicaments to convince me to do things that make no sense or that seriously violated my aesthetics. She never respected my boundaries. Whatever was mine was public property, from coffee mugs and tissue boxes to curriculum and manuscripts of my own writing. She had severe and completely arbitrary opinions about what I should wear (nothing to do with the dress code of the college), and once came after me with a pair of scissors just like Karen did in order to trim my long hair.

There was also the issue of evangelism, in the case of my supervisor, not for religion, but against it. Similarly, when the state changed academic standards (and I disagreed with them), she was more concerned that I espoused the right point of view instead of just trusting me to be competent on my own. She had a seven- year influence on me, just under half the time Karen did. Karen damaged my ability to stand on my own in so many ways. Dorothy damaged my ability to ever come into my own as a professional in the college. She never allowed me to function independently of her. She always made sure that I knew – and that others knew – that I was too weird to present the right image, that I didn't say things with the right "polish." Intellectually, I know this is not true, but emotionally, I can't get past it. Harm was done. I will forever be distrusting of women who assume authority over me, who think of me as a project.

It's really hard not to get caught up in someone else's crazy. It is especially hard when he/she is in a position of power. Because I was older and had read so much, I was a little bit more able to resist Dorothy's influence than Karen's, though not completely. And while Karen was bipolar, and therefore would sometimes "attack" for no reason and without warning, Dorothy would do the same because she was an alcoholic. With both of them, it seemed that there were two different personalities that would suddenly switch places. The two women were so similar I called my supervisor by Karen's name on more than one occasion. But thankfully, Svengali, Dorothy was not.

    I wasted so much time on Karen. I also spent my trust on her. She promised to teach me magick, but never actually knew enough herself to teach me, although she sure thought she did. That's the thing I wish I had known. Just because someone says he/she is an expert on something doesn't make him/her an expert. Those who boast don't usually live up to their self-promotion. I wish I would have made her prove herself instead of blindly believing in her. Had I done so, I might not still feel so cheated, so ashamed. Still.

Promise Me

Sometimes non-witch families attract demons or may in fact create them, most likely accidentally, but demons nonetheless. The families' dynamics provide the mechanism for the entities to manifest, and at least one member will serve as a vessel. For me, the experience involved Robin, my second husband, and the legacy that spawned him. The red-eyed demon was the manifestation of a colonizer's evil. A colonizer provides the perfect energies to create or attract a demon. Colonization is a takeover, whether it involves countries, academic territories, ideologies, or marriages and families.

A colonizer is the kind of person who feels entitled to and therefore lays claim to the resources of others. On an anthropological level, he/she is also the type who imposes his/her own culture on the subjugated one, who will erase any presence of the original. On a personal level, he/she will break those in his/her vicinity utterly and without remorse, will reprogram his/her victim(s) according to an arbitrary and, for the colonizer, an expedient set of "truths." A colonizer can be the abuser of whole peoples, but for most, the process begins at home.

It was Daniel, the father of my second husband, who was the colonizer, and who was responsible for the demon that destroyed me. He was a colonizer on both a large and small scale. I met Daniel shortly after my return from my nearly disastrous sojourn to the desert Southwest. I had thought about going back to school for a PhD in something related to theology, an academic study. Daniel was a professor of religious philosophies at a good university, one that had the kind of program I was looking for. So I visited the department and was directed to his office.

When I went to talk to him, however, I was not prepared for how dismissive and condescending he was. I said I wanted to learn about what is true and what is not, and about evil and how the religions of the world dealt with it, and he simply blasted me: "They don't say anything about evil. There's no such thing as truth. That's juvenile. You'd be wasting your time and mine." So I gave up on the idea of another post-graduate degree and left. Some months later, I took a job at a different university, and there, I met his son, Robin, and in the ensuing years learned something about evil that, indeed, I would not have learned from studying religions in a classroom or library.

Robin didn't start out as a vessel for the red-eyed demon. At first, he was something else, an otherworldly being, yes, but not yet a demon. In fact, he passionately struggled against the demon that authored Daniel's legacy for as long as he could. I met Robin at a literary symposium at the university where I taught. He was a student, an undergrad, not *my* student, but from another department. Robin was nine years younger than I. He was beautiful in a supernatural way, which for me, was extremely unfortunate because, for all sorts of reasons, mundane and abstract, I have always found that humans were never as appealing as non-humans. One look at Robin, and I was doomed. He was also a bit of a psychopath with no sense of right and wrong and no concern at all for trying to appear as if he had such a sense.

Robin's first conversation with me was about how his father was making him go to counseling. A year earlier, Daniel had an affair with one of *his* grad students and thus brought an end to his marriage with Janet, Robin's mother. Robin was furious with Daniel for hurting his mother. "A marriage is forever!" Robin said vehemently. The counseling was intended to make Robin more accepting of the situation, convince him to get over his anger. I didn't know it then, but sure do now, that sending dissenters in for reprogramming is what Daniel did regularly. The "expert" was supposed to adjust Robin's thoughts according to an acceptable script. Robin was fuming over the presumptuousness behind that idea as well. I found his intensity fascinating.

Besides the appeal of his beauty and charm, Robin was familiar to me. I knew him, recognized him immediately though it took me several months to realize where I'd known him before. The spirit in him, his fay spirit, his unearthly soul, however I could describe it, had followed me into this life for reasons I have only recently figured out. I did not encounter him in the interim between lives (as I did the black-eyed entity), but as a disincarnate entity hovering over and near a trunk (that held ritual implements) in my witch grandmother's basement when I was a child. My grandmother would see him too. "He's waiting for you," she would tell me. He stayed there until I was exactly eight and a half years old, and then, abruptly, he was gone.

Eight and a half years is exactly how much younger Robin was than I. When I was that age is exactly the time my family completed the plans to move out west toward to the western edge of the Great Plains. That exact time frame is when Robin's mother knew the pregnancy would hold (after more than one miscarriage). Then, decades later, there he was, wild and dramatic and completely uninhibited. Robin had never for even one moment contemplated leading a conventional life. He was perfect for me, as by the time I met him, I had made the same choice. But in the end, one of us had to be viable in the real world. It would not be him.

My nine years with Robin can be divided into those before he "died" and those after he "died." Robin was a Type I diabetic since toddlerhood. He didn't take care of it or himself. As soon as I came into his life, I began going with him to his doctor visits and learned a great deal about how to deal with diabetes and a diabetic. In the time I knew Robin, most of his diabetic episodes were due to sudden and extreme blood sugar lows. In the beginning, however, they were infrequent, and we partied as if there were no tomorrow. We drank; we smoked pot; we nearly annihilated ourselves making love, often violently and with a great deal of drama. It was the most hedonistic, rich, indulgent, most unrestricted time of my entire life. It was a long, complex, extravagant, delusional feast of the senses.

To maintain it, I supported Robin. Robin would not work, and certainly not while he was a student. He made his money selling pot. He would take the rent money his father provided him, invest it in a large purchase, which he would then break down into carefully weighed snack baggies and sell to most all of his fellow students in the theatre department. To assure his success in school, I wrote papers for him, read and summarized books for him, and kept him fed. I cleaned his apartment pre- and post- parties. I paid for our movie outings and whatever else we did. When Robin lost his entire rent investment because his wholesaler died, ironically, of alcohol poisoning before delivering the large bag of greens, I paid the rent. He never thanked me; it never occurred to him.

Robin was a celebrity, of sorts, on the campus, though. The parties at his apartment were legendary. His short stories earned him recognition as a horror writer of some promise. But his masterpiece in those years was one of his plays. It became the central production for the department that year. The play was about a young woman trying to individuate, self-actualize, against the pressures of a society that values money instead of people, that demanded conformity to all sorts of ridiculous demands. It encapsulated all the arguments Robin had had over the years with his father. It was about a young person saying, "Please, value me for who I am!" It was about railing against the masks we are all made to wear.

The night before the play opened, Robin became extremely ill. It was, he said, as if he were being punished for trying to deliver his message. Flus and other such illness that a normal person can survive could kill a brittle Type I diabetic. With the loss of consciousness, the other symptoms (diarrhea, vomiting, dehydration) became untreatable. I carried him to the car and drove him to the hospital. He recovered enough to sit zombie-like watching the opening night performance on the stage.

The play was the summary of the entire conflict that Robin would ultimately lose in his life. It's not that he ever conformed; instead, he absolutely refused to do so. But he was never able to succeed in his nonconformity (was never able to be the successful filmmaker or writer he aspired to), and because he was unable to become viable in the real world, he would over and over have to submit to the stipulations society or his father imposed on him and that he found loathsome in order to survive. He didn't have the discipline or stamina to fight is way out of dependence. Therefore, he psychologically remained a furious, self-destructive teenager.

The dissolution began when Robin graduated from college, for then, Daniel decided to end his "support" of his son as if he could just say to the damaged Robin, "OK, you're on your own now." He and Robin had always had a volatile relationship, but at this time, it exploded. On the phone with his father, Robin screamed and shouted, punched a wall (cracking a couple of knuckles), declaring that he would never get a job, that life shouldn't be about working; it should be about being happy. No, he would not work. He would steal, beg, and beat whatever he needed out of everyone who had it. He would have done exactly that. His rages throughout his entire life overruled any sense of self-preservation or potential legal consequence.

If Daniel was not going to rescue his son, then I had to. There was nothing in my codependent little brain to tell me otherwise. So,

Understanding Evil: My Soul Contract

Robin became my responsibility, and I took him on as much to save him from himself and from Daniel as to keep him near me, to make myself indispensable to him. I felt that if something were to separate me from him, I would stop breathing, shrivel and die. It was unthinkable. My fear blinded me to the beginnings of the horror story. I knew he was beyond redemption, yet I lived in a visceral symbiosis with Robin, fearful that my life would end if I lost him. He would in the next few years cost me everything I owned and my identity as well.

It is hard to explain why I allowed this situation to occur. On one level, I can say that I was predisposed to Stockholm Syndrome because of my mother. On another level, I can say that there was a charm to Robin, an exciting amorality, a fearlessness, a stage presence that was beyond powerful. The later, however, could be due to the former. I don't know. My death wish can also not be discounted as motivating factor – conscious or unconscious.

There was also something else – Robin's non-humanness had a similar feel to the demon from my family, an entity I was preset to desire long before I could even walk. (See essay "Serve Only Me") The truth is most likely "all of the above," as that is the nature of the universe – overlapping Venn diagrams, "as above, so below," and all of that. There are many ways to tell the same story.

So, when the next point in the plot had to take place, with his father's reluctant help (Daniel couldn't stand being embarrassed by his son), Robin moved to a town 45 minutes away. He wanted me to follow. Yes, I had to move too (because, as absurd as it sounds, a giant cottonwood tree fell and destroyed the house I was living in), but I wanted to stay near my then well-paying job. We fought and fought. Finally, he bullied (really truly bullied) another friend of his into moving in with him as a roommate. I drove up several times a week (leaving my cats behind and by themselves) to be with him. He didn't want to come to me because his "stuff" was in *his* apartment.

Robin took a job touring and managing a theater group for a few weeks, but could not stand being away from me. He would call me collect, drunk and weeping, every night, hanging on for hours – collect! – threatening to kill himself if I hung up. He wouldn't let me hang up and call him back. My phone bill one of those months was my half my paycheck. Then, when he discovered that the owner of the company was broke or a crook or both, and the paychecks all bounced, Robin completely lost it.

Daniel had to rescue him. He made Robin go on a "rehabilitative" program of two jobs, an exercise routine, regular check-ins with either him or with Robin's mother, and counseling. That worked for a while, but Robin became more and more unhappy. The fact that his emotional catastrophe had forced him into an attempt at normal life made him feel defeated. It wouldn't last. And then, he lost his jobs because, one, he was always late and, two, because he ended up nearly comatose, again with a flu.

Before he blacked out, again, in a mess of his own vomit and diarrhea, he called me, weakly saying, "Help me," before dropping the phone. I couldn't reach the roommate. I had no choice but to drive the 35 miles to his place to take care of him. I called the doctor, who gave me some instruction, but in the end, after I cleaned up Robin, cleaned up the kitchen (thinking the illness was due to food poisoning—and it might have been!), bedroom (so much laundry!), and bathroom, I gave up. By then, I thought Robin would have recovered enough to speak to me, to help me help him, but he didn't.

His roommate finally came home, and he and I carried Robin out of the apartment, put him in the back of my car, and dropped him at the hospital. Food poisoning can be lethal to even a healthy person, let alone a brittle diabetic, so I had no choice. From there, I called Daniel and told him it was his turn now. I had been up for 36 hours and couldn't do more.

I missed my classes that day. I called the department secretary after the fact to explain, but everyone was angry with me. Robin himself was a full-time job and had been for some time, interfering with my ability to function as a teacher. My own life, too, was out of control. My father, at that time, had begun his lengthy death of emphysema, and the resulting corrupt family dynamics simply added to my hysteria, alcohol consumption, and extreme behaviors.

Yet, that year, at the university, I organized an entire two-day symposium of about thirty local poets. Robin and I had been arguing and arguing over time I spent working. We fought over his insistence on dropping acid (because afterward I would have to clean up the disaster of his being unable to tend to his diabetes for the hours of the effect of the drug). The argument that broke everything had to do with his choosing to go see a Star Trek movie instead of coming to my performance at the poetry symposium. I broke up with him. But he threatened suicide, came to my apartment, tried to get in the back door, and got himself arrested. Daniel had to rescue him again, getting him out of police custody and into counseling, again.

I tried. I really tried to stay apart from Robin that summer. But he never let up. He called and begged. Then, something happened to me at work. That summer, I had no classes to teach. My contracts were for the school year, and until then, I usually managed to wrangle a couple of summer composition classes to teach. Not this time. So, I took a job as a bartender. A month into that job, I learned that my paychecks all bounced (interesting parallel to Robin's situation), and had to threaten the bar owner with prosecution.

Then the unthinkable happened. The DJ from the bar was sent over to my house to . . . to . . . he said something about showing how much he and the boss cared for me. I don't know what he was thinking, neither my boss nor the DJ, but the big uneducated lunk attempted to rape me, but I fought back. His solution was to hold me down in a chair and masturbate all over me, telling me we would visit me again soon. The police told me to quit my job, but I couldn't, so, for the three weeks before the school year began again, Robin came and sat in the bar during my shift to protect me. The DJ kept his distance, but I was just freaked out. Robin had found an in, and I chose him, the devil I knew, over all the other monsters that had it in for me. For a while, this devil even seemed civil.

Robin then moved back to the town I was in, in fact, into the same apartment building. He enrolled in an art school (to put off student loan payments from his undergrad loans) and commuted to classes every day for exactly one semester, then stopped. Something had gone awry, and he refused to continue. Angry outbursts began to become commonplace again. One night, he went on a rampage, punching fourteen holes in the hallway of the apartment complex, waking up everyone in every apartment, trying to smash his way into my place. When he succeeded in getting in, he attacked me, until the police carted him off to detox, from where I collected him the next day.

Daniel interceded again. With his help, Robin and I moved into an apartment in the city an hour away. I began teaching at one of the community colleges there, and Robin, instead of working, began a venture with a sleaze-ball friend of his, creating CDs of soft porn photos of various young women. The two of them invested money in producing the CDs, setting up a website to market them and so on, but the sleaze-ball friend's checks for his share of the venture bounced. He mollified Robin by providing a supply of cheap pot. Robin forged documents (signatures, totals, dates, whatever needed changing) for the sleaze-ball friend. We somehow managed to pay rent and live, barely, but we did.

Until that move to the city, I kept my relationship with Robin a secret from my family. They thought I had broken up with him for good. In fact, I was told that if I ever saw him again, I would be kicked out of my family, couldn't come to their home, couldn't see my dying father, would never be allowed to retrieve my belongings or be welcome at the holidays. So, whatever I struggled with to keep Robin, I did alone, and did it while maintaining a pretense that I was over him and my life was going well. What a terrible, insane tango my life had become.

Daniel then decided to purchase a home in the city for Robin and me to live in. The agreement was that Robin would do technical and promotional work for Daniel's international music studio (to which he imported people from all over Africa), and the money paid to Robin from the studio Daniel could write off as "advertisement." Robin, then "returned" some of the money to cover his own health insurance and a minimal (around a hundred dollars) amount for his "living" expenses (pot). Daniel wrote the loss of "uncollectable" rent off on taxes. I did not know about the tax fraud going on – Robin essentially helping Daniel launder the money, deducting it twice, as advertising expense and lost rent expense!

My responsibility for our maintenance was everything else: gas, electricity, internet, cable, phone, groceries, trash, water, gasoline, landscaping costs, car repair, clothing, veterinary costs, Robin's diabetic supplies, cigarettes, alcohol, and everything else. I shopped as cheaply as possible. He didn't even help me carry purchases into the house (for that would mean putting on pants and shoes). I did all the housework and cooking and shopping and yardwork, all entirely by myself. We went out to eat only once every two weeks, when I had a paycheck. That was it; that was our life, for four years.

In the first few weeks of that time, my father died. A few months later, Robin and I were involved in a terrifying high-speed car accident on a mountain highway. Robin's car was totaled. We had finally gotten the car road-worthy. That meant getting the "boot" removed from the wheel, which was the result of Robin's deciding he didn't want to go through the bother and expense of getting his vehicle legally registered. Daniel traded us every penny Robin had in savings for a replacement car.

Then, a year after we moved into that house, Robin had an incredible seizure (not like the smaller ones I'd become accustomed to his having) and literally died in my arms. He stopped breathing. After all the trouble I had gone through to keep us intact, he couldn't just be taken like that. All I could think and say was *No, No, No*, and to wherever it was that Robin's soul was slipping away, I threw my own soul in afterward to retrieve it. I connected with something and pulled it back. The body reanimated, and at the hospital, it was determined he had broken two vertebrae in his back during the event, but he would recover. What I didn't realize right away is that I had brought back something other than Robin. Enter the red-eyed demon. It had been around long enough to be familiar with Robin's life history with mine, and was just waiting for a chance to jump in.

The very first thing I chose to do when we finally returned home, after getting Robin settled in bed, was to clean up the blood that had sprayed everywhere in the living room from his biting his lip and tongue during the seizure as there had been no chance to deal with it before we took off after the ambulance. With my spray bottle and rags in hand, I set about the task, then realized that the blood was gone, all of it. Not even one speck remained, not on lampshades that should never have come clean, not on the fabric in the framed artwork which I had assumed was utterly ruined, not on the window shades, on the floor, the sofa cover, the throw cushions, the coffee table; even the *paperwork* on the coffee table was clean! My shirt was covered in blood, but the blood in the living room had vanished in the hours we were at the hospital. I knew then that all was not quite right. The red-eyed demon had made itself welcome.

When I drove to the pharmacy to pick up the pain medications and other prescriptions, I felt my heart simply crack open. I pulled over into a grocery store parking lot and, once stopped in the farthest corner, rolled up the car windows, screamed and cried and screamed, wordless bursts of agony. My Robin was gone. Something still breathed in his body, but he was gone. The grief had nearly split me in two.

Several changes in Robin's physical being confirmed my suspicions. The look in Robin's eyes was completely unfamiliar to me. In those first days, the spirit in his body acted like someone who had just bought a new car and wasn't quite accustomed to driving it yet. Initially, I assumed it was due to the trauma of the event. Yet, clearly, his body was taller than whatever (the demon) was animating him was used to. He looked at his feet with uncertainty, as though they were farther away than he anticipated. He stopped wearing his contacts, as if he didn't remember having them. His hernia magically healed itself. He suddenly developed a pot belly. Somehow, he smelled different. This was not Robin anymore.

The three years that followed nearly drove me mad. As arguments became more insane and more frequent and escalated in intensity, I did everything I could to keep matters under control. Incense, candles, pentacles in the windows, sage, salt, evocations of the elementals, spirit-trapping bottles in the garden, ritual circles of stone and brick in the garden, gargoyles, anything. I paced the house, creating circles of energy.

And I made a doll, the doll of all dolls. I tried to call the original Robin into it (as my grandmother had done with her first born). "Child of my heart," I called the doll. I tried to stop its ability to speak the terrible things he was saying, to do the terrible things he was doing by binding the little totem by stitches and string until the doll was virtually alive, but Robin was no more under control. His rages and craziness were boundless. No doll could ward off the vortex that opened up.

In addition to the arguments, Robin's diabetes directed much of our life, mine anyway. Robin, when he slept, slept like the Dead. If he dropped for the night (or even for a nap), there would be no waking him. No matter what obligations or appointments were scheduled, if he fell asleep, they were pretty much cancelled. No noise, no alarm clock, no shaking, no involuntary bodily functions, no amount of light, no shouting, nothing could rouse him till he came out of the near coma on his own. Except sometimes he didn't come out. In that state of unconsciousness, his blood sugar would often fall below the point where his brain could function enough to bring him around. No self-preservation trigger, no survival mechanism was intact enough to prevent the blackouts.

On a few occasions, when he was awake, I could tell when the blackout was imminent. I would have just moments to get some sugar in him before (a) his eyes rolled back in his head and he dropped like a stone to the floor or (b) he started an argument that would end with either (a) or (c) I would try to get him to accept some sort of sugar, which he would refuse until (a) or (b) or (d) the argument would escalate into a catastrophe of violence. The challenge for me was to notice the smallest changes in his speech patterns, and suddenly myself become "hungry," in order to get a quick fix of food into him. The result for me was, needless to say, weight gain.

However, when Robin had the blood sugar lows while asleep, all I could do was try to trick his body into accepting enough sugar in order to rouse him. The efforts took well over an hour each time, for the attempts had to be subtle, in small bits and/or sips or he would react as though he were being attacked and smash the juice bottle (with the bendy straw) or smack the tube of glucose (or cake icing) across the room and flail at my face. Each time, my own adrenalin spiked dangerously. I risked injury (for he was actually quite strong in these states), risked having to call the paramedics, risked having his episodes keep me from going to work. I was a virtual slave to his condition.

The episodes grew in number from one every couple of months till the time of my eventual flight when they were happening two to three times per week. Every morning was a crap shoot as to whether I was going to be able to have him functional or not. Later, he would say that I didn't see him as more than his disease and that these dramas didn't really exist. They did. The demon in him found my weak points and exploited them mercilessly, then placed the blame, the accusation of misread reality on me, on my perception.

This twist was the core of the abuse pattern. Robin began acting like his father. It was the classic abuser begets abuser syndrome that happens in so many families, but this one had an additional special supernatural feature. Daniel and Robin's mother, Janet, were divorced, so Janet sometimes talked to me about Daniel's behaviors. She and Daniel had argued often and intensely. Daniel would continue the arguments late, late into the night, keeping Janet up for hours, talking, talking, shouting, repeating his case over and over, rephrasing his case, on and on until she gave in. She told me he wouldn't let her sleep until she conceded.

Robin learned the pattern all too well. Only he wasn't as educated as his father, who, with his doctorate in religious studies, had a vast body of knowledge to draw from for his sophistry. Robin didn't have such a background or vocabulary, so his arguments came out more circular, more confused and confusing than Daniel's, *and* more ferocious, as Robin had never learned to be civilized. He became a screaming, drooling, spitting, arm-waving, furniture-kicking, life threatening monster.

Inevitably, the pattern concluded with Robin, once again, being arrested. I had spent the afternoon trying to repair the towel racks in the bathroom. He had pulled them all out of the walls. My repairs weren't pretty, but they worked. Instead of helping me, he waited until I was done and then went into a tirade for destroying the value of his father's house with the ugly work I had done. It culminated with his upending the coffee table, sending the hundreds of items on it flying, and eliciting from me, a stream of wordless screams.

The neighbors reported the disturbance in our house. I called Robin's mother and, while the event was in progress, let her listen to the insane tirade over the phone. I wanted her to know what I was experiencing. I held the phone up as he screamed and screamed and ran back and forth knocking things over in the house. Even knowing his mother was listening to his torrent of abuse did not deter him.

The police, of course, made the situation worse. They took him to jail. This time there was no detox to which to detour Robin, no Daniel to call to the police station to bamboozle them into releasing Robin into his custody (Daniel was on the way to his mother's funeral in another state). And without getting into a long criticism of the police, I'll just say that they were bullies just as much as Robin. Their idiotic behavior nearly caused kidney failure in Robin when they refused to allow him his insulin until they "were done with him." They made a big, threatening deal about the battle axes and scythes on the wall (which were all light-weight plastic and foam, made in China, Halloween costume props), demanding to know instead why we kept dangerous weapons on the wall, pulling them down just to make sure. Freaking Keystone Morons!

The cops broke items in the living room as they snooped around. They dumped out my sewing kit that I kept under the sofa, knocked over a lamp. They rummaged about until they found something "juicy," which, of course, they did. They confiscated all of Robin's pot pipe collection – about twenty prized artifacts – a loss that sent Robin into a massive depression. To get Robin free took all the money we had in the world. I couldn't press charges as I had nowhere to go (it wasn't my house, and my family would never have taken me in at that time) and nowhere to put him (again it wasn't my house). So we had to prove in court that he "didn't mean anything" by smashing up the living room, and then pay a fine for the minimum pot supply – all via a costly lawyer.

The worst part of the entire episode was that Robin would not admit that what he had done was wrong. He saw the entire event as an opportunity to really lay into my psyche. He, with invigorated enthusiasm via the keep-me-up-all-night method and threats to harm himself and worst of all to end our relationship if I did not concede to his viewpoints, battered me with rhetoric. His world view was going to become mine, no matter what it took. He was going to convince me that he was right.

Life had to go on, though. A household- with 5 cats in it too!- had to function. To begin with, he did not want me *doing* any housework. He, himself, never, never, never washed one dish or towel or floor or toilet in the years we were together. Ever. Life was not supposed to be about cleaning the house or working in the yard. He did not want me grading papers at home because home was not the place for work. He was bound and determined to get me to give up all these "stupid activities."

My only solution to the situation was to take advantage of the fact that he slept twelve to fourteen hours like the dead. I got up early and frantically ran around the house to do what needed to be done before he woke up, furtively doing chores as if they were crimes. Since even running the lawnmower right underneath the bedroom window wouldn't wake him, I could do that as well. The vacuuming, though, would take too many hours, and would always earn me some sort of punishment for me that night, sometimes a self-induced insulin reaction or a tantrum, say, over something as mundane as chicken wings.

Yes, chicken wings. After one day of my working in the house, dinner was a bit late, but I was ready to completely focus on it in time to prevent an episode of low blood sugar. Robin, in retaliation for my wrongdoing, didn't want anything I proposed to cook. He wanted chicken wings. Well, that was the one, the only one, of the usual foods I did not have any in the freezer at that moment. So, now, I had a dilemma.

The grocery wasn't that far. I could go quickly and get some. He didn't want me to leave the house and leave him alone. Another option was for both of us to go a very nearby restaurant that specialized in chicken wings. He didn't want to leave the house. We could order delivery from that restaurant. He said that would take too long. He wanted chicken wings now. I offered all of the alternatives I had in the freezer or cupboard, foods he usually liked. No, he wanted chicken wings, but would not let me go about procuring them. If he couldn't have chicken wings, he didn't want dinner, never mind his plummeting blood sugar. The fight went on for hours, until I was ready to hang myself, and he finally agreed to a sandwich. Where Robin left off and demon began would have been indeterminable except for when the red light shone in his eyes. It flickered in and out during this exchange.

Still, I tried to maintain our home. But the more I did, the more Robin rebelled. Many days, he never left the house. He would get up (or I would struggle to restore him to consciousness), smoke pot, drink coffee, spend the day at his computer, surfing porn, playing games, doing some work for Daniel's music studio website, enter contests (by creating big-boobed female characters for a game), smoking more pot, until dinner time.

Understanding Evil: My Soul Contract

Every few months, he would wear out a joystick. The broken ones sitting on the top shelf in his "office" looked like a graveyard of giant deformed, defunct electronic penises. The ceiling was coated with coffee from when he accidentally tipped himself over while in his reclining office chair (playing a game in which monsters attacked) with a full coffee cup in hand, the contents of which he launched right up into the ceiling fan as he was trying to right himself, thus distributing the liquid in a full circle above his head.

All this drama, he enacted while naked but for his bathrobe. He took a shower only every few weeks, usually when he had a doctor's appointment or we had a get-together with his family. That way no one ever knew about his lack of hygiene, but me. To me, when I complained, he said that taking a shower was a waste of time. The smell was unendurable. I ended up buying several bathrobes for him, so that I could at least wash one every day, spraying the mustard and grease spots and skid marks with stain remover before nearly boiling them in hot water. He would drop his robe on the floor when he went to bed, and before he got up the next day, I would confiscate it before he put it on again for a second day, which he would if I didn't. His finger and toe nails were always filthy. His long hair was always heavy with oil and his unkempt bushy beard full of food crumbs. I couldn't stand for him to touch me. I didn't want anyone I knew to see him. Whatever beauty he had had was profaned. And his eyes had that peculiar red light shining from them more and more often and for longer periods of time.

Nothing in our lives worked the way it did for other people. He would not participate in the things that needed to be done. Robin refused to go shopping with me because, he said, stores were "scary." So, I went alone to the grocery, to the discount stores. When the dishwasher broke, I carried it downstairs and out of the house by myself so the new one could be put in. I organized everything in the house. Since he never opened his mail (every day, at least two or three envelopes from creditors would arrive!) and got angry if I threw any of them away, I bought plastic containers to store all the notices of lawsuits and threats, just rubber-banding them by type and piling them in the containers (four large tote boxes of it before I left him).

I took on the neglected yard. I took down old fencing in the yard, moved tons of rock to fill in where water threatened the foundation of the house, trimmed bushes, planted trees and roses, created a garden of perennials, all without his help. I watered and mowed grass and raked leaves and shoveled snow, all on my own. Someone had to. He would tell me in those last days that we could have hired someone if I hadn't been so stubborn. We never discussed it. Besides, hire someone? With what?

"You care more about the house (or yard or "those student papers") than you do me," he complained, and the fights would begin. They would go on for hours and hours (that last year, I perhaps had two to three hours of sleep a night). Often, the evening ended with his falling asleep, drunk, with a full drink in his hands, one that would soak the sofa when it slipped from his grasp. During the night, I'd lay a blanket over him, and the next day, pick up all the wet padding and blankets I started to keep on the couch to absolve the spills, replace them with a new set, wash the rum-soaked pile in preparation for the next night of psychological torture for me. And I had to do it all without his catching me at it.

What we fought about most, however, – the humiliation still turns my stomach, and as I sit here typing, I feel waves of nausea – was that I was not letting him show me how much he cared about me. For instance, to let him show me properly, I was supposed to be naked when I was at home, when I cooked, when we watched television, when I did laundry, when I vacuumed. That way he could sit to the side and "admire" me.

Understanding Evil: My Soul Contract

To defend his position, he absurdly cited one of those obnoxious, popular cartoons, where the wife was so desperate to get the husband's attention, she posed in doorways at his workplace in revealing lingerie. "See," he said, "here, I am willing to pay attention to you, so you don't have to beg like her, and you reject it. Every woman wants her husband to look at her!" Then, because I had worked as an art model for three years in the past, he added, "You sat naked for all those artists! You owe it to me too!" It was no use telling him that that had been a decade earlier and very different circumstances! It was for art, not disgusting lechery.

In order to be allowed to keep my home, I had to give in. If I didn't adopt his view, he said, that then he was in the wrong marriage, and I was going to have to go. There was no way out of the dilemma. I had put so much work into the yard. I had my cats in that house, all my belongings, my essential papers. I had no savings. The credit cards were maxed out. I would rather die than go back to my family (in the end I had to anyway). I was trapped. So, I gave in, told him what he wanted, and complied with the behaviors he demanded. I had to paint the bathroom and bedroom naked. My identity, my self-esteem never recovered. I was dead. I figuratively became the madwoman in the attic.

I did not think I could become less, have less value or substance, but, of course, that was not true. For, then, my Luca cat became ill and died, much too young and in particularly difficult circumstances. With her death, I became undead, beyond dead. Soon, I could no longer work effectively. I could not face a class of students with any sort of dignity or self-respect or even accountability anymore. When my department chair asked me, the answer to why I was not doing a good job was too shameful.

I was isolated and caught in a potentially lethal game of madness. At home, at night, Robin's and my sexual connection had become extremely frightful. What used to be fun, the bondage and role-playing suddenly seemed to me to be the way I would die, tied up and helpless, either at the mercy of his cruelty, or with him passed out cold from low blood sugar, and potentially never waking up again. I taped razor blades to the backs of the nightstands, and tied a string to each bed post from which dangled a small knife so that I could reach at least one tool in an emergency. One way or another, I was going to be able to free myself – and protect myself if need be. This was not how I wished to die.

When Robin began accusing me of making certain absurd promises and not keeping them, I was once again made fully aware that Robin was no longer Robin. His memories were someone or something else's. He repeatedly mentioned a big flat rock up at his father's first home that he claimed I had agreed to let him tie me to for sex outdoors in the mountains. I had no idea what he was talking about. We had never had that conversation. There was no rock like the one he was describing. The home in question had been sold years earlier. Robin would never engage in outdoor sex. Nothing fit. It was as if someone or something else was speaking through him. There was. The red-eyed demon born of his family's dysfunction. These were the fantasies of an entity that was not Robin.

The three and a half foot snow storm was what finally did it. I had to shovel it all myself. It was so heavy. A spring snow. It utterly smashed to pieces both of the beautiful apple trees in the front yard (one had already been damaged by the neighbor who chopped half of it off to get his stupid RV next to his house). I shoveled and screamed and cursed and cried for half a day, just to make a path to the cars. Every muscle in my body felt torn.

As I shoveled, I saw movement a few feet in front of me. Out of the blue, a pair of geese had landed in the wreckage on the lawn. They weren't afraid of me in the least. A voice (the mysterious voice that has in extreme situations addressed me) accompanied their landing, telling me I had to get the cars freed, drive up to the college, and quit my job. In the middle of the semester! So I did. There was no redeeming the situation anymore anyway.

The quitting was terrible. I still had to grade about a hundred essays before I could hand over the job to someone else. My mind was barely able to function; it was total mush. I wrote an apology to my students, and in it, full of anguish, expressed that a soul knows when it is faced with ultimate slavery, and that I had finally understood that I could no longer function in my life as it was. It was not a suicide note. It was a statement of insight that I hoped would justify my decision to them as well as inspire at least a few of them to reconsider their own paths before they became confined. I had lost all hope.

My life was a living hell. Escape was imperative, one way or another. When I started the tedious, grievous process of unburying myself from that house, I didn't know how I was going to accomplish my exit – feet first or in a moving van, suicide or outside rescue. It really didn't matter, but either way, the removal had to be streamlined, my presence thoroughly erased. I could not leave anything behind that could be used against me for magick spells or anything that could be used to document my mental state. For Robin would sooner have killed me than let me go. For Daniel was not alone in his greed and power lust.

Daniel brought another perpetrator into the mix, an African storyteller, who knew something about demons (he called them djinn) and magick (albeit it from his cultural perspective). Toward the end of this fiasco, when Robin's family realized I was really leaving, they sent the storyteller to try to convince me to turn my entities and magick over to him. "Give me your power," he said on the phone like a mantra, over and over. "I can help you be happy," he said. "Give me your power." I told him I would rather throw myself into a fire. "Give me your power." He wanted me to give him my entities, to let him direct them. He wasn't talking about the demons, but about the others I had with me who were my allies. He, even with all his grinning charm, could not persuade me.

For months, I focused my energy on a wholescale clearing of my existence. I had a room in that house that was my private altar room. It was unimaginably full of my collections of magickal supplies and artifacts. I had covered the walls with black fabric and hung a curtain over the doorway so that the room was closed off from the house, but the cats could still come and go as they pleased. Everything had to come down.

My altar room was my stargate into the other worlds. It was where I, by myself, conducted all my rituals and spells. (Robin had promised to work magick with me only long enough to trap me into our hand-fasting, then never resumed even one ritual with me). The room was where I kept all the remains of past spells and materials for future spells. In it, I burned incense, made offerings to the Dead, did tarot readings, communicated with spirits via a cursed mirror. It was in this room that I made the doll and then kept the doll.

To be free of my nightmare, I knew I had to dispose of every single item in it. I could leave nothing behind, and I couldn't take anything with me. If my exit were to be by suicide and I left any magick implements behind, they would be desecrated somehow. If my exit were to be by flight and I left any magick implements, they and the energies in them might be used against me, to curse me, or worse, to haul me back. Or again, if my exit were to be by flight, and I took any magick implements along, the energies in them might act as a beacon for magick to reach me, for the storyteller or Robin to find me. Everything had to go. Everything I loved. Everything I had believed in. Every single thing.

Intuitively, I knew I was fighting something preternatural. With so much fear in me, I was on overload every moment. I hadn't by then figured out how all the pieces of the truth fit together. All I knew is that my freedom and my soul were at risk. Every item from my household or my magickal room that I took in my hand, I would consider with the following question: "Is this worth my life?"

During my purge, I burned things, tossed things into rivers and lakes, buried things, scattered them on the old wheat farm I had used for decades for ritual back north, mailed things back to their original owners, gave things away as gifts, set furniture on the sidewalk with "free" signs, took boxes of stuff to the second-hand stores, filled up the trash, pile after pile, till my altar room was entirely empty. Robin said nothing except to joke with his father that one day he would find himself out by the garbage too.

I am still amazed to this day that he never once asked me what I was doing or tried to stop me. How could he not think the situation was strange? But then, I was never a person to him, never had a soul or needs or a destiny of my own. My interests and desires were insignificant. I was property, an object, an appendage. I was even less than that to Daniel. To him, I was a commodity, like lumber or livestock, a tool to use.

A year and a half before I left Robin, Daniel came to the house with a lease for me to sign, just me, as my last name was different from his, because he was applying for a second mortgage and had to show income from the property and to prove he didn't have family living there. I was hesitant. "Oh, don't worry about it," he said. "It's just to fool the bank." So I signed it. To justify the second mortgage (a portion of it), he sent contractors over to the house to replace the windows. I had to deal with these messy gorillas trudging dirt all over my home for weeks. I had to lock the cats up over and over because contractors don't care about people's pets. The "home improvement" caused so much stress. Also, it would have been better to have included central air conditioning in the project, but no. Windows. In every room of the house, including my altar room. I had to have disrespectful clumsy strangers in my altar room.

A few months before I decided to leave Robin, I went to speak to Daniel to ask him for help with his son. I told him what was happening in the house, what I was experiencing. We talked about Robin's propensity for violence, and how many times in the past, Robin lost control and demonstrated unpredictable and completely over-the-top reactions when frustrated or disappointed (aka, intermittent explosive disorder). I recounted the chicken wing incident. Daniel responded that Robin was indeed good at creating unsolvable dilemmas, good at holding people as emotional hostages. Like father, like son, I would realize later. It seemed, though, that we commiserated. Such was my impression. Daniel agreed to help. His help, however, consisted of his finally setting up the pool table in our basement (which only provided Robin another activity to demand I conduct naked!) and to have Robin's sister drop off some bills (that he thought we should start paying). That was all the help Daniel gave me.

A few weeks before I actually did so, I told Daniel that I intended to leave Robin. My purpose was to ask him to help me find a way to do it safely, for my sake and Robin's. To my surprise, he indicated that I was out of my mind for wanting to leave such a beautiful situation, and that I should seek some mental help. Just like in a bad movie script, Daniel had thought this through already, and began laying the groundwork for having me committed. He was going to assure that I literally became the madwoman in the attic. He started hinting about maybe getting money from my medical trust fund so that I could "rest," and Robin could be paid to take care of me. Daniel's plan was to place custody of my existence into the hands of his monster son! Rather than just let me go, he wanted access to my medical trust fund. But he did not want to deal with Robin's temper were I to leave. He did not want his son back. Taking away my freedom, my sovereignty, fulfilled both motivations. He, like Robin, wanted what he wanted and would take it, no matter what.

I was out of my head with terror. So, not only did I have to destroy my altar room, I had to clear out my papers and books and anything laden with meaning throughout the entire house. I had to reduce and organize. All my personal letters and journals, medical records, and reports of my futile attempts at psychological counseling over the years had to go. Those could not fall into "enemy" hands. My transcripts and diplomas had to be moved somewhere safe. The amount of paper I sorted was staggering.

Some items, I *had* to secure. The box with my remaining jewelry, blankets that my grandmother had crocheted, memorabilia from my childhood, and such, I loaded into the car in the very early mornings, driving loads to my mother's house an hour away and returning before Robin ever knew I was gone. Many of my books were intended for my brother. So, I separated those thirty crates out of the eighty crates of my books and stacked them in a different location. I thought, if I could get Robin out of the house for just a few hours and get someone to pull up with a truck, I could manage to get what was important out of the house and be gone. If . . .

I was ready. I renounced the hand-fasting ceremony, gave back my "wedding dress" and the binding cords to the Goddess, burying all of the materials at the farm I had been using for rituals for decades, feeling Her give me permission to separate from Robin. I prepared the cat carriers. I bought rolls of trash bags for my clothing and vital papers (a trick I learned from some of the literature from the women's resource center at the college). I took all the contact information for my friends and family from the refrigerator door and address book. I even cleaned the oven. It was a symbolic act. And I burned the Robin doll in the garage, at four in the morning, to be sure I would not be interrupted.

My destination was supposed to be a house my brother, Rudyard, owned back in my "home" town. It was, however, due to terrible renters, uninhabitable. A contractor had been hired, but as many contractors are everywhere, he was a lazy crook, took weeks and weeks, and in the end didn't finish. My emergency was not Rudyard's emergency. In order for him to even consider trying to save me, I had to negotiate with him, and that was at first as impossible as negotiating with Daniel. I was supposed to abandon my cats. Not an option. I was supposed to live with a roommate. Not an option. I was supposed to hand over my credit cards. Not an option. Yet, if I didn't get out, I was going to have to end my life. But I was not going to bargain away any more of myself to survive. There was almost nothing left as is.

At this time, also, a windfall came my way, or so it seemed. The administrator of the trust fund, for some reason, asked me if I had been paying health insurance. Of course, we had. He decided that it was better for the trust fund (explanation to follow) to help me pay insurance rather than pay for medical expenses without it. He made me the offer of paying half of the premiums we had paid (to cover my share) over the two past years. Retroactively. That meant $4,000 dollars. It would have been enough to rent a moving truck, rent a room. I thought the medical trust fund, cursed money that it was, was actually going to save my life.

Then the unthinkable happened. I don't know if the impetus came from my mother, her evil lawyer (who made the will of his nephew, who was a friend of mine, "disappear"), or my brother (from whom I had the year before wrested control of the fund, giving it to the bank to manage instead), but Rudyard called me to tell me that because I accepted that money, I was likely going to be charged with a felony. The way the insurance was paid was automatic withdrawal from Robin's account.

Since I could not produce checks that I had specifically written for the insurance, I was, according to Rudyard, committing fraud by accepting the money. Legally, though, money in a marriage is communal. It wouldn't have mattered, Rudyard said. Long after the trauma was over, I did confirm with an attorney and an accountant to verify that I was right, and that if anyone were to have gotten in trouble, it would have been the administrator, not me. But then, at that most vulnerable time, I was blindsided.

Right when I was in the most dire straits, in danger of losing my liberty (in a psyche ward) to Robin's family, or my life itself to the red-eyed demon that was almost entirely in control of Robin, I was suddenly in danger of losing it to my family (in actual jail). Rudyard put me through a "mock" trial, asking me over and over, "Did you write the actual checks for the insurance?" And I would answer, "No, but . . . ." He would never let me finish my explanation, asking again and again, "Did you write the actual checks for the insurance?"

He was condescending and merciless, my own brother, telling me that even though he was ashamed of me, and disappointed in me, he would try to keep me out of prison. He let me know that I absolutely deserved to be locked up. In order to help prepare me for "what the prosecutor" would put me through, to mount a "defense" for me, he demanded to see the insurance policy. I made the hour plus drive immediately to drop off a copy, and a long note of pleading for his forgiveness. He didn't even bother to read it, just let me wait and suffer and nearly lose my mind. For three weeks, I lived with the constant fear that at any moment, the police would come to the door and take me away. It was unbearable.

Because it is important to the whole picture, here is the story of that cursed money. The history of it alone guaranteed that it had something some terrible energy or entity attached to it. When my uncle died, our family inherited well over a million dollars from his estate. How he acquired that money is still a mystery; his miserliness alone could not explain it. He did not have a high-paying job, nor did he make much money trading stamps. What he did have was a questionable relationship with an occult group that he had joined during WWII and the many trips he made to South America with secret packages over the years. We never knew more than that.

Before he died, though, he wanted to start sending us the $10K per family member gift per year. This was a year after my father's death, a year and a half after Robin's grand mal seizure. Rudyard got his disbursement directly, but my uncle sent mine to my mother to hold for me. When I called him to find out why, he told me that it was because he wasn't sure of my character. My mother had told him that I had organized a gang of boys beat up my brother while we were in high school, and he couldn't quite forgive me for that. It was the first time I had ever heard the accusation – about something THAT NEVER HAPPENED. "She lied!" I screamed into the phone, but he stuck with my mother's portrait of me. I told my brother what my uncle said, but he did NOTHING to stand up for me. If the situation had been reversed, I would have fought for him like a maniac. But he didn't want to risk his access to the money or his position of power.

I tried to reason with my mother, but she wouldn't

give up the lie. She didn't want any family money to be used for Robin. I begged Rudyard to get her to let me use some of my portion to at least pay off my credit cards. He said he might, but only if I turned my credit cards over to him until I "could prove that I had learned to be fiscally responsible"! I was in my forties. He was treating me like a recalcitrant child. I told him to forget it. I was so humiliated. In the meantime, it was *he* who was living well beyond his means, something he would continue till he had blown his way through his entire allotment of the inheritance and then on top of that had run up hundreds of thousands in debt.

To deal with that first $10K disbursement, my mother found that crooked lawyer to write up what she called "idiot tax papers" that I was supposed to sign so that she could put the money into an account for me. What a naïve "idiot" I was indeed back then. When presented with the papers, with my mother, the lawyer and his office assistants hovering over me to intimidate me, I signed them. They didn't look like tax papers, though, and when I told my accountant what they were called, she flipped out. What I had been duped into signing was a general financial power of attorney. She told me exactly what to do to get it reversed immediately.

I made the hour drive and presented the papers to my mother the next day and then went home. It was Thanksgiving. I decided to invite her to my home. It was then that she said I was no longer welcome in the family, and that she was through with me. Again, my brother did nothing to intercede. That was it. I was banished.

I went outside to have a cigarette (I smoked a lot then), and standing there in the snow and cold, I noticed a stray branch on the juniper bush closest to the stoop. I pulled it loose, then noticed another, and pulled it loose. Finally, out of breath and freezing, I stepped back onto the porch to look at my work. What a pile of dead stuff I had pulled out of the junipers! I stood there in the quiet and suddenly became aware of a strange sound – a heavy dripping sound. I looked down at my shoes. Blood. Then I looked at my hands. They were completely raw and bleeding, torn by the rough and sharp branches. I couldn't even feel the damage.

When I went back to school to teach, my hands in bandages, a Native American student of mine, took one look at me, and said, "Something really bad happened to you. I have something for you." He went out to the parking lot to get it –a pair of smoky quartz crystals (a palm-sized rock). He said it would help absorb the chaos and pain I was feeling. I accepted it gladly. It would be very important years later.

The separation lasted over a year. My uncle died during that time, and the inheritance came in. My portion, according to his will was to be put in a trust fund, to be used for housing, transportation, medical or educational purposes, with my brother as administrator(!) with the ability to invest is however he wished! It would have allowed him another opportunity for him to abuse his power over me given to him by my family under false pretenses. Well, he had already given most of his to the martial arts school and generally wasted the rest, so I could not let him have access to mine. We had a terrible, terrible fight over it, but he relented and turned it over to a bank to administer, with an abridged version – medical and educational use only. Doing so cost me thousands in fees, but preserved the bulk of the original deposit. It almost cost me my relationship to my brother entirely, but by then, I couldn't even look at him for all the betrayal. It didn't matter.

Just for the record, Rudyard never apologized for what he did to me at any stage of our relationship to that money, but he did, after he left the martial arts cult, release the trust fund to me directly. My mother never knew what happened to any of the money. She did not know that the prodigality she accused me of had been perpetrated a hundred times more by my brother. I never told her. I protected him even when he wouldn't protect me. The wound still aches, but I have let go of ever expecting acknowledgment.

And just for the record, he is no longer the person he was then who was so cruel to me. He has changed due to extreme circumstances in his life during which he faced the threat of prison for years due to false allegations made against him because of people he had done business with. I was stunned by the karmic retribution – and ironically, I paid tens of thousands of dollars to cover his fines so that he could maintain his career. I do not regret it. I learned about how profound and complex forgiveness can be.

So, with all of that history, I have since then decided to blame the cursed money itself and the influence of the martial arts cult and guru for Rudyard's cruelty. But at that time, I was utterly and completely terrified and devastated. I signed off the phone call during which the mock trial had occurred and collapsed in the garage where I had gone for some privacy. At that point, I hoped Robin would just go ahead and kill me.

But here I was, with the threat of going to jail or being committed both hanging over me, and with Robin likely to just kill me in a fit of frustration. I would have let him too ... except that I had promised my Siamese cats I would save them, wouldn't leave them. And I couldn't leave my brother either. My love for him was agonizing and complicated and occult as anything else of importance in my life.

My time was running out. In the end, when Daniel finally figured out that I was really going to leave, he arranged a spontaneous family intervention, where I had to face all of them, Daniel, Janet, Robin, Robin's sister, her storyteller husband, and the child they had produced together. They all descended on me at once. They all presented their unified position that I should not leave Robin, that they would all "help me to see things the right way." I tried to have a friend come sit with me to support me, but Robin attacked him and pushed him down the stairs, so he had to leave. So, I was alone with the Inquisition.

The way that family spoke indicated that unless I acquiesced and promised to stay with Robin, they were going to have me hauled off right then and there for a hospital stay for "my own good." I read the subtext. They were ready to make that call. Robin's health, they said, couldn't take the stress of my leaving, and he had already lived long past the years that had been predicted for him. I had to stay. How could I endanger his life? Besides, no one else would ever want anyone as crazy as I was. I should stay. They loved me. All of a sudden?

Understanding Evil: My Soul Contract

Daniel had evidently coerced all his minions into compliance. He roped all the players together to pull the carriage of his totalitarianism. They had all been made to drink the Kool-Aid, and they outnumbered me. So, I agreed to go with their plan. Just like a prisoner of war agrees to what his/her captors say to end the torture to buy time to find an escape, I said I changed my mind. I would try their plan. I had learned that means of survival with my parents. This was not my first rodeo.

It was astonishing, though, in its scope. A schedule for my existence was going to be prepared – by Daniel. He was going to take over every aspect of my existence. Just like that. My visits to family and friends were going to be regulated. Robin and I were to spend two nights a week going to movies or other places together, so he and I could reconnect. We were going to be sent to a marriage counselor. Robin and I were to open a joint banking account. My conversations with my brother were to be limited because he had clearly brainwashed me, and I was just supposed to let him know that although I appreciate his offer to help me, I would be staying with my husband.

I was supposed to start *allowing* Robin help with the housework and not keep him from it. Yes. I he claimed I was keeping him from doing his share by doing it for him. And so on, so forth. *And* we were going to have a dinner at my house, cooked in my kitchen, as a way to celebrate our newly established union – in other words, they wanted a victory dinner, to gloat. Since they had all decided that whatever was mine was theirs, my kitchen was of course open to them. The entire family was going to participate in gaslighting me together. And the house my brother said would be open for me was not ready.

I almost imploded. This was hell. I was cornered in hell. These people speaking utter gibberish were my wardens. It was also the hottest summer on record, temperatures around one hundred for weeks without a break. We had no air conditioning. Two cans of tomato sauce in the kitchen bulged and split. The cats were lying on wet towels to cool off. Between the heat and my absolute state of cortisol overload, I was extremely ill. This was going to be the end of me. I was going to be erased, slowly and painfully, my entire identity rewritten by these people who for some reason decided they had not only the right to do so, but the obligation to bring me around to their way of thinking. They meant to crush me.

To make matters worse, Robin never, for one waking minute, stopped talking, trying to persuade me that he had so much to teach me and that I was throwing my life away if I left him. Repeat, repeat. Day after day. Hour after hour. Telling me what I should value, how I should think, what I should believe. Talk, talk, talk, talk, talk. Without cessation.

There was also pressure from the agreement I had made with my brother. In accepting the offer of a house to live in, I had made a promise to get myself out of where I was. But these people were going to prevent me from keeping it. The storyteller kept telling me, "He's your brother; he'll forgive you." *No, no, he would not.* Things between me and my brother in those days were such that if I didn't make good on my promise – no matter what I had to fight my way through – I would be a villain, would have betrayed him, and he and I would be through. How much of that came from him directly or was invented by mother I still don't know and certainly didn't know then. What I did know was that I was being drawn and quartered by everyone I knew. I contemplated poisons I could concoct at home . . .

A few days later, that is, after a few days of constant, hour after hour of droning non-sense, of Robin's litany of why I should stay with him, how much I had to learn from him about love, about what I good life we had together if I could just see it, he let me alone for a few minutes. He did so in order to call his sister to complain that I wasn't obeying him the way Daniel had told me to. Well, I fell asleep, until someone woke me. A man in ancient Roman battle garb (helmet, sword, armor, etc.) stood before me. He took my hands and said, "It is time." Yes. Yes, time, yes.

The spirit walked me out into the backyard, from where I could see the planet Mars (actually in real time) redder and larger and closer to the earth than it had been in sixty thousand years or so. The spirit told me that he *was* Mars, and he had answered someone's request to help me (I had indeed asked my best who was also a witch to contact my dead grandmother for assistance). My grandmother sent Mars! For two hours (Robin thought I was on the cell phone to someone, as he saw me outside talking and gesticulating as if in conversation), the old God and I talked, argued, and finally came to an agreement. I don't know now what the terms were. I can only speculate.

Four days later, my life as I had known it was over. The previous evening, I, still pretending I would go along with the family plan, the subject of the cats came up. He said I couldn't have them, not even my Siamese, and that he would get rid of all of them. My cats! My cats! Then, that night, Robin insisted I sleep (a) naked (which I hadn't done for a while) and (b) in a position he chose *for* me, that suited his need to sleep with his arm around me (something I never tolerated from anyone in my life). I lay awake the entire night, and though he did sleep, for once in his goddamned life, he slept lightly, so when I got up the next morning, he jumped up immediately too. I was never going to have any peace, ever again. "The marriage is over," I told him.

At this point, I was willing to risk his trying to murder me. I could not go through another night like the one I just had. It didn't matter anymore. "I am going to take the movies back to the rental place," I told him, "and we will talk about it when I come back," but instead, I loaded up my three Siamese cats (I could only carry them, but they were mine years before Robin), took them to a friend, and then went to the police to ask for a twenty-minute move out assist. At least this time, the police were helpful.

I begged my friend with whom I had momentarily left my cats to come to my house and help me load my belongings into my SUV and his. The trash bags were the best idea ever! My clothing and those papers were vital to my survival. I had to leave my computer, but I kept the data disks. I had to leave my all my kitchenware (a full, functioning kitchen that I had built up over the years), my linens, and all the other household items. I had already taken my tools (for these had been my father's) to my supposed new home. I had to leave the other two cats, a sorrow that still clutches at my heart when I run across the memory. But I got out.

As I removed my belongings, Robin acted as if I were misbehaving. He got on the phone immediately to his father and his sleaze-bag friend/pot dealer/cohort in fraud. But by the time Robin's entire family and the friend arrived, I was gone. The sleazebag friend told me later that when the family got there, the first thing they did was go room to room, opening drawers and boxes to take an inventory of what I left behind – to count their spoils.

The house I was to live in was not finished. I would have left Robin much sooner, before the crisis hit, if the house had just been livable, but my brother was in no hurry to make it inhabitable. And it wasn't. The toilet, which had been removed to replace the flooring in the bathroom, was still on the back porch, no doors on hinges, the kitchen counter broken. I had to run for my life and had nowhere to go.

Therefore, my mother had no choice but to take me and my three Siamese cats in. We found ourselves standing on her doorstep with nowhere else to go. It turned out that as much as I had never wanted to return to my family, they were the only ones who could stop Daniel and Robin from completing their mission, which was to have me declared mentally incompetent so they could prevent me from leaving. To get to me, Robin's family would have had to go through my mother and brother, and that was not going to be easy. My mother didn't let me out of her sight in those months while the court proceedings were going on until the divorce was final.

 Robin pestered his sleaze-ball friend to keep calling, trying to convince me to see a psychiatrist. He, too, had been convinced by Robin and Daniel that I was insane, that my family had corrupted my mind into believing that Robin was bad. Robin's family was concerned about my well-being, he said. Robin loved me! I was flabbergasted. Months before I left Robin, I had contacted said friend in order to solicit his help too, not just Daniel's. We had talked for a couple of hours, and even agreed that if someone were to do to his daughter what was being done to me, he would become homicidal. He promised to talk with Robin the next time he made a pot delivery. Then HE FORGOT the entire conversation!

 The same fate befell the conversation I had around that time with the friend who helped me move. He *also* could not recall the discussion. He said helped me because he thought that Robin had thrown me out of the house, not that I was fleeing for my life. For he didn't remember one word I had said those months before either, not until I recreated the entire day, reciting details for him: the trip to the archeology exhibit (I recalled exact items in the cases!) and the visit to the bookstore (the exact book titles we debated, the pastries we bought at the coffee shop). Those peripheral physical images brought the rest back to him. He said it was as if the entire verbal exchange between us had been fogged over, become resistant to detection. Then I knew what had happened.

 It was a glamour. The demon had cast a glamour. Daniel's

demon in Robin had silenced me, had made my words either vanish or be misunderstood. Janet, who had witnessed Robin threaten and shove me at a family gathering once, who had listened to his screaming over the phone the night he was arrested, who had watched Robin throw my friend down the stairs, looked me right in the eyes and said she didn't know what I was talking about when I said I couldn't live with Robin's violence anymore. Robin's sister, who had confided in me that she was sometimes afraid of her brother, stared at me blankly when I reminded her about that conversation. There were moments that I doubted my memory, felt that uneasy "floor slipping out from under me" sensation. Surely, I didn't imagine all that happened!

It is not unusual for a family to rally around the abuser in its midst. But they can't change people's memories! I was alone, screaming my own truth, that I knew was THE truth because I had confirmed it with others – and then, the ground shifted.

Nor is it unusual for them to repress their experiences and reconstruct their realities (and then try to reconstruct whoever threatens them) any way they possibly can in order to maintain their internal structure – and to protect their monster, lest he turn on them. Which monster? Daniel? Robin? In this case, probably both, but what became abundantly clear was that not one of his parents wanted to take Robin back. Daniel, in fact, had a vacant downstairs apartment in his house, and would not even consider moving Robin in there. Though everyone in the family insisted that Robin should never live alone, no one was willing to take him in. They were all terrified of Robin and would do anything to protect themselves.

So, they were all, en masse, gaslighting me in order to maintain their own delusion. Denial. Denial. No matter whom they had to throw under the bus to hold their little drama together. The demon either helped tweak reality in that family or just surfed along as they tweaked it. But typically, the abuser's gaslighting doesn't extend beyond the immediate household. A family's reinventing truth is usually contained within the abuser(s)'s immediate sphere of influence. This was bigger. The rest was the demon's doing. It made sure I couldn't call *anyone* for help. It made sure that I had no defense as the nightmare descended on me.

As far as seeing a psychiatrist, though, I have to say, again, that I was protected, for in my plan for escape, luckily, was I stopped at the nearest women's resource center at the university where I had taught years earlier. In that brief meeting, I learned something extremely important: the last place a woman in as traumatized a condition as I was in should ever go is a psychiatrist's office. He/she would take one look at me and know that I was in dire straits, and conclude from my hopelessness, my anxiety, my desperation, my terror that I was unstable, and I was. But I wasn't crazy! Any potential intervention or even a recommendation for one would have provided Robin's family with ammunition to use against me.

My freedom, my sovereignty, might have been forfeit on the spot. Also, the record of the evaluation would from then on exist as fact and could be used to weave the very sort of web in which Daniel was trying to capture me. One never escapes psychiatric evaluations – they remain on insurance and medical records forever. Robin, as my husband, might have used it to prove that I was not competent enough to file for divorce. I am so grateful to the woman in the resource center who warned me that seeking psychiatric assistance would have been the worst decision. I was told to wait, to not go near a shrink until I was stable again. As much as I wanted to talk to someone, I didn't do it. It was the best advice I could have possibly been given. How many women have been spirited to asylums for disobedience?

Robin wanted me back with an unrelenting ferocity. Much to his surprise, he couldn't get the judge to force me to communicate with him. Therefore, he took it upon himself to write letters to everyone he could remember that I knew, for I had left him no addresses or phone numbers of my friends or family. He managed to find a few on his own: an old professor of mine, my best friend, my first ex-husband, my mother, my brother, the friend who I believe is a dragon incarnate. In those letters, he claimed that I was being brainwashed by my family, that I was throwing my life away, that I won't be happy until I return to him, that if they cared about me they would convince me to come home, that there was so much he could teach me, that I was just letting it all go to waste.

These letters were pages and pages of accusations, faulty analyses, deranged, obscene rants, as well as some bizarre sexual content in which he described his desire for me. A marriage is forever! It was, therefore, he claimed, impossible for me to leave! My freedom didn't actually exist in his mind. It is interesting that every single one of the recipients was disgusted by the letters, and not one of them could get past the first few paragraphs before the imbecilic premises made them cringe. The demon's power to glamour did not apply to Robin's writing.

I did convince Robin's sleaze-ball friend to bring me my computer, the books destined for my brother, and my cooking pots. So, at least I had what was most important. Robin tried extortion: to exchange other household items for chances to meet in a coffee shop so he could tell me his side of the story. He sent me an email with photos of himself and the two cats I left behind to show what I was missing, what I was giving up. He hunted through old cell phone records to find phone numbers of my friends, found two, called them to tell them I was in danger because I didn't know what I was doing, and they should tell me I was wrong.

It took mediation to resolve the financial issues in the divorce.

Understanding Evil: My Soul Contract

While Robin wanted *me,* Daniel wanted my money. In his mind, I had to pay for my freedom. He produced the lease I signed, trying to bill me for years of rent unpaid. But since he had never "tried to collect" before, and I had proof of my having paid for all the other expenses as per the agreement he and I had made when Robin and I moved into the house, the request was dismissed.

Daniel wanted me to provide Robin maintenance, for it was my income that had supported us. Well, those geese and the voice that came with them had advised me well. Because I quit my job right then and there, enough time passed for me to be considered unemployed for just *exactly* long enough to disqualify the demand for maintenance. If I had finished out the semester, I would have had to come up with money for Robin.

Lastly, Daniel still wanted half of my medical trust fund. This trust fund, the cursed money that it was, was not something I could access without going through the administrator at the bank. It was only to be used for approved medical expenses for me, an arrangement, while unfair to me in general, protected the funds from Daniel's greedy grasp. Daniel may have thought that whatever was mine was his; the court disagreed. Daniel received no monies.

I was granted the few belongings I requested be turned over to me. In his last petty attempt to make himself a victim in this situation, Daniel asked that I provide Robin an accounting of cost for each item on my list. The judge told him, "No!" And Robin, as his very last, final interaction with me, refused to turn over a cutting board I had asked for as I had bought it long before I met him. Fine. Gavin, my first husband, came with me to retrieve my belongings and to make sure Robin didn't kill me.

The home I was originally supposed to live in sold (of course after my mother and I spent a lot of time and money fixing it up), and I ended up in another of my brother's properties – half of a duplex. I didn't want it, but there I was, and soon, once I had a full-time job, purchased it from him. I moved in, however, before the divorce was finalized and was afraid I'd be found through public property records and hauled off by Robin as he threatened. But fate again protected me. The piece of property didn't appear on any county records due to a clerical error, which was not realized until tax assessments were mailed out. It seems that a man in another city was erroneously attributed ownership of the duplex during the time Robin (according to his sleaze-bag friend) was trying to find out where I was. For some reason, I was worth saving, and the universe saw to that.

The divorce papers came through, and I never spoke to Robin again. I never wept over losing him. I wept over losing my home and the two cats I couldn't carry with me. But not over Robin. Those tears spent themselves the day he "died," and the weeks that followed. Besides, there is no Robin to speak with. The entity in his body has no self-awareness beyond its own desires. Trying to have meaningful dialogue with him was like talking to a robot that was programmed to say the same words, make the same speech over and over, no matter what one said to it. It would be no different now. I'm assuming no new way of thinking would ever emerge from him. I'm assuming he would just have another tantrum.

Not that the original inhabitant of the body qualified as benign. Not even from the beginning. Janet, his mother, said that already at just a few months old, he would look at people angrily and scowl. Then came the diabetes at three years old. That did not help his disposition. But he developed a sense of humor of sorts and passed as human.

What took over after the grand mal seizure death had no potential "human" switch that could be activated from the inside or out. It was pure ego, pure "I want," pure "I'll pulverize you if you don't do as I say." It was and is incapable of empathy or mercy. The look in the eyes was never the same as before the seizure that created the opening for a new passenger. There was no mischief left in them, only hatred. It had the heart of the colonizer.

The red-eyed demon is the manifestation of Daniel's legacy. Families give birth to demons to by accident more often than by intention. The energy passes from one generation to the next. Daniel's parents, for instance, were the type of Christians who believed that homosexuals could be forced into being heterosexual if the entire community participated in their conversion (group brainwashing). Even though he dispensed with the religion itself, Daniel could not help but be affected by the culture of it, one which accepted that the "righteous" had the "right" to coerce deviants into submission. Daniel became the vessel for an ideology that not only allows but encourages the strong and privileged to bludgeon the weak or unconventional. His sense of entitlement became hegemony incarnate and produced a sentience (demon) to which he ultimately sacrificed his son.

The body of Robin, I believe is still alive. The entity in it posted on Facebook a year or so ago his wish that everyone on his/her birthday should be allowed to kill one person. I cannot imagine he is fully self-supporting. I assume he will always be Daniel's burden, though I wonder what will happen when Daniel dies. Maybe Robin will die first. His body *is* the one with diabetes.

It is now over fifteen years since my flight from Robin. I've wondered countless hours what purpose the experience served in my evolution in this life. What I decided was that the original spirit, the one that waited for me in my grandmother's basement, was indeed fay, and indeed took on or was granted the life of Robin for a deliberate and complex purpose. Maybe the original fay soul felt that if we joined forces against Daniel, we could win. We didn't. Or did we?

But it seemed that Daniel, who truly thought of himself as an unstoppable force, met, in his own son, an immovable object. In battering himself against his son, perhaps he has learned or will yet learn to reassess his own insufferable modus operandi. Since Daniel failed to honor the original soul in the body, he must now serve the demon that took its place. Robin will never be independent.

Maybe the nature of their (father and son or father and demon) relationship was the other way around. Maybe Daniel was the immovable object. Only Robin was a not so powerful a force. Maybe the original Robin lost his right to occupy the body because he chose to try to change Daniel instead of maturing himself or removing himself. Maybe all possibilities are true simultaneously. There is never only one explanation.

For me, the original Robin provided me a chance in this life to experience something extraordinary, to be near his fire, to connect with another physical body with such passion and compatibility that all barriers or illusions of separateness dissolved for priceless moments. He was a precious, exotic pet, to some degree soulless (no human soul), a confounding muse, a divine flame that danced on the stage like nothing earthly ever could. There was a terrifying infinity in his eyes. Then, he was gone, his place usurped by the manifestation of Daniel's ambition and custom of privilege. It is interesting to note that Robin's seizure occurred just weeks after trust fund had been established. The trust fund had its own demon. Maybe one spoke to the other.

Either way, Robin would never return. I would never know that kind of a connection again with anyone. In a way, I died with him, remaining here as a ghost to complete the rest of my mission. My goal before incarnation was to establish this life as my last life in human form.

Understanding Evil: My Soul Contract

I am tired. But before I departed permanently, I had wanted to learn (and then report) about how evil works on this plane. I wanted to write my conclusions into a dissertation of sorts – these narratives and their culminating thesis.

A dissertation. That's what I called it in the seventeen page letter I sent to Daniel (with a copy to Robin's sister) after the divorce was final. The purpose of the letter was to point out his duty to support Robin, as he was the one most summarily responsible for making and then breaking him. He was, after all, the father, literally and figuratively. He had the education and the physical health and the monetary resources that Robin did not have and would not ever have. Daniel was the perfect colonizer.

After three years, I did send Robin (the demon in him) a letter, too, actually a book of letters. I assembled about 60 pages worth of prose for him: a copy of the letter I had sent to Daniel, a copy of the letter I had sent to Janet (to accompany a set of photos) right about the time Robin was being moved out of the house I shared with him into a condo that Daniel owned, a copy of a letter I had written to the sleaze-ball friend, and most importantly, all of it the truth I wanted him to hear from me. I had them all spiral bound and mailed to the new condo address (the family had no choice but to move Robin closer to them) I was able to find online. Then, I burned all copies of anything that remained at home and deleted all the files from my computer. As far as I know, he still lives in that condo.

The part of the "treatise" I wrote to Robin directly consisted of two versions of the story, one a "this world" explanation of what happened between us and one an "alternative world" explanation of the same plot. That's how this drama played out. Two versions running simultaneously. Here and there, a duel between this world and the other. That's how evil that involves both supernatural beings and humans simultaneously works.

Two worlds that overlap but that are still separate.

I am fairly sure Robin received the letter, but have no idea if he read it. But it doesn't matter now. It served its purpose. It became a very preliminary outline for my theory about evil in the world. It was the first time I laid out parallel interpretations of the same events occurring simultaneously as mundane and metaphysical. In writing it, the light dawned, so to speak. The mechanisms of evil were suddenly definable, the mysteries of it accessible.

In this life, on this plane, in the interaction with Daniel's family, and in my after-the-fact analysis, I came to understand patterns of human behavior that produce the colonizer/abuser, the way those patterns are passed on, and all the attributes: the entitlement, the gaslighting, the brutality, the extortion, the greed, the power lust, the hegemony, the brainwashing, the moral relativism, the violence, and lust for destruction. Daniel was the product of a legacy that promoted bullying; he became a bully with a great scope of influence. Because his son was unable to become a mature productive adult, he destroyed him; his son, in turn, destroyed me. Somewhere in this progression, the bullying spawned or attracted a demonic entity.

When Daniel had to deal with the fallout of his betrayal of Janet, he was furious. He didn't think there should be fallout. Friends they had had as a couple turned on him for his cheating on Janet with that grad student. They wouldn't invite him to their homes anymore (though they invited Janet). "How do you think that makes me feel?" he said. When I told Robin that he had hurt me irreparably, that he had broken me, he said, "How do you think that makes me feel?" After all, he had done nothing wrong.

Robin didn't stand a chance against Daniel's sophistry, the relentless propaganda meant to outline a life plan Robin that found repugnant. Robin didn't stand a chance against the relentless devouring maw of the demon. When Robin's seizure presented an opening, the ugly changeling hopped in. My only hope now is that, deprived of me as a target, it will turn on its maker. Perhaps it will punish Daniel in ways that Robin could not accomplish on his own. For now, the entity is stuck in a human body, one with terrible health concerns, a life with very little sovereignty. It must be furious!

Yet, through these terrible circumstances, a gift was given me by the universe or by the original Robin himself. I was allowed to reenact a set of circumstances very much like those of my last life so that I could reevaluate them. In that past existence, an evil man had taken away my two children, and I could do nothing to save them either. I was born grieving their loss and laden with guilt over my failure to protect them. Was he one of those children? I don't think so. I think he, by choice or by chance, took on the role of surrogate, or just hitched along and having a similar agenda, latched on me to fight in the same crusade – against a powerful and evil patriarch. I just had to survive first and then figure out what happened. I think I did this time.

Ironically, because I fully and finally came to understand that I didn't have a snowball's chance to save Robin, I came to understand that I could no more have saved my children in that other life. Repeating the dynamics gave me the insight I needed in order to forgive myself for a tragic loss I perceived as having been my fault. It was no more my fault then than now. Some forms of evil are so powerful and complete, so pervasive, that one single person doesn't have a prayer trying to defeat it. It takes a village. For the evil has a village at its beck and call. I had no village, then or now, not a human one anyway.

I still, foolishly, when I'm sad or afraid, find myself saying, "I loved you, Robin" to the universe, as if he can hear me from the other side of death, as if some justification for all my pain could be found in that declaration, as if I can be absolved for my part in all of this. For I did love him, and then he died. Then I tried to keep him with me in a doll as my grandmother had tried to keep her first born son here in a doll (See essay "Believe Me"). Did he forgive her for keeping him bound here for years beyond his death?

Is Robin waiting somewhere again for me? Will he forgive me for trying to keep him with me on this plane? (it wasn't for very long …) I think the answer for me is yes because I think he let me know that he is back in the, I guess, fairy realm from which he had come to me. A few months after I burned the doll, and was by myself in my new residence, I woke one night to a presence in the house. In the living room, on the sofa, I found him (a vision), reposed as if in a final resting position, dressed in a silvery tunic, with his eyes peacefully closed, his arms folded over his chest, and oddly enough, a slender sword at his side. It was like seeing a hologram of his funeral in that other world. I believe he was letting me know he, the soul I knew originally, had gone home. The divorce at that time was not yet final, so I'm assuming he wanted to make sure that I knew that the body of Robin was inhabited by something that was not Robin, and that it was all right to let go.

All the time I have spent so much worry on what might happen when Robin's body finally dies, thus releasing Daniel's demon, I never considered what might happen when *I* died. Will I see the original Robin again? What if I do? What if I don't? These thoughts didn't even occur to me until the writing of these words. They feel very strange, as if just uttering them is making the ground beneath me seem less than stable. They feel very sad.

The evil I learned about through Robin's family came from the red-eyed demon it produced that took over Robin's body when his spirit broke.

Understanding Evil: My Soul Contract

A walk-in. An entity that had lurked about waiting for the opportunity that the grand mal seizure and my ill-advised actions provided. My last vision of Robin was of his standing in the living room he and I had shared, glowering at me with the red glow in his blue eyes. Humorless, hateful, furious, merciless, vengeful, lurid, avaricious, terrifying red. I hope when it's finally free of flesh that I am unfindable, protected, or no longer palatable. What a thing to wish for!

Join Us

One of the inevitable experiences in store for anyone on a metaphysical path is the encounter with a recruiter and his/her fanatical agenda. I can guarantee that at some point in the journey, one of them will show up, along with his/her minions and propaganda. I've had several such experiences. The most pivotal one occurred when I was in my late thirties. I really should have been more careful, but even the most outrageous can appear subtle at the outset. At the time, I thought suspicion just would have seemed farfetched and made me look paranoid, but now, I'm thinking paranoia isn't always a bad thing.

The whole thing seemed to start so casually, but I now know it was far from casual. The male half of a neo-pagan couple, Darren, really *did* hunt me down, and he might have eventually found me anyway, but his doing so had been made a lot easier by a certain student of mine. During those years, I taught various levels of English courses at various community colleges in the state. It didn't really provide a living, but it also didn't *not* provide a living, so it's what I did. One of its benefits was a certain degree of freedom other jobs wouldn't allow. It allowed me the space and time to live my unusual life. It left me unprotected from and, therefore, open to a whole world of experiences.

This particular semester, I had my usual course load to teach, time slots chosen, students registered, rooms assigned, and books ordered. However, a few days before the semester began, the department chair called to say another instructor and I had to trade sections of one of the composition courses because a particular student who had taken the

101 course with me demanded I be the teacher for the 102 course. The student said he would quit the college if his request weren't met. I was dumbfounded. Department chairs ordinarily do not bend to students' arbitrary whims; this young man wasn't anyone with influence, not political or financial anyway; and I couldn't imagine why he wanted me as his teacher – I could barely remember who he was at all. Yet, so it went.

The switch in classes put me in another building at a different time. It worked out in spite of everything. The other instructor and I luckily had chosen the same textbook, so the students were fine with the change, and the room was much more to my liking. When I called roll on the first day, the kid who instigated the switch asked me, "Do you like the change of course I arranged? It is my gift to you." The phrasing, somewhat archaic, and full of innuendo, implied a great deal more than it stated.

The voice had a familiar sultry tone to it that could not have melted out of the kid's mouth. It wasn't human. Here, after more than two decades, was the black-eyed demon, the most terrifying of all my demons, and it had asked the question with the seductive depth that I knew too well. I could feel its music in my bones. But all I could do under the circumstances was answer affirmatively and move on. The kid said nothing more, just smiled and leaned back in the chair.

The old proverbial "my blood ran cold" couldn't even remotely cover what went through me as the realization hit home. It was the taunt, THE taunt, the one that would precede another terrible entrapment, the one that announced a coming doom. Not again. Still, I could do nothing but conduct business as usual and wait, stuck in the constructs of the mundane world, with tenuous job security and a volatile home life. Demon or no, I had a class to teach; I needed a paycheck; and I couldn't very well explain my situation to anyone.

Join Us

From that very first day, I established a habit of visiting the campus grind immediately after class, standing out on the deck with my steaming coffee and a cigarette or two or three, as such was my habit then, waiting for my next class. Also, from that very first day, Darren made himself known to me, with criticisms about my smoking, with marginally witty small talk, with the "gotta have coffee" comradery he used to start our relationship. That initial encounter with that student had rattled me enough to allow Darren an "in"; I took comfort in speaking to someone who seemed normal and harmless and close to my own age.

It didn't take long, however, for subsequent conversations to become less comfortable. Darren relentlessly focused on our sometime getting together to have a real talk, say maybe, about my pentacle and what it means. About a month later, I finally gave in, hoping to stop the pestering, and agreed to meet him in the lobby of the library to talk at length, mostly because I had to talk to someone about what had happened that day that first day of class.

The day of my agreed-to meeting with Darren, about a month into the semester, that kid came in late for class. For half an hour, he said nothing, just sat still and watched me move around the room. Maybe I was talking about semicolons, maybe about notecards, who knows? Then, in the middle of my lecture, I simply stopped talking, my breath momentarily halted, for I had caught sight of the demon, of the bottomless blackness of demon's presence, in the kid's eyes and froze. Just as I did so, the silver chain from which my pentacle hung around my neck broke with a tug from some unseen force. I caught the pentacle as it fell, stared at it in my hand, and looked back at the kid, utterly speechless.

Here I was, in public, out in the open, and there was the black-eyed monster, present and menacing, just a few feet away from me. It knew I couldn't say anything and give it, and therefore myself, away, so I just stood there. It isn't as if I could have just explained to my class that my lecture had been interrupted by a demon, sorry. My paralysis ended when suddenly the kid packed up his books and jacket and bolted out of the room, and I never saw or heard from him again. I put my pentacle in my pocket and continued.

I was so glad to be meeting Darren that day. I had to talk to someone about what happened in my classroom! The conversation, however, was disturbingly unsuccessful. Darren derailed my narrative again and again. We were not, apparently, going to talk about demons. He wouldn't even use the word or indicate he had ever even heard it before. He cut into my sentences, talked over me, found something in the school newspaper to point out to me, all in order to deflect my every attempt to return to the topic.

For all intents and purposes, Darren had had demons brainwashed right out of his consciousness. That he became as agitated as he did was surely a sign of his reprogramming. He wasn't allowed to talk about them. He couldn't even use the term. The whole situation was bizarre. When challenged, all he did was glare at me and say I wasn't making any sense; he couldn't understand what I was talking about. It was absolutely infuriating! Eventually, I became too frustrated to continue.

In the four years of my interaction with Darren and his wife, Marla, this absurdity (among others) was never remedied. A discussion of demons would never occur. Our interaction was and still is hard to justify, especially the question of what I was thinking by participating in it. They were, they told me, part of a coven. Darren had been brought into the practice by his wife Marla, who had had a "teacher" who had initiated *her*. Their role, as presented at first, was to help people on the path. They even had a non-profit "church" complete with website for their endeavors. There was a nauseating and almost militant "greater good" tint to everything. Darren had "found" me for a "reason." I would "learn a lot" from Marla. She would teach me about the Goddess and Her ways. Not once did either one *ask* me what I already knew or what my magickal goals were.

I sure didn't take any of it seriously; I had no intention of "learning" anything from Marla. I was quite aware most self-promoted gurus are full of excrement and ego and perhaps some mental illness. Mostly, they were power mongers. Also, I didn't need a teacher. I was by this point in my life in "magickal grad school," so to speak; I just found it unfathomable that someone would try to put me back in "magickal grade school." They thought I was a novice because I hadn't been trained by *them*. The hubris! The audacity! To them, what I knew, or thought I knew, couldn't have been real, I was told, because I hadn't been properly prepared. Besides, my way was reckless and out of bounds. I was not to talk about it. *Not to talk about it?* Who *tells* someone who is educated – and nearly forty years old – he/she is *not allowed* to talk about something? I couldn't believe what I was hearing. What were they thinking? More importantly, what was *I* thinking?

My relationship with Darren could have a quite simple explanation. I just thought I had found a friend who was capable of understanding the world beyond the mundane and who was funny – I mean, he *was* funny. I *needed* a friend who was. I was steeped in conflict with my family; I was in an abusive marriage; and I was completely isolated from the few friends I had left. But still, the distraction caused by all of these circumstances doesn't fully justify my lack of common sense.

I suspect the situation was just so weird I thought I must be missing something, misunderstanding something. I couldn't believe it was really happening, but clearly, it *was* happening, so all I could do was engage in denial. It's what people do. When faced with the outrageous, they put on blinders, ear plugs, gas masks, and helmets. I was no different from anyone else in this respect and, therefore, when I found myself in odd circumstances without quite knowing how I got there, I didn't run.

So when Darren, for instance, decided one afternoon to pressure me into having sex with him, I had to wheedle my way out of the situation carefully. He had, under the pretense of having to feed the dogs, ushered me into his home before I realized it. He delivered an interesting line of reasoning in order to obligate my compliance: (a) he was a servant of the Goddess; (b) servants of the Goddess should have a good grasp of sexuality; (c) he hadn't been able to develop an expertise because he had been raised as a conservative Christian; (d) I had lived a free and richly sexual life and had all kinds of experience; (e) I would be serving the Goddess by educating him. Right.

I listened to his speech, thinking, "This isn't happening!" My body was simply a resource to be acquired, an object. Holy crap! Not only that, Darren failed to consider was how, without a doubt, my husband at this time would have *killed* me. But, the most important element in the plan, however, didn't even occur to Darren for one instant – my sense of aesthetics. I didn't *want* him! He was an OK companion, but I found him physically repulsive. I stuck with the "potentially being killed" excuse and extricated myself from the situation. Since it never came up again, I let it go. It slipped into that amnesia of denial.

What almost concluded the friendship a few months later was an argument about my jewelry. I regularly wore on the average four silver chains, each with a pendant of a pagan symbol, among then, of course, my pentacle. Darren insisted I no longer wear my jewelry because by doing so, I was advertising my pagan sympathies, calling attention to myself. It was bad for all pagans. He even went so far as to say he couldn't be seen with me if I wore it. My predictably rebellious response was to add on a few more necklaces, so I veritably clinked when I walked. We fought about it quite viciously at least half a dozen times. If I wanted the opportunity to become part of something good, he said, I would have to present myself correctly, would have to give up my preposterous habits.

This whole episode demonstrated to me Darren still thought of me as a project. The argument was not about the jewelry, not really; it was about my refusal to submit to the authority he imagined he had over me, over *me*. It never dawned on him he had no such authority, nor did I *need* his permission to do, well, *anything*. I rejected dogma, of any kind, outright. I was a sovereign entity. I acknowledged no hierarchy. The Goddess and I were on speaking terms for quite a while already, but heretically to Darren, She and I were partners in a mutual venture. It was as if I were a cat, but Darren and Marla were determined to treat me as though I were a hamster because that's how they had classified me. How dare I act like a cat!

No matter how many ways I tried to make my position clear, it was if I my words fell into a vacuum. The divide between our paradigms was unbridgeable, but that didn't stop me from associating with Darren or Darren from continuing to assume a role I had never agreed to acknowledge for him. It just didn't seem anyone would actually be so delusional, and certainly not so delusional as to act on the delusion, as he and Marla inevitably did.

The rift over the jewelry didn't last forever, though. Once Darren and I ran into each other after a few weeks of non-communication, I just resumed our comradery. My life was sliding into the abyss anyway, but again as before in my life, I chose the devil I knew. It still didn't occur to me that I was being set up. And I still, however, to this day, can't quite decide where to place the blame.

But at that time, I began to share my problems with Marla.

Again, I was offered advice that really wasn't very helpful, but which was presented as some great and powerful wisdom. When I divulged to her how bad things were for me at home with my abusive husband, she handed me a sprig of lavender. If I just waved it over my bed, it would calm the energies because lavender was sacred to the Goddess. *Just wave it over the bed!* My husband, Robin, was a psychotic monster, by then fully inhabited by a demon. Robin had always been violent, drug addicted, prone to destructive outbursts, willing to risk his life (and others') in fits of misbehavior, but once the demon showed up, Robin turned into something truly treacherous.

The fact that Marla so clearly misread the situation goes to illuminate how off her perception in general was. I was living with a classic abuser, made exponentially worse by his unearthly passenger. *Just wave it over the bed!* That was all she could come up with. If she had said set fire to it and stuff it up Robin's ass when he was passed out cold from alcohol or one of his diabetic episodes, I might have thought her advice useful. It would have at least proved she understood the magnitude of my predicament. *Just wave it over the bed!* Aagh!

The only real assistance I received from Darren in dealing with my husband was his being a witness when Robin's family attempted an intervention to keep me from leaving. I convinced Darren to come to my house for the meeting, as I was going to be completely at their mercy. He got on a bus and made his way to me, but then Robin attacked him as he came in the door, knocking his coffee out of his hand and pushing him down the stairs. I gave Darren the key to my car so he could sit outside and call the police if necessary. When the intervention was over, and I had lied my way into buying myself some more time to escape before the family would have me committed for being "obviously insane," I drove Darren home, and gave him two twenty dollar bills to keep in his wallet – in case I needed him to come back, he could take a taxi and be there quickly.

Luckily, I gave him the money, for two weeks after I moved the 60 miles away, Darren needed a ride to the veterinarian for his cat, and called me, wondering if I could get to him in time to take the cat to a 7:30 AM appointment. Getting him to the appointment meant I would have had to get up before 4 AM, shower, waking my mother (with whom I was staying to hide from Robin until the divorce was final) in the process, driving 60 miles, picking up Darren and the cat, driving another 40 minutes to the veterinarian, waiting through the appointment, driving 40 minutes to drop Darren and the cat back home, then driving 60 miles back. He just expected I would make the drive without question. Trade a favor for a favor. I told him to use the forty dollars for a taxi. Today, I am pretty sure the request for my driving to see him had nothing to do with the cat.

A couple of months after my move, when Darren invited me to Winter Solstice ritual, after I finally freed myself from Robin, I thought, "All right, I'll get to see what this is all about." Darren led me to believe there would be people for me to meet, and we would have a nice dinner after the ritual. He even suggested I dress nicely. I still remember how stupidly I looked forward to being acknowledged as a colleague. That's what I thought the invitation meant.

When I got there (and to get there, I had to drive those 60 miles), I was totally shocked. As soon as I arrived, a candle on a stick inside a paper cup (to protect it from the wind), a photocopied script for the ritual, complete with a little history of the God and Goddess, a general benediction, the lyrics to a little "merry meet" song. Because I had been misled into believing this was to be an indoor event, I was inappropriately wearing a long skirt, make-up, and fancy sweater, and shoes not meant for treading about in an outdoor park.

Adding to my confusion was the fact that I was the only one who showed up! Darren said the invitation had been made, and if people wanted to come, they could come. Marla, it was explained to me, was offering an opportunity for people to share. It was completely open, he said. If they decided not to come, that was OK too. The dozen or so candles sat sadly in their paper cups on the plastic camping table. The photocopies remained pinned down by a paperweight. Darren and Marla both must have been so embarrassed, disappointed at the flop of a turn out. Didn't they have a coven?

We chit-chatted till the moment of sunset. It was time! The ritual, absurdly (to me!), proceeded with the reading of the history of the Goddess and God, like an informative sermon, the singing of a little song like a hymn. Then Marla, Darren, and I lit the candles, holding them toward the setting sun, and repeating after Marla the words to an encouragement for the sun to return again from the long night. We reiterated her words like a congregation repeating phrases uttered by the preacher.

Marla claimed that she, as priestess, had the power and duty to make it happen: "You can do it, Sun. You can do it. I command you to return. I give you the courage to return." As if the Sun depended on her urging and entreaty for its ability to rise again and begin making the days longer once more. Of course, what would it do without her? Clearly, it would get lost out in space. Thank goodness for Marla.

This was my first experience with this kind of ceremony. I was, of course, utterly stunned by how much the script resembled a standard, simple-minded Protestant church service. My group rituals had always been collective raisings of power to promote a common agenda. A mass spell. Or a cooperative parting of the Veil. Or a party with the elementals. Not a religious service. Not even close. I might have used the sabbats for their energies, but the rest was free-form, wild and visceral, perhaps hedonistic and dangerous. There was no template for the procedure, no trappings; everything was organic. What I saw in this event seemed juvenile and scripted. I was embarrassed for them. For what they intended as much as for the train wreck the event turned out to be.

But here was Marla all teary-eyed proud of herself. She said she was so happy to be introducing me to Sabbat ritual, sharing the most profound experience with me! By the conclusion of this particular Yule, I was so mortified for Marla I was speechless. This, THIS, was the sacred knowledge that would transform my soul? Then, to top off the sham, dinner was a visit to an all-you-can-eat buffet at a Chinese restaurant. That was the sacred celebration.

Why didn't anyone show up? One would think a coven would actually *show up* on such an important day. My guess is that everyone else had more sense than I. Now, I never met the coven *as a coven*. Occasionally, we would "happen upon" a member here and there, in a bookstore, in a mall. I would find myself introduced and like a piece of livestock at market assessed; then, the individual(s) would nod some sort of signal to Darren and walk away.

I did meet Marla's "teacher." What a toad! He was short, fat, balding, dumpy, smelly, with thick crooked glasses and pants that were too short. His mundane world expertise was computers, but he clearly was not making a lot of money at it. I met him when he agreed to reformat one of my brother's old computers for a friend of mine. Again, I didn't even think about what information was on that computer; I am doubtful my brother erased anything or even thought about what might end up in the wrong hands. Hopefully, nothing important . . . .

The delivery of the computer to my friend, though, became a prime opportunity for Darren to suggest to my friend that her two young daughters ought to be taken from public schools and brought into the coven, to be trained while young. Darren just assumed a trade was taking place. The exchange was the technical assistance with the computer for access to the children. My friend, understandably, kicked Darren and the toad out of her house.

The toad also loaned Marla, who still had a driver's license, his car to drive me and my dying cat on one of the worst nightmare trips to the veterinarian in my life. My Luca cat was only three years old, but had developed pulmonary edema and her heart was failing. She needed twice daily medication for just the few more days it would buy her. I didn't know what to do when I was told Robin's aunt was planning a four-day family get-together, and we were obligated to go. I had no more freedom with Robin's family than my own.

Darren came up with the idea that his veterinarian, because she was a witch, was where I should take Luca. He just didn't let up, so, after much persuasion, I agreed to have his veterinarian, whose office was across the entire city (the 40 minutes mentioned earlier), take a look at Luca to see if the cat could be boarded with her. On the day of the appointment, Darren and Marla talked me out of driving myself; I don't remember why. All I cared about was Luca.

When I met the veterinarian, I realized she was clearly someone of more importance than Darren let on. According to my after-the fact analysis, Darren was involved, in a service capacity to a powerful coven, to which this woman belonged and perhaps led. The "coven" Marla imagined she was forming by collecting souls like mine was small potatoes. Something about the vet seemed cold. Darren had overstepped a line by bringing me to her. She had a better sense of who I was than Darren did.

But here we were, I with the cat I loved more than any cat I had ever loved needing a veterinarian. The vet listened to Luca's heart and stepped back carefully, saying the cat was just a hair's breath away from . . . she didn't finish the sentence. She would not be able to board the cat. Well, I paid my bill for the visit (more than I had planned on) and got back in the car to go home. I sat in the back with the cat carrier on my lap.

Suddenly, Luca began to have such a panic attack that I opened the carrier to put my hand in to comfort her, but she shot out, and then dropped onto my lap, dead, urine spilling everywhere and her weight suddenly limp and still. I started screaming, *No, No, No!* But she was gone. The last few minutes of her life were in a crappy car, in a cat carrier, with people she didn't know, and on the road, not with the other cats she loved!

I carried the body inside when I got home. Marla and Darren didn't want to come in because of Robin. They said the air in the house was too full of THC from Robin's habit, and they couldn't risk breathing it in in case they might be subject to a drug test. That was the reason they gave. They just dropped me and the dead cat off in the driveway and left me to my fate and my grief. Neither called to check on me for a couple of weeks.

And, Robin, well, Robin screamed at me for hours about what I had done to the cat. I had killed her! She died terrified, in a stranger's car, and it was my fault. The loss of Luca broke me. In retrospect now, I realize if she would have died in my house, I would have taken my own life on the same spot in the months that followed. Things with Robin were by then on the road to the end, to a potentially murderous end. That the cat died in transit, and since I wasn't paying attention to the road, I would never be able to find the exact location again,

Before Luca's death, during the months of her illness, a few other events took place, helping to prepare the path for what finally did follow. At that time, I played with the idea of going back to school, maybe for a PhD in mythology or literature or myth or folklore or whatever I fantasized might actually exist as a possibility. The thought came about due to my running across some interesting books in the campus library while I was waiting for Darren one day. When he arrived, I shared my "finds" and ideas with him. Immediately, he started voicing plans for my degree being useful to the school he and his associates were thinking of creating for young pagans. I could be a teacher in this proposed school and share the gifts of knowledge I was given. In other words, any resource or accomplishment of mine would be put to use for the greater good.

The same theme emerged when I drove him out into the plains to the old wheat farm my first husband's family owned and which I was permitted to use for my private rituals. Darren immediately began citing its potential as part of his great plan for a large pagan community. "What a great place! We could put an altar there, and use this space for a circle." I had brought him here because it was my sacred space, and I wanted my entities to meet him, and I wanted to share my "world" with him, not as a piece of real estate for him to colonize. He wouldn't let up even when I told him it wasn't *my* land to sell or donate. "Don't worry about that," he said. "We'll work it out." I have no idea what working it out meant.

Among all the other goings-on, perhaps to check on the progress of this drama, the black-eyed demon made another visit to me those years, also during the months of Luca's terminal illness, when Mark, an old lover, came to visit me. As we sat in my house talking, he acknowledged the cat's imminent death, talking about the expression on her face. His tone of voice was clinical, impatient, and full of disregard for me and the cat, for our souls. Usually, he would at least make an effort at pretense, especially when trying to win me over. He was, instead, a bit robotic. Though I thought it odd, I didn't make an issue of it, for we were heading out to a restaurant, then a stroll in the indoor mall, as it was too cold to walk anywhere else.

When Mark stopped to use the mall restroom, I sat down on the benches in front of one of the department stores to wait for him. I happened to look up when he came out of the restroom and caught a glimpse of his eyes. The gaze wasn't Mark's. He walked over to me and said in that voice that was also not Mark's, "I will wait for you." At that future time, when I was going to leave Robin, he would be waiting, he said. But I *had* no plans for leaving Robin at that time (not till after Luca died). I was going to stay until one of us was dead, even if the end were facilitated by my suicide. "I will wait for you," he repeated. Then, suddenly, the demon vacated, and Mark complained about the effect of the greasy food on his intestines. Yes, indeed, all Mark again.

It upset me enough to tell Darren about it, forgetting what a lost cause that would be. Of course, he had no comment when I told him of the demonic visit. After three years of our friendship, he would still not engage in discussions of such concerns, let alone my most significant past experiences, my relationships with my magickal partners, and the legacy handed to me by my witch grandmother, for instance, or, needless to say, my demons. None of that mattered, he said. I needed to learn from Marla. She was a "wolf" and was wise and would guide me. Well, I wasn't going to go back to her for any more sprigs of lavender.

In the process of separating myself from Robin, I had a lot of magick to do – and undo. However, when I burned the doll (my doll of all dolls!) I had made of Robin, Darren became furious. Why didn't I tell him first? He said he thought I understood I was to do no magick unless it fit my "level," unless I cleared it with him first. Level? What level? WTF? I was not a novice! I didn't need his permission! I was a free entity! It was just like my first grade teacher's scolding me for the I'd I had only been given permission to read the first twelve pages. Who does that?

Understanding Evil: My Soul Contract

"But whatever you do affects us. It reflects on Marla's abilities as your priestess." My *priestess*? *My* priestess? Again, WTF? At what point did I get drafted? That doll was none of Marla's business. It was *my* sacred artifact, *my* creation, *my* responsibility, *my* fate, yet she thought it belonged to her, that *I* belonged to her. Soon, however, came my catastrophic flight from Robin, and it took precedence over any concern I had over Marla's perceived jurisdiction.

Shortly after burning the doll, I left Robin, and for a brief time *did* connect with Mark. The demon did, in fact, "wait for me." I had moved 60 miles away from Robin and my home leaving my entire household behind, having been able to keep only three of my five cats with me. I had to wait months for the lawyers to work out the rest of our separation. But I maintained correspondence with Darren and Marla. They constantly pushed me to come visit, to move in with them, to continue my progress "on the path." I did not comply because I was busy with Mark until that ended.

My relationship with Mark didn't end well either. After nearly two decades, I figured out that to Mark, I was never going to be anything but a pet, that he fancied himself upper class and I was never going to be his equal. In truth, he was a failure and was reaching for me a last resort. So, he tried to trap me into a marriage with him, but without revealing to me that he had become impotent. When I realized his deceit, I sent him packing for the last time. Darren, however, didn't want me to leave Mark. Instead, he wanted me to work it out. He'd never even met Mark! We fought again, but not for long, for in the middle of that struggle, Darren and Marla committed their final trespass.

Who would have thought these two buffoons, with their junior high school drama version of an old earth-based religion could do what they ultimately ended up doing? And why? The answer lay in my family's history and a relic – a dagger. My family is from Eastern Europe, the former Yugoslavia. They were Germans who had settled there more than a century and a half before the war. Their ancestors had drained the swamps and were farmers. They were mostly Lutherans, but some of the women were witches – midwives, herbalists, and more. Sometimes, I jokingly say some of the Grimm fairy tales were based on my ancestors. Most every myth contains a kernel of truth.

During WWII, everything, needless to say, went by the way of chaos, slaughter, politics, and fate. My uncle, though he resisted as long as he could, was eventually drafted into the fight. Many of the German speaking people were forced into service, especially if they met the prerequisite physical characteristics. Nothing could protect my uncle as Hitler's armies were reduced in number by the Allies, and the recruiters scoured the villages. The Nazis took everyone they could. Once in, the unwilling draftees had no choice but to participate in the atrocities and the thievery. My uncle ran away as soon as he could.

Somehow, though, my uncle, it was rumored, though never proven, and in circles outside my family (for we didn't hear of it), ended up with at least one artifact, specifically, a dagger. A certain legend from Tibet (which the Nazis combed for relics and magickal implements) described a certain set of daggers that allowed the wielder to control demons. Again, no proof, and all those involved are now dead, the bodies cremated, and the estates long dispersed. The lure of the dagger, however, persisted. Apparently, also, a popular female science fiction writer used the legend for a novel. Darren and his crew had come across it, had done some research, had put two and two together and evidently come up with a theory, a dramatis personae, which included me as I was the descendent.

Although their efforts are not covered in history classes, it is true various covens in Great Britain focused their magick on protecting their home, the earth, humanity from the Nazis. But Darren indicated the work was still going on. The duty had passed to current covens, among which, he hinted, was the one he was associated with. He would never be specific, though, always, instead, talked in vagaries. The dagger, however, would be useful.

My uncle was still alive when I met Darren, but died about a year or so later. He had accumulated quite a bit of money in the bank, and had no children, spouse, or parent, only my mother (his sister) and my brother, Rudyard, and I. However, I was deprived of my share of the inheritance because of my black sheep status, my mother's evil, and the general cowardice of everyone else in the picture. When I made an attempt to stand up for myself, my mother ended any and all communication with me, changed her locks, and took my name off any family related property. Darren seemed to be my friend during this drama.

While I was still with Robin, a pivotal event in my family's history took place. Before my uncle died, he confessed to Rudyard how back in Europe, immediately after the war, and for reasons he did not reveal, he took up with an occult group (which he didn't outright name – how annoying all the vagaries are!), and said from that moment on, they had run his entire life. There were trips to South America. There were meetings at the UN building in New York. There were break-ins at his house. He hated those people, he said. But the one thing he still wanted to do was induct Rudyard into the group. He said it was so that he and my brother would recognize one another in the other world, after death.

So, on his deathbed, my uncle began the ritual, tracing the secret signs on the palms of my brother's hands, and then making a phone call. As he spoke to the person who answered, he became more and more agitated, and finally in exasperation hung up, saying he can't do it. My uncle died within three days, but Rudyard fell seriously ill with a pneumonia that lasted weeks and left him weak for months. I was terrified a connection with the occult group had been made anyway on the astral. I was unable to do anything to help.

To get some information, I went to the metaphysical bookstores. Did they have anything I could read about this sort of situation? What I got was worse than nothing. The crystal-powered, glassy-eyed, frizzy-haired, patchouli-drenched, muumuu-clad morons who worked there informed me that nothing would happen to my brother if he didn't allow it, that evil has no effect on people if they don't believe in it. I wanted to shout at them, "Are you fucking kidding me!?!" Idiots!

So my brother was in trouble, and I could do nothing. For during those months, I was completely exiled from my family. The only person to whom I could speak about such matters was my brother, and he was clearly in peril. I voiced my distress to Darren, of course. I was just blithely feeding him information, trusting him.

Then, months later, and despite my living those 60 miles away, Darren decided to cash in on my worry for my brother. I had told him of my problem, and lo and behold, before long, he claimed my uncle had come to him in a vision. It seems he told Darren he had some things to say that might help my brother. So Darren and Marla were going to arrange an opportunity for my uncle to speak to me, to see "if he comes through." Sure, anything to help my brother, I was game. They didn't have a car, as Darren had had several DUI's. So when they decided to do it right away, I had to drive the 60 miles down, pick them up, and drive another 20 miles to a park near the inner city.

The only explanation I was given for why we were heading to this park was that it was here that my uncle had contacted Darren. This reason wasn't even logical, and why would my uncle talk to Darren and not to me directly? The rest of the Dead in my family have always felt free to come talk to me. Why this roundabout communication? And why Darren at all? They didn't know one another. But it was late and dark and cold, and I was strung out from all the stress in my life (the divorce from Robin was still not final). In short, I was an idiot, at least in retrospect. Here I was, alone with these two in a park I was not really familiar with and that was not exactly in the best of neighborhoods. I briefly wondered if anyone else was there in the shadows somewhere watching the show, but I didn't ask.

Marla seemed oddly cold. In all our previous encounters, she acted maternally, full of concern. Maybe she was angry I didn't allow her to do my taxes even though she was a certified accountant. Something had told me not to put my finances into her power. Maybe Marla was upset with me because I wouldn't allow her to take me shopping to show me how to dress better. I had told her I *do* know how to dress for success, but I had *chosen* my casual "costume" at this stage in my life for a number of reasons. The discussion finally turned into an argument every time. How dare I reject her expertise? Again, never mind that I was by then forty-one years old!

Maybe she was angry that when I left Robin, I didn't move into the room she had prepared for me (in her filthy hoarder's house!), but moved, instead, in with my mother, who, while she may have been the cause of the worst misery in my life, had begun speaking to me again, and because she wanted me back in her clutches, I could count on her warding off anyone (as in Robin and his family) who would try to take me from her again. I had essentially slipped past every trap Darren and Marla had set for me. Except one.

What Marla *said* frustrated her was that I insisted on taking my purse with me into the park. "Someday, you'll learn to travel light," she lectured me. *Travel light*! How ironic coming from someone who was several inches shorter than I and over a hundred pounds heavier, wearing a grease-stained sweatshirt – and eating a bag of Funyuns to boot! I tried to tell her I took my purse with me because I didn't know the area. It looked a little sketchy. I would not be able to justify my foolish behavior to my mother if my car were to be damaged by thieves AND my purse were to be taken as well. By taking my purse with me, I was making sure *both* of these situations could not happen simultaneously. But Marla said I would never come to develop any power if I continued to behave the way I did. Really? Again, the absurdity. I really should have left them in the park in the dark and driven home, but no, I was committed to going through with the final folly.

As we entered the park, Darren, all of a sudden, was interested in whether I could see what was "over here" and "over there." For four years, I had been talking about things I perceived around me and was told to be quiet. Now, I found myself suddenly subjected to a "test" of my abilities! Fine. I described the spirits lurking about. "Very good," he said. "Why do you need to know?" I asked. He had no answer for me.

Farther in, toward some wooden picnic tables, Marla asked me what I sensed about the place. I told her I could feel the residual energies of weddings having taken place there. "That's very intuitive for someone who is just beginning on the path." Just beginning! I was choking on my outrage by this time, really tired of the mistaken identity thing going on. But I never had a chance to expel my fury.

I was led directly to a table, sat down, and as I watched Darren take out his ritual sword and begin casting a protective barrier, I slid right into oblivion. My last thought was to send a psychic distress call to my dragon protector, my friend Jack. But it was too late. On the way home, Darren expressed his astonishment at the "something big" that tried to get in the circle. Do I *ever* regret not informing Jack of the event well ahead of time! But I still say that until the exact point of my unplanned departure from the here and now, I had no idea how bad it was about to get. It just didn't seem possible.

Instantly, once in the designated perilous siege, I found myself manifested in the woods of Central Europe, near a makeshift military camp, sixty years in the past, watching a German soldier drag a body from a swamp, watching him take it to my uncle (who was a young man) who made him return it to where he'd found it, watched my uncle kill two other young men and slide their bodies under a table that stood over an opening in the earth from which emanated a pulsing blue light. The table had a particular symbolic shape, revealing the occult group to which my uncle belonged. My uncle had taken a dagger from the table to stab the men, a double-bladed tool of ritual, with an inlaid set of stones forming a creature, which was moving its wings, squirming about in the handle. Then, in the vision, my uncle, incredibly, spotted me, and came after me. I jolted myself into the here and now. I think I screamed.

How long I was under, I do not know. That I had been set up was incontrovertible: I had been unceremoniously yanked from one time-space continuum and thrown into another, without a flight plan. Did they have any idea beforehand of my ability to travel out of body? Did they know ahead of time where and/or "when" I would end up? Did they plan it? Maybe the episode was some sort of test of me. I should mention here that I narrated the entire visit with my uncle out loud, with prompting from Marla's questions and direction. She had been able to listen in on my entire adventure. Maybe I was just being used as a time-telescope.

When it was over, I was freezing cold, but I couldn't move. I had been psychically ruffied. Something had been done to the location, some sort of portal had been opened up, and no one warned me, either because they thought I "might not have understood," or I didn't rate high enough for the "need to know" to apply, or, what is more likely, because they thought I *would* understand and simply didn't want me to have a choice.

They had not, however, expected me to remember what I'd seen. As soon as I came out of the trance, Marla asked me if I remembered. Of course, I did, I told her, and then, in apparent panic, she grabbed me with her fat arms and said she was going to block my memory of what I'd seen to protect me from the trauma of it until I was "ready to deal with it." With no respect for my sovereignty, she began murmuring something and aiming her first and middle fingers at my third eye. She was about to mindfuck me! Holy shit! I wriggled free just in time and nearly fell on my face as I stumbled out of her reach. If she actually had any power to affect my memory, I don't know. I don't think so, but she did, however, clearly assume she had the *right* to affect it. Of all outrageous reasons – for my own good! Somehow, her imagined authority gave her the right. The horror still floors me!

Or I could look at it another way, yet. Marla heard all the details of everything I saw as I was seeing it; she witnessed it through my reporting. She got her prize, and so the next step was to take it from me. Either way, it felt to me as a rape. My mind belonged to me! My memory was my sanctuary. I almost threw up, reeling from the attempted penetration. I was dizzy and out of breath. "See," she said, "it's too much for you to remember right now." Marla assumed I was reacting to what I had seen, not to what she had done! She was interpreting her observations in such a way that they confirmed her conclusions. What a biased nightmare!

Marla was *not* trying to protect me. She was trying to take control over me. Whatever she and Darren had planned was not what happened. What was supposed to be helpful to my brother had clearly not materialized. That enticement had been a lie. What I saw instead, I guess I was not supposed to see. I can only guess that it had to do with the connection I had inadvertently made. The iconic shape of the table symbolized not only the occult group to which my uncle belonged, but also the occult group, which Darren had let me know was interested in him as a potential member. If his proposed invitation was true or not, I'll never know. It might have been a story he used to try to "bait" me. It might have been an accidental slip of confidential information. I see no need to name the group here, as it would serve no purpose to do so. These esoteric groups are all equally suspect in their motivation and methods anyway. Which one I believe (or was led to believe) was behind these events is irrelevant.

What was relevant to me was that I had been betrayed and utterly violated as much by Darren and Marla's arrogance as their stupidity. It was an incredibly dangerous fiasco. As far as the dagger, who the hell knows? Darren insisted we go get food and talk. I thought being out in public would be a safe way for me to "ground" myself and would allow me a chance to collect myself before I drove the 60 miles home, so back to the Chinese buffet, we went.

Marla kept trying to convince me to let her liberate my memory. Darren finally told her to be quiet, that since I remembered it all, he might as well ask me about something. He wanted me to identify the souls of the men in the vision, not the bodies, but the souls. Was one of them so and so, whom we had met at the bookstore? Was one of them that guy who went out to eat with us downtown? What was the other one like? He wanted to know their identities in the previous past life so that he would know them in this one. His interest sounded very much like my uncle's agenda for my brother.

On the way home, Marla cruelly teased me about how my soul was dangling out the window of the car instead of staying in my body where it belonged. When my phone kept flashing, Darren took it upon himself to answer my mother's twentieth time to try to call me. "*Alles ist in Ordnung*," he said to her. She'd been trying to reach me for hours. Maybe that's why Marla wanted me to leave my purse in the car. My phone was in it! I did turn it off, but then forgot to turn it back on. Darren finally saw it light up, and answered it, but my mom didn't know who it was on my phone saying those words, just this disembodied male voice speaking to her in German. She freaked out, until I grabbed the phone from Darren as I was driving and made up a whole set of lies about bad phone reception and whatnot so that I didn't have to deal with her wrath when I finally made it home.

In the next few weeks, I emailed him long letters expressing my sense of betrayal, explaining why I felt violated, and repeating what I had told him over and over in the past years – my demons were jealous demons, especially my family demon, and that what he and his wife had done to me will cost them. They were now marked. He wrote back long responses, which didn't seem to show any comprehension of what I had written him but repeatedly insisted I must let them educate me in these matters. Finally, on the phone, I told him I was going to have to spend some time away from him. He wanted to know exactly how long I would need to be out of contact. He wanted me to provide him a schedule. I told him I couldn't say and hung up. That concluded the association.

I was a bit afraid he'd come after me. Robin had. Why not Darren? But he didn't. When I felt restored enough and had found a partner with whom to share my magick, four years after I had ended the friendship with Darren, I sent him a letter, snail mail to the house. It was an invitation to reengage in dialogue, mainly to clear things up, as I was finally in a better position in life than when I fled from Robin. I never heard back in response to that letter. Four years after my first letter, I emailed Darren a second one, having found his email address on

Facebook, and this time, he responded.

Apparently, the arrival of my first letter brought an unlucky event. Darren, who was an electrician by trade, had 5,000 dollars in tools stolen from a house he was wiring. Immediately after reading my email a few years later, he totaled his car – actually, he said it totaled itself by turning into a curb at full speed. In the email, I had asked him if he was still with Marla. I asked if she was the impetus behind his search for the dagger or if they were both pawns of another institution. He ignored the question. Instead, he gave me another one of his signature lectures, as if he had not understood one word of what I'd written.

Darren's unbelievable metaphor was that he was a bone Marla and I were fighting over like dogs would. "He's mine. No, he's mine," he imitated the imagined conflict. Both of us wanted him, he decided, for different reasons and were trying to convince him to leave the other. He was going to stick with Marla, though, for he's committed to her after all, and . . . drumroll, please . . . the fact that these terrible things (thievery and car wreckage) happening to *him* was proof *I* still don't know how to control my energy, that his bad luck showed I was still dangerous. Dangerous. Wow. What a bad girl, I still was!

I realize now, how, due to luck or contrariness or both (certainly not due to any good discernment on my part), I managed to evade every attempt the two of them made to try to bind me, get me into their control. I didn't get away completely unscathed, but I did get away. They had been recruited to recruit me. I wonder what price they paid for failure to bring me into their coven. I wonder what cost my demons will still exact from them for messing with something (me) that didn't belong to them.

The biggest "what in the hell?" of all was the fact that when I contacted him those years later, Darren no longer had any idea what dagger I was talking about. He didn't remember the book or the history of the British covens or my uncle. Maybe Marla "zapped" it out of his memory. Who knows? He *did* take his contact information down off Facebook, though. Had the search at that time been instigated by yet another demon? OR my black-eyed nemesis?

I will also never know what the true purpose of the visit to the past was. Obviously, my uncle did not contact Darren. Darren and Marla contacted *him* – or tried to – perhaps not as effectively as they wished to. They wanted something from him – the dagger, his memories, something. There was nothing for my brother. That was simply the bait. They treated me like a game piece to be moved here and there without regard for me, for what I was.

It could have been so different if they had ever looked past the false identity they put on me. If they had treated me as a colleague, we could have worked together and perhaps found answers for all parties involved. If they had only asked me as a friend to go on this bizarre "mission" for them, I might have done it, maybe, but at least, with a plan, with my being fully informed, under my direction. If they had only listened to me.

Nor will I ever really know why I allowed the entire thing to happen. Retrospective self-analysis informs me my head was deep in the sand. But explanations are fairly simple. I was painfully lonely, though, and in such despair. I wanted to trust them, so I ignored the obvious signs and my doubts. Also, in *my* paradigm, people couldn't possibly be so overtly ludicrous or so blatantly unconscionable, so I told myself I must be misinterpreting them or the situation. Since I wouldn't do such things to someone else, I couldn't imagine someone doing it to me.

But reason and logic were not exactly at work here. For me, it was a particularly challenging situation, as my "crazy meter" had long ago been broken by my family. My father was an alcoholic, my mother was a monster with a cruel heart and mind; my fifteen-year mentor had proven herself bipolar. I was, therefore, accustomed to arbitrary commands and unthinkable extortions. Since my family was toxic, I had no good sense when it came to strangers. I wanted to believe these two were my friends. I needed to believe someone was my ally. Still, somewhere deep in my core, I should have known how perilous Darren and Marla were, not because they didn't really believe in what they did, but because they *really did believe* in what they did. There was absolutely no reality check going on. Blind faith, no matter what flavor, makes people commit atrocities and exercise ignorance with abandon.

Luckily, neo-pagan groups are almost never like the ones in question here. But this one, in many aspects, behaved like a cult. I think the neo-pagan presentation was a cover. Darren and Marla found me when I was vulnerable and alone. They tried to gain control over my physical life – where I lived, what I wore, my finances, my friends. They wanted me to submit to a hierarchy that placed them between me and the "top" (They, and *only* they, had a handle on the real "truth." They were the only means by which I could attain that truth.). They were doing what they do for my own good – or worse yet, the greater good. They spouted their rhetoric rigidly – and demanded my conformity. They closed their eyes and ears to anything that didn't fit their rhetoric – and expected me to do the same. They employed a catalogue of threats – namely exclusion. They adhered to the practice of withholding information. They found an "in" to my family. These are all the standard characteristics of a cult (or for that matter, any sort of proselytizing organization), with a classically maniacal tunnel vision. Either way, both employ an assortment of minions: inquisitors, charismatics, and – recruiters, whose job it is to find devotees to feed the machine. I almost ended up as food.

I do have to say that recently I attended another Solstice ritual. The neo-pagan coven who hosted the event created an experience that was at once silly and fun and in moments, moving and beautiful. It was a nice social event. Everyone respected everyone else, and the sense of community was authentic and loving and very earthy. There was the regulation script and photocopied programs, yes, and a few parts of the ceremony were a bit embarrassing, but as a whole, it was OK. Not what my soul craves, but OK.

Lastly, there is still the matter of the black-eyed demon and his/its purpose in this set up. That demon's only goal in any interaction with me has been to destroy me. Its purpose in this matter was to make sure that Darren and Marla would have the opportunity to run me right over. He/it twisted my words, misrepresented my nature, complicated my loyalties, put me into situations where I had no control over my destiny. And then, he/it sat back and enjoyed the spectacle.

Understanding Evil: My Soul Contract

Believe Me

Here among all these discussions is where I can perhaps create a bridge between my experiences in this life in which I've been a victim and experiences in which I've been a bit monstrous myself, either accidentally or deliberately. For as much and as often as I've had things happen to me, I have also known incredible power to use in my life. The truth that may account for both extremes might explain the paradox. While the previous and the following narratives indicate warnings about the behaviors of other types of entities and/or humans, this one is about what I am. It, hopefully, identifies my own true nature as I've chosen to reveal it and what that might mean to someone out there stepping into the occult.

Before I even begin this, let me say that I am sure that what follows in this particular essay will sound like absolute nonsense. I aware of that. But this project is for those who already have a mind that's open to what I say. To someone who has never experienced some kind of occult interference or attack or weirdness, I have no doubt what I'm about to say will sound dubious. That's OK. The things that I describe here are extremely subjective, more so than anything else here in this volume. They should be taken both literally and metaphorically, but not dismissed outright. This essay covers a lot of ground.

Now, it may seem strange for me to issue a warning about myself, or rather about someone like me, but it would be dishonest of me not to. I and those like me can also be dangerous to the unwary. I have referred to myself over my lifetime as a witch, a rogue witch perhaps, but a witch nonetheless, but that has only led to my becoming frustrated when people assumed witch meant Wiccan, which I am not. I have adhered to the calendar (the wheel of the year and the lunar cycles), yes, but only as a practical and, in some ways quite beautiful, way to live. It's nice to have an every six-week reminder to check up on friends and take stock of life. I refer to the deities, yes, in my mythology, as well, but I have no religion.

I have also called myself a dollmaker, but that has always been a monumental oversimplification. I mean, I do make dolls, so in a sense, that's true. But for the scope of this essay, I will use the term necromancer, at least as I chose to define it. The term has been misused and misunderstood, but there is no substitute for it that isn't in some other way misleading. Necromancer. No, that does not mean I bring corpses back to life. Sorry, Hollywood. My definition is a composite subjectively synthesized from several sources. I need a term for what I am, so necromancer it is. It may or may not be exact.

Someone like me is, first of all, no matter what the circumstances, a living amplifier. Our presence expands and enhances supernatural forces in our vicinity. If someone can sort of see ghosts on his/her own, if that person is near one of us, he/she can see ghosts vividly. If a ritual has the potential for power, it can become a super ritual if there's a necromancer involved. One woman who was present at a few of my Sabbat rituals gave up trying to recreate them on her own, saying that they just never reached the level she wanted without me there, and she just felt too disappointed to continue trying.

This aspect is extremely dangerous to novices. There have been instances when someone has asked me to be a part of a ceremony or go along on a venture, not realizing that my presence would supercharge whatever was planned. Even the most common practices are not conventional when *I* do them. I go all in, no pretense, no caution, no fear. It took me a long time to realize that that's not how others approach things. Though this sounds extremely prideful, it's not; it's a warning: If a necromancer steps in to a situation, those involved will get more than they bargained for. Especially if the necromancer is like I was when I was young, when I didn't realize how extreme my energy could be. I caused a whole lot of trouble that I hadn't meant to. It took several conversations with very astute people after magickal catastrophes for it to finally dawn on me. Oops.

Necromancers also can psychically traverse the barrier between life and death. We can act as go-betweens because we are on the threshold between here and there. We can, at least partially, animate (to impart life to) that which ordinarily would never (but perhaps must) live. Of course, we talk to the Dead. Or, should I say, the Dead talk to us. We have a relationship with the Death Angel (also incredibly misunderstood). We can keep the souls of the Dead earthbound, or release souls that have been so bound. We can make deals with entities. In fact, we have (at least I have) our own entourage of non-corporeals. We amplify their sphere of influence too. We allow them to find residence in our belongings and homes. And, of course, we make – and animate – dolls.

Because of what I am, I've had issues with the neo-pagan community and those associated with them. They may say there's no such thing as necromancers. Of course, many neo pagans will also say there are no such things as demons either. These are the same fools who say that there is no such thing as evil, and that nothing can ever harm someone if he/she doesn't let it. Ha! Or worse, some have their own form of the Inquisition, and say that entity work such as I have done is evil and that I should be stopped. Witches persecuting witches! Who would've thought?

My grandmother (my father's mother) was a necromancer before me (she was also an herbalist and midwife – which I am not). Before her, there was another, and before her, another. That is not to say that family legacy is required for a necromancer to be. I'm fairly certain that it isn't. It just works better as the infrastructure for such a specialization to develop. I believe, though, that necromancy is innate. One is born with it or not. It can go through family lines, but doesn't need to. My brother, though of the same blood, never had the gift. He had his own.

As a necromancer, I came into this world knowing, seeing, and being able to do things that defy the mundane. I was never a novice though it would have been nice to have had some guidance with it. But I don't think there's a way to train someone to be it. It is not something one can learn from scratch if the seed isn't already present. I wouldn't even know how to teach the art. Even if I could, I'm fairly certain I wouldn't want to. But those who might cross paths with one of us might want to know what they're in for. It's only fair.

First, I will begin by talking about dolls. One of the first doll spells I cast was when I was five. My brother, Rudyard, at that time four, had been poisoned, as secretly indicated by other members in the family, by my grandmother. She knew her herbs. Why she wanted my little brother gone is part of the bizarre nature of my family dynamics, and truthfully, I'm not sure I can fully explain it. It seems, though, that his soul nature was not acceptable to her, while mine was evidently prized. But it must have been more than that, that he was a threat somehow.

Why doesn't matter. What I knew in my little five-year-old heart was that my four-year-old brother was really sick, paralyzed. I knew his sickness had been done *to* him. Doctors were unable to help. I was nearly out of my mind with helplessness and terror. Then, something in me rose up, and said, "No." It was the "No" that issues commands. My doing what followed would change my life forever.

I took two of my little "troll" dolls (those with the long brightly colored hair) and gave one my name and the other Rudyard's name. I did then what I would do many times in the decades to follow: I breathed life into them. Then, I bound them together. In doing so, I ensured that what would befall one of them (one of us) would befall the other. If my grandmother or her coven wanted him to die, they'd lose me too (I knew they would never let that happen.). Since I knew it was there, I turned to one of the entities that she had follow me around and revealed what I had done. Then, I stayed at the living room window waiting for her come to the house. It was snowing. But she came. She visited only a short while, but before she left, she gave my brother something to drink. His recovery began within a few hours.

A little over forty years later, I had to recreate this very spell in order to release myself from it. I had finally become aware, after it happened yet *again*, how many times the direction of my life took coincidental turns that benefited Rudyard, sometimes to the detriment of mine. How the timing of these incidents was simply uncanny. In this case, half of a loan I had secured for home improvements ended up going to him to cover one of his crises. "How was this happening?" I had been asking myself for a long time. "Who would do this to me, to put me or my resources exactly where he could call on me or them?" "Who could have that kind of power?" Then it dawned on me. *I* did. *I* do. How ridiculous is that? The irony!

Another of my significant doll events took place when I was just three years old. I had a special doll. She had wavy blonde hair and a huggable body. No one seems to remember who gave her to me, but I had named her Kylie. Now, Kylie was not a German name, and the only language I spoke or that anyone spoke to me was German. We did not watch television. Yet, for some reason, I had chosen the name Kylie, much to everyone's shock and amazement. I think that was the name of my child in another life. How I loved that doll.

One day, that doll disappeared. It was the same day my grandmother had stopped by for a visit. She had been carrying a large shopping bag in addition to her handbag. No one ever confronted her about it, as it seemed absurd to accuse her of taking Kylie although I think my father knew. He grew up around a lot of dolls.

I was heartbroken. Later, someone gave me another doll, one of those that looked very real, had eyes that opened and closed depending on the posture of the doll. I named her Kylie as well, but she was never Kylie. I never saw the original again.

When my grandmother died, it had been maybe seven years since I'd seen her. Due to the toxic dynamics of the family I grew up in, I was not able visit her when she was dying of cancer. Then, of course, I was not allowed to go to her funeral, as my family was afraid my grandmother's coven would "get me." (I still sort of wish they had . . .) I was, however, asked what I wanted of hers that could be brought back on the plane. My answer was, "The dolls." I was very sad when I realized Kylie was not among them. She is still out there, most probably in the hands of whatever remains of my grandmother's group. But the others that came back proved themselves significant nonetheless.

At the time the dolls arrived in our lives, many miles from where they had been stored for so long, my family owned and lived in a small motel in the rural town near the Great Plains. We had kitchenettes that would be rented by the week. In one of them, a single woman was staying until she could find a job and relocate. Two nights after my parents and brother returned from the funeral, and with them five of my grandmother's dolls, the woman caused a great disturbance at the motel in the middle of the night. Karen, the psychic who had insinuated herself into our family, (See the essay "Trust Me") was in the unit next to hers and called the office to say that something was wrong. My father went to investigate.

By the time the situation was concluded, the police had been called, as well as an ambulance. The woman was put in a straitjacket and taken away. She was screaming, "They brought the evil here. They let it come here!" Inside the kitchenette, we found the strangest scene. It looked as though the woman had been involved in a physical altercation with someone. Furniture was toppled, small items tossed about, and the Gideon Bible lay on the floor absolutely destroyed. All around the kitchenette were blue streaks from the crushed binding, on the walls, the bathtub, the kitchen counter, the window sill. It seems she was trying to kill something with the Bible. All she managed to kill was the Bible.

My father looked at me. "Which one was it?" he asked.
I told him which one. It was the largest one, one that had been among those that had pinned me down during the ritual in which I was "promised" to my grandmother's demon (See the essay "Serve Only Me") when I was three or four years old. My father went to the utility room where we were keeping the dolls temporarily, grabbed that particular one, a metal trashcan, and some gasoline. In the alley behind the motel, he put an end to the trouble maker.

Of the remaining dolls, only the one we came to call the Lazlo doll carried any significance. It was perhaps the most significant of all. Karen took an interest in it and asked to keep it in her kitchenette unit so that she could "read" it. Within a short time, she came up with the name Lazlo. It was only when she said the name to my parents that my father revealed what he knew. I don't know if he was testing Karen or hoped no one would figure out the truth, but he didn't say a word until the name became known. Either way, my father spilled out the rest of the fantastic story for the first time.

Understanding Evil: My Soul Contract

Lazlo was the name of his older brother, a child who died at six years old (when my father was only a baby) because of a congenital defect that kept the plates in the skull from closing properly. My grandmother could not let go of her first born, was inconsolable, and acquired the doll as a vessel for the child's soul and kept it with her, her whole life. When, thanks to the Yalta Conference, the entire family in the former Yugoslavia was rounded up after World War II (all the German-speaking people were called into a "town meeting," and a fence was drawn around them, and that was that!), she even escaped the camp to retrieve it, getting past the guards and wire, and returning without being caught.

The doll came with her when they eventually made it to America. There, she kept it in the bottom drawer of the dresser in its own "cradle." My grandfather had teased my mother when she was pregnant with me, saying, "You don't need a crib; you can just keep the baby in a drawer." My mother, at that time, thought he was being mean to her when he was actually being mean to his own wife, my grandmother

So, the doll housed the juvenile soul of my uncle. I have no way to explain why, not even so many years later, but I loved the doll. Something in my heart ached for it – perhaps my innate desire for the company of the Dead. I convinced my parents to let me have the doll, and I took it home. My husband, Gavin, and I lived in a townhouse a few miles away, and I kept the doll (and all my stuffed animals) in the spare bedroom. It was my special connection to my grandmother, to the other world.

My mother was furious. She hated my grandmother for "ruining her daughter," and so she hated that doll. I had no way to protect the little Lazlo soul from her psychic venom. The doll's light began to suffer, to deteriorate. The doll literally tried to get away. It would wander out of the bedroom toward the stairs, where it sat at the top, glaring at anyone coming up. I would put it back into the small room, but it wouldn't stay. Day after day, the loving presence became more and more menacing. I could not protect the child from my mother. Gavin, who usually good-naturedly referred to the supernatural shenanigans in my vicinity as "Slimer" (from the *Ghostbusters* cartoon) activities, finally said, "You have to do something about that doll."

So, I took the doll back to my father, weak and devastated by my own grief. "Here is your brother," I told him. "Release him." And so, the Lazlo doll met the same fate as the doll that had caused the havoc weeks earlier. However, with this one, I heard it screaming until the flames reduced the vessel to ashes. The creepiest thing about the whole event was that the hands didn't burn. They stayed intact, obscene little jewels in the blackened debris.

I have no more dolls in my house. My second Kylie and two other dolls I retained from childhood stayed in my mother's house until she sent them to distant family she had found (after decades of not knowing where they are) on the West Coast when I was in my late forties. The Madame Alexander and other dolls I had begun collecting, I sold. I allowed no more dolls into my home. This was not a grief I could ever risk again. Or a danger I was willing to chance.

I did, however, *make* dolls for specific purposes. I kept an entire doll making kit in my supplies. It contained fabric, stuffing, different colors of doll hair, various embroidery threads, coils of wire, and so on. I kept scissors and needles in the kit to use only for making dolls. I also had the automatic habit of collecting what I might call tidbits, memorabilia, or artifacts, from the moment I met someone (anyone), at least if I had reason to believe he/she would be significant in some way. The collection would include hair, hair pins, signatures, receipts, buttons, coins, cocktail napkins, theater tickets, threads, souvenirs of get-togethers, photos, things touched, anything. I would store all of the material for potential justin-case scenarios – in case I needed to protect myself somehow – or in case the subject needed protection from some outside force. That's how I personalized the dolls.

I didn't make many dolls in my life, but when I did, the circumstances were without exception dire. In anyone's life, there are moments when one is helpless to save oneself or someone one loves by conventional means. When the law is no help. When the medical/psychiatric professionals are no help. When colleagues or friends are no help. When family makes the situation worse. When prayer is useless. That's when a doll is called for.

When a practitioner of any sort makes a doll, the creation takes on a supernatural energy. The doll becomes the "this plane" subject on another plane. A sort of quantum entanglement occurs. Magick is just a form of physics we haven't learned to understand yet. Anyone can make a doll and have it serve a supernatural purpose.

Here, I must say something very important. Actual physical dollmaking is not a defense against demonic evil. Dollmaking is for dealing with humans, whether they are acting alone or at the behest of demons, but not the demons themselves. Demonic evil is immune to most sympathetic magick. To think otherwise is great folly.

When a necromancer makes a doll, a part of the necromancer goes into the doll – as well, sometimes, as do other spirits. It is a different product from a vehicle for sympathetic magick. It is actually alive. More than a golem. It makes the doll an agent of the necromancer's will – or the embodiment of the necromancer's pain. Or, in the case of my grandmother, it becomes the vehicle for a disembodied soul. The necromancer can put the soul or part of the soul of someone dead – or of someone living! – into a doll or other container. (yea, Harry Potter was not the first to discover that!) The necromancer can also use this "power" for acquiring and maintaining an entourage of entities, for *these* might provide some defense against demons. The entities can inhabit statues, masks, stuffed animals, mirrors, even boxes – anything.

I had a few special entities. I had a gargoyle (housed in a faux granite foam replica) and the spirit of a dead bride I collected to keep him company. The gargoyle was my protector, and his bride was my friend. The gargoyle (whose name I knew!) would amuse himself by occasionally throwing things at people, but mostly he liked to be my guardian. He circled the house and returned to the foam sculpture I had purchased to house him and watched the door. The bride wore my special scarves and amethyst and garnet beads. She would sometimes leave the faux skeleton I provided her as a vessel and come sit beside me on the sofa to watch TV, the mist of her shrouded corpse for company.

I am not the only one who witnessed these goings-on. Because I am what I am, an amplifier, my friends were also able to see beyond the Veil and be witnesses. "Who is that with you?" "Did that gargoyle just turn to face me?" These friends also were visited by some other members of my entourage. In particular, one, which I called my Watcher, would not only pursue me threateningly, but followed two of my friends, one as she was leaving my house, appearing in her car, and the other at her home, after I dropped her off after visiting with me.

My Watcher was huge, flowing, black, and menacing when he went to assess my friends. I am certainly glad he approved of them! The creature might have been an egregore, a thoughtform formed through generations of my family's magickal alliances, that had developed its own consciousness, one that had been with me life after life (to what end, I don't know). One of the last times I saw it, it was looming behind me, behind the sofa where I was watching television. The visit was a year or so after my divorce from my second husband, and I was feeling lonely and bitter and powerless, and here was this thing menacing me further. By then, I had just about had it, tired of being bullied by mortal and immortal entities alike, and maybe I had had enough whiskey in me too, but I turned around and shouted at it that if it wasn't there to help me, it had to go. I never saw again, at least not it in my house.

One of my friends also caught a glimpse of my grandmother's demon, as it waited for me in my car. He was making my car, which was luckily not running at the time and not occupied, rock back and forth. It was the most astounding sight. My friend and I looked around to see if anyone else was seeing what we were seeing. Luckily, there was no one. But she was shaken. Its eyes in the near dark evening were luminous and beyond sinister. We stood on the sidewalk a long time, unwilling to move toward the car until he dematerialized. Had she not been with me, would she have seen it? Would it have even been thee?

Another friend was paid a visit by the black-eyed demon. She saw him one night as we walked in a park in the winter darkness. Soon after I stepped into the public restroom, I heard her screaming my name from outside. I told her who it was after she fully described him. He was very tall, with long black hair, and mesmerizing eyes. He was as beautiful as he was malignant. That's how I knew whom she had seen. It still spooks her when she talks about it. But his business was with me, not her.

So, necromancers make dolls and have unearthly associates (both allies or enemies). But we also commune with the Dead. My grandmother started me out early with this. She often took me to the cemetery near her home. That was not really unusual. It was a quiet place, with grass for a toddler to play. But once there, she would place me on one grave, then another, setting me near the headstones. "Is he still in there?" she would ask. "What is she saying?" "How does it look in there?" "Tell me about her dress."

Believe Me

My grandmother knew that some of the souls lingered near the bodies, that some had moved on, and most importantly, that I would know which was which. She must have been encouraging or assessing my ability, proclivity, obligation, inclination – I'm not sure of the exact word to use here (maybe all four) – to let myself, my spirit self, out of my body to sink into the ground, down into the coffins. She was training me, letting me learn about what I am.

Letting my astral self permeate the ground like water is something I can still do though I don't push my luck anymore because I could easily, at this point in my life, find myself unwilling to emerge again. The imagery of Death is comforting to me, familiar. It is home. It was always home, decades before the Goth thing ever became popular. It's a difficult fantasy to satisfy. At least, at Halloween, the haunted houses I visited would fill a deep craving. The fake bones, skulls, tangled roots, dusty crypts, broken beams, head stones, rusted iron, chains, crumbling brick, and petrified crows, all the paraphernalia of the season calm something in me that is otherwise frantic. It's like coming home. The urge to lie down in the sets and never move again has sometimes been overwhelming. In another life, I swear I must have spent a lot of time in graveyards or catacombs – a kind of crypt keeper, I joke with my friends. Death to me is not just a conclusion anyway. I believe in reincarnation, as well as ghosts.

But I also know the Death Angel. The first time I saw him, he was lurking around my grandmother's basement before my grandfather's death. A decade later, he was looming behind and over a fellow high school student – right there in hallway of the high school – in the alcove of a third story window. The young man was unaware of his stalker, who nodded his head at me under the hood of his cloak, then vanished. I still feel guilt for not telling someone, but who would have believed me? The following week, the boy drove his car into a tree, by all accounts deliberately.

Why did the Death Angel deem it necessary to tell me!? I was not the boy's friend. He was not even in my grade; his twin siblings were. Then, a few months later, the boy's father, for some equally unfathomable reason had me called to the principal's office where he asked me if there had been any warning of his son's imminent suicide. He asked *me*! I had no idea what to say. Tell him about the Death Angel? Not a chance! I said I was sorry I didn't know anything that could help. I said that I'm sure it was an accident. Finally, he let me go. How in the hell did he pick me to ask? What did he know about me? Had someone else seen something, said something? I will never know.

At least the last time the Death Angel showed himself to me, the visit made sense. He appeared right before my mother's only friend's death, standing behind my mother in the living room one evening shaking his head. My mother was talking to me about her friend, who was in a hospital on the East Coast. My mother was standing in her living room, having a conversation with me, but unaware of the entity near her. That night, the friend died. Something of my mother's sanity went to the grave with her friend. As horrible as my mother is, she is not immune to loneliness. The Death Angel had let me know the loss would be significant.

My ability to negotiate with Death is as much a mystery to me as to anyone. An event concerning my second husband, Robin, demonstrated to me that necromancy is less what I do than what I am. Robin was never exactly a benign person, but still, he was mine. When a grand mal seizure due to low blood sugar broke his back and stopped his breathing, and he was literally dying in my arms, I chased his soul into wherever it was heading as it left his body and brought it back (See essay "Promise Me"). The maneuver was automatic, instinctive. It happened without pause or thought. I wish it had. For what I brought back was not entirely him. But the body revived. I had cheated the grave of *that*. What a disaster!

Messing around with the Dead is not something I recommend to anyone. Some of the Dead are vampiric, some demonic, and all are unnatural if still hanging about. It costs something to interact with them. The price could be anything – stuff, energy, relationships, etc. In my extensive reading on the occult, I have come across two, and only two, books that authentically instruct the reader in how to interact with the Dead, how to get the Dead to be servants. I have long since given the books away and don't even remember the author of one, but I think of them sometimes and wonder what doors they might entice people to open. Woe be to anyone who tries to enslave the Dead! That causes all kinds of grief, even for the professionals.

I have only met a few other necromancers. One affected me the way I might have unknowingly affected others. He was the only one up till that time outside my family who acknowledged the forces that I wielded. Francis, a friend from grad school, and a mystic of his own making, he had a better grasp on what I am than I did. In our poetic musings, in response to his question once about what I was doing that afternoon, when I answered, "Waiting for Death to find me," he shouted at me, "Don't you ever say that! Not you! The spirits listen to *you*!" To which, I just laughed then. In my mind, I wasn't really extending an invitation. Death was already with me. I actually didn't start using the term necromancer for what I am until decades later. My contact with Francis was catalytic and, yes, I can say supernatural, and it revealed to me the extent to which I could employ my power.

Toward the end of the drama of my strange relationship with him, he fell into the clutches of a group he claimed he was "not at liberty to tell me" about. I assumed it was a twisted sect of some Mid-Eastern religion, as that had been his fascination for some time, but he had also spent some time near Mount Shasta and with whatever went on there before moving back to his home town in the Rockies. I do not know. What I do know is that the aspect of him that to me was his sovereign self was at risk. He was giving it away. I could not allow that to happen. "They" (whoever "they" were) couldn't have it! Was I about to make an arbitrary decision about someone else's fate? Yes. No apologies. He was one of my own kind. It just seemed like doing something like that was a matter of honor and loyalty to kin, soul kin. But we were not really friends. Maybe slightly adversarial colleagues.

I drove well over three hundred miles to see him, but he would not let me see where he lived. We had dinner, but I had to stay at a motel. But before we parted, I took the aspect of him that was in peril with me. On the way home, I made a stop at the site of some ancient sacred ruins in a state park. That is where I interred the part of his soul that I took. I wrote him a letter telling him what I had done. The only way he would get it back would be to honor it properly. He did eventually give up his other pursuit, but there was no more friendship left for us. Did he ever go reclaim that part of his soul? No idea. I had told him where it was....

In another life, I am certain, he messed with *my* soul. I know he pulled such an aspect of it out of the ground where *I* had hidden it. He retrieved it in order to resurrect it. I remember being pulled from my happy grave, my peace disturbed. I remember, also, another life in which he killed me – on the altar of the Aztecs. I can still see his eyes as he cut into me.... We had a lot of soul history between us.

Did I have the right to do what I did? I don't know that "right to" applies. I think of it more as an obligation, but "supposed to" might not truly apply either, for that would suggest a set of rules. There are no rules. The necromancer aspect of me is an independent agent. It functions spontaneously and according to a system of motives that are not of this world (which I am sure sounds full of hubris or sociopathy or delusion . . .). Necromancers like us have our own rules for interacting with one another.

It was complicated. The first time I began associating with Francis regularly, I came down with a pneumonia that nearly killed me. The second time I spent a length of time with him a few years later, I developed pneumonia again. Something was poisonous to me. But Francis affected not only me. He spun a web over his surroundings and trapped young women as though they were flies. He would leave them devastated and confused. Two (not just one, but two!) of my professors who were aware that Francis and I knew one another, called me into their offices so that *I* could somehow explain what had happened to *their daughters*, to help them understand what this unattractive, near-destitute Francis had done. All I could tell them was that Francis had a hypnotic effect.

The strangeness that connected us manifested over and over. Before one of our graduate classes, I gave him an amethyst stone pendant to wear, one of a pair, the other, which I wore. In the middle of class, he suddenly found it burning his skin, tore it off, and threw it at me, much to the surprise of our classmates. When he stayed down the street at the house of a friend's parents for a few days, my white Angora cat, my familiar, climbed up to the second floor window to stare at him. He complained about the spook in the window when I talked to him the day after. I enjoyed his discomfort. Later, when he was staying in an apartment rented by the same friend, I dreamed of the place long before I ever visited it:

> In the living room with shelves of books from floor to ceiling, he stood, facing me. I couldn't touch him from where I stood, nor could I hear his breathing. But

the symbiosis was there. It pulsed between us, pushed at the walls of books so that they rocked. The place was gray and reeked from cigarette and candle smoke.

Between us, a woman materialized, an elfin princess, a shadow of Francis himself, only pregnant and wobbly. "What does she want?" he asked furiously, me, as if I would know. "Let her have her name" I said, "Please." "Name?" he whispered, "I don't understand." "Let her go," I demanded. It was as if Francis had the key to her becoming real. Without a name, neither she nor her child could be. But all Francis would do is look down at his hands. "I will take on the price of this," I told him. "I'll do it for you."

The instant I made the promise, the fairy woman vanished, and the shelves began to rumble and fall. Behind Francis, the walls cracked, and what had been pushing against the room from the outside came pouring in. Blood. Warm blood. I was suddenly soaking in it, wading it. It had been waiting for the cue. Then, there was no end to it. It splashed in a wave against one wall down the shelf where Francis did nothing while books floated in the rising surge above both our heads. He just stood there and let himself be submerged while I fought my way to the top of the bubbling deluge. I had saved the fairy woman from him.

I told Francis about the dream, and he said I should stay away from him, that he would only cause me harm. When his house burned down, I dreamed it as it was happening. I saw the sword he kept under his bed blackened with ash. Was the sword from the present or the past? (the fire was in the present). It was symbolic, nonetheless. I think maybe he blamed me for the fire.... These images are what my rivalry, my history, with him were like. They exist on this plane and another simultaneously. We were both necromancers. There was never going to be ordinary interaction between us.

Francis wanted me to live up to my potential. I just never had the right training to use my necromancy wisely. I ended up overdoing things. Sometimes, I let loose on an offending muggle with far too much force. Those people who say that spells don't work on someone who doesn't believe in them haven't met me. One friend of mine finally, gently, pointed out that I had a tendency to use the equivalent of a magickal Howitzer to kill a small annoying mosquito. I could be a little bit scary.

Without my grandmother to do so, there was no one to train me to use my abilities more effectively. There were, however, many whose mission it was to dissuade me from using. But there was no one who understood how the process worked in order to make it (and therefore me) less chaotic. I might have been spared so much pain. But then again, I might have become more of a target. A lot of maybe's.

My abilities as a necromancer have attracted all kinds of trouble from both the Dead and the Living. During my first year of college, I found myself in a den of Death, an Old Hospital (See essay "Come to Me"), where the trapped souls clawed and shouted at me. I think some of them clung to me for years and years. If all the "experts" who stepped into my life to "teach" me had only helped my clear myself of the hangers-on, I might have had a better chance at avoiding trouble. But no, they were all more interested in molding me, rather than freeing me. The truth is the Dead cling, sometimes in fear, sometimes in love, sometimes in fury, even in confusion. Entity attachment can happen to anyone, but is more likely to occur to a necromancer. It's like a Pied Piper effect.

Understanding Evil: My Soul Contract

My abilities, therefore, enticed a certain neo-pagan couple (See essay "Join Us") into tricking me to visit a time in the past to track down people from this life in their previous incarnations. I'm sure at least one of those souls took note of me in my brief visit and recognized me in this this incarnation. It would explain the instantaneous hostility from their "friends" that otherwise would make no sense. But this is what happens. Once someone finds out about my ability, he/she wants to use me as a weapon or a spy, unless, of course, they just want to crush me. Then, while they might succeed, they also enter dangerous territory, not necessarily from me directly. I don't control or command all the spirits that are around me. They are with me of their own volition, for their own purposes. They will deal with people who trespass in my life in whatever ways they see fit. That is how it is.

I have to say, also, that I don't do ghost busting, except under special circumstances, especially not for muggles, and absolutely not for Christian muggles. That never works out well. Except, maybe, if they are already dead. During the time my brother was a realtor, one house just wouldn't sell, no matter how many open houses he held. Finally, he realized that potential buyers were being made uncomfortable by a spirit in the house, that of a child. My brother knew the story of the previous owners. They moved after their ten-year-old daughter died of leukemia (in the house). The child had been told (she revealed to us) that she was waiting for Jesus to come get her. Her mother and father had told her that Jesus would take her to heaven. So, she wasn't going to go until he came for her. In this special case, I helped my brother open a portal to let the child's spirit move on. She would otherwise have been waiting there forever, thinking Jesus was going to show up. He was not, of course.

I also don't allow foreign (not of my own design) dolls to be brought into my house. That is also how it is. But as with all of the lines

I draw in the sand concerning my life, someone always has to try to cross them, even when I warn them not to. In the end, everyone is damaged.

When an old acquaintance from my first year in community college ran into me again twenty-five years later, we had coffee together and talked about my crazy life. The next day, he came over with a "gift." Determined to prove to me that my injunction against dolls was unwarranted, he brought two ten-inch dolls for me to keep in my apartment. Unbelievable! In spite of all I had told him, he placed the dolls on the shelf, and refused to leave until I admitted he was right, that the dolls were harmless. These dolls were different, he insisted. He had filled the dolls with love, he said.

Completely taken aback by the invasion, by what immediately took possession of them, and by his suddenly, forcibly keeping me in my apartment, I started drinking heavily (stupidly!) as the only response I knew to episodes of PTSD. Soon, I was too helplessly drunk to leave myself, and wouldn't have anyway, as my cats were in my apartment, and I was not going to leave them. I was for all intents and purposes trapped. This was not the first time someone, trying to convince me that my truth wasn't valid, had trapped me in my own apartment with the intent of keeping me there until I "converted." My nightmare of nightmares, and here it was playing out again.

Could I have called the police? No. I was too drunk. I didn't trust cops. If I explained my issue with dolls, I was pretty sure they'd haul *me* out of there and leave him with my cats. So I kept begging, sobbing, pleading with him to take the dolls back. My hysteria grew and grew. It was a volatile time in my life with my brother, with Karen, with some very important friends. I couldn't have this guy's meddling in my universe on top of everything.

So, I did what I have had to do several times in my life. I pretended to agree. I forced myself to calm down. I turned the energy to a different kind. I invited him into my bed (because I knew it would disarm him and let me drain some of his energy) though I could already feel the dolls becoming inhabited by unacceptable spirits. Then I shoveled him out the door, bagged the dolls, got myself together, and drove myself and the dolls to the home of my "wolf" (one of the only two shapeshifters I'd ever known) friend, someone with power (and no annoying morality), and together, we burned the dolls.

When my old acquaintance came by the next day, my wolf friend was with me, so he stood in the doorway demanding I give him the dolls back. "And who's this Adonis?" he gestured at my wolf friend. I answered him by stating that he had violated my home and disrespected my beliefs, that the dolls were gone, that my Adonis had helped. It took my former friend a while to understand that I had destroyed the dolls. He wouldn't be getting them back.

I told him to go. He was truly distraught, as though I had betrayed *him*. Maybe I did – I could have just put them outside my door – but I reacted with an action that to me seemed equal to his violation. There was nothing I could do to remedy the tragedy. He left, cursing me furiously and weeping. About a year later, I saw a news broadcast on the television about the use of prisoners from the county to pick up trash along the road. The camera focused in on some of the inmates' faces. There he was among them. He looked terrible. It seems he was the one confined now. Coincidence? Maybe. Probably. Or did one of my entities make his punishment fit his crime (of trying to imprison me)? That is the pattern. I felt both ill and vindicated.

I wish people would believe me when I say my entities do what they do without my input. They act on my behalf, and of course, on their own behalf. Sometimes their and my agendas are in conflict. Sometimes the two agendas are the same. The neo pagan couple who tried to use me for their nefarious purposes found that my entities would turn their lives upside down for their transgressions (thefts, car accidents, and so on). When my wolf friend eventually turned on me, stealing from me and threatening to devour me, he ended up toothless (literally) and homeless. The payback is occasionally befittingly awesome. Even those closest to me are not immune to retribution. The exchanges might be as simple as one of my non-corporeal followers becoming annoyed with my mother and on impulse giving her a swift kick, sending her flying while she was making her bed, to complex and far-reaching acts of vengeance. The reach of my entities is probably where the greatest danger lies.

Whoever wants to participate in some sort of magickal endeavor with a necromancer must be honest with himself/herself. No self-deceivers, no charlatans, no self-aggrandized interlopers. Or there will be consequences. The most important advice for someone coming into my magickal sphere, to any necromancer's secret world, is to approach with a pure heart. That doesn't mean "good or socially acceptable" motives (if someone is coming to a necromancer for something, that's probably a moot point anyway), but transparency, reverence, honesty, respect. Lies people tell themselves will come to light. Visitors to my world need to be self-aware, or I can guarantee that my entities will know the guests better than they know themselves. They should never try to test me or teach me without first knowing what I know. I have had far too many meddlers try that already. I react poorly to that kind of trespass.

To that end, it pays to remember that I *do* collect materials for making dolls. It is second nature. It has sometimes come as a shock to people when they have found out that I didn't maybe see them as an exception. I collect stuff to make dolls. That's what I do. And that should translate into a most stern warning for someone starting a relationship with anyone who engages with the occult. Until one knows or learns to trust the other person, it is best to keep track of one's leavings. Just about anything can be squirreled away for later use.

Then there is the issue of covetousness. If someone comes in with a sense of entitlement, thinks he/ she is privileged to what he/ she hasn't earned through devotion and sacrifice, my entities will know and act accordingly. *I* will act accordingly. Dabbling is a worse offense to me than abuse of power.

A colleague of mine at the community college, Sherrie, was someone who had a huge fear of missing out on what was rightfully hers if she thought it should be. She took an interest in being pagan because I was pagan. Once the fact that I was pagan became known to her, she thought being pagan too might offer her something better than her Christianity. She was shopping around. But Sherrie had once been on the road to being a minister, so the indoctrination had pre-set a world-view in her, and it affected her approach to most everything else she attempted.

In addition, she already had a pattern of the "grass must be greener" behavior. She had already bought a specific kind of sports car because I owned one. She had already acquired another cat because I had more than one in my house. She had already convinced herself that as soon as she finished her master's degree, she would instantly have a tenured position at the college because, since that's what I had, it was only logical and fair that she would too.

So, overnight, she decided she was pagan. She read *one* book on paganism, had *one* experience of seeing a ghost, and *one* experience of being able to feel the energies of pendants she was choosing from in a store, and suddenly, she considered herself one of us (me and two of my witch friends). All of a sudden, she acted as if she were an expert. Automatically, she assumed that she could now be a participant in my rituals. Besides, she was a good person, she told me, and good people are rewarded.

Without realizing what she was doing, Sherrie was overlaying the tenets of her Protestant world unto the pagan world, assuming that the same principles applied. These included, for instance, that there is an open door policy. Well, sure, anyone can take up a pagan belief system. But not with me. It *is* a free country. But not in my backyard. Churches welcome anyone, so of course, if she wanted to join my "congregation," my group, she would naturally be permitted, just like that. After all, she had completed all the requirements. She had also shown the appropriate "signs" of being "elect" by seeing that ghost and feeling the energy of that pendant. She had made her "testimonial" by saying that she believed in supernatural beings and forces, and had proved her devotion by reading a book. That meant she qualified. Truthfully, the three of my pagan friends that she knew and I never did a group ritual together, only had the occasional Sabbat dinner, to one of which I invited Sherrie as well.

Suddenly, Sherrie felt it was her place to educate us! She began with her discovery of a cat tarot deck – and would we "like to live with the images" for a while to see what they inspire? As if she could aid us in our spiritual growth with her newly acquired expertise. She could use her gift toward our enlightenment. A cat tarot! With the Temperance card about alcohol consumption instead of strength, and the divinatory layouts called such names as "the kitty litter spread" and "the catnip sprinkle." And did I know Hello Kitty is really Bastet! Oh, how profound the archetypes are! There wasn't one opening into which she wasn't going to insinuate herself. Nothing was sacred or safe. I thought I was going to kill her. But she was a colleague! I was going to have to deal with her at work.

Also, a part of me just couldn't quite accept this was really happening. I mean, no one behaves like that, at least no adult. So, I kept associating with her. Still, I never allowed her to participate in any of my rituals, which for the most part were lone ones anyway, because I could not risk adulterating them. The night of one private ritual with my magickal partner, Riley, she walked her dog close enough to my house to tell me the next day that she could smell the fire in my backyard. She had to steal her bit of it anyway. Unbelievable! It wouldn't have surprised me if she had been peeping in through the fence.

One day, when Sherrie was at my house, a storm was coming in. My inclination, as the weather was impending, was to meet it head on. It was just what I did. Stupidly, I brought her into my circle in the backyard with me, my sacred circle!, because I wanted to experience the raw elemental energy of the storm, and the rare opportunity would pass quickly. I just brought her in as a matter of being a good hostess. For, in those sacred confines, the cold, slicing wind and frozen rain were not the enemy. The interaction is instead joyful. I should never have let her have a taste, but I didn't know what to do with her. Tell her to stay inside while I went out to stand in my circle? Send her home abruptly?

My circle was a place of power. I had put hundreds of hours into selecting the location, preparing the soil, creating the physical circle (the stones and gravel and brick circumference), and raising and maintaining the spiritual energy in it. It had seasoned over four years, four turns of the year, seasons of intense cold and extreme heat, and my daily, nightly pacing, round and round. The result was a portal of amazing magnitude. My backyard was mine and mine alone, no dogs, no children, no husband, no neighbors. It was truly sacred space. I should never have let her experience it, but I wanted to feel the storm, and I couldn't figure out how to exclude her. There was a time limit for the experience. I wish I had just let it go, foregoing it rather than spoiling it with her presence.

A few days later, this silly woman decided that it would be nice to have all of us over to her house one weekend so we could help her put a circle in her backyard. As if it were simply a landscaping feature! As if creating a circle would be like participating in a quilting bee! I told her I would never reveal the means by which I had created and activated my circle to someone who isn't pagan. And certainly not for a circle placed where it would be subject to contamination by her dog, her son and his unruly friends, her small grandchildren, her husband, and her neighbors!

Because I refused, she thought I was being selfish, denying her this wonderful thing, when a truly spiritual person would've shared. Again, another Christian concept: who would keep a potential follower from finding God? The truth is she didn't have at her disposal all the elements/components necessary to make it work anyway, but that isn't the point. She was not pagan. Never would be. Not by my definition. "But I'm trying," she whined. Like the student who says, "I tried really hard on my essay," or "I'm a good person," and, therefore, deserves an A. She had put me in a position where to keep her happy with me, I would have had to let her into my secret world. My real pagan friends, actually, NEVER asked me how I charged up my circle. They either knew from their own study or experience, or simply had respect for the sacred nature of the thing not to try to own it.

When I told her that she had to first reject the vestiges of her Christianity and had to learn the principles of magick, she was crestfallen. She just couldn't understand that the two were incompatible. She just thought making a circle in her yard would give us something we could all share. It was something our club could enjoy together. That was the exact word she used. Club! She was hurt that I was trying to exclude her from *our* club. There was no club! When I told her *No!* about the circle, she consoled herself by thinking that it just wasn't time yet. That if she just proved herself a little more, she would be let in on the secret. Holy crap!

Understanding Evil: My Soul Contract

Talking to her was like standing on a floor where the tiles kept shifting.

Sherrie had a way of filtering all information coming into her brain to fit preconceived notions (yes, we all do that to an extent), but hers in particular allowed her to think everything was negotiable. When, for instance, in casual conversation, I once mentioned that I can tell if someone is taking psychiatric drugs by the look in the eye. People who take anti-depressants have a sheen in their eyes – like another colleague who was present at the time. People who take anti-psychotics have a cloud in their eyes. At least that's how I perceive the effects.

Well, Sherrie takes anti-psychotics. After a few days, Sherrie came up to me to ask if I noticed a difference in her, that she was trying to be "less cloudy." She had apparently gone off her meds. I tried to tell her that I hadn't said cloudy, that I had said *cloud*, and that the cloud caused by the drugs had nothing to do with her character or disposition; it just was what it was. She had misconstrued my observation into a judgement. She has learned (or perhaps it was a manifestation of her mental illness) to rearrange the playing field of truth to suit her needs, so that no matter what, she could try to claim advantage.

Since then, Sherrie has managed to sabotage every opportunity she might have had to raise her daily existence above the mundane, to raise her social status even marginally closer to one she clearly thinks she deserves, to experience the extraordinary. She finished her degree, but then made herself utterly unemployable in her field, by filing complaints against chairs and deans, quitting in the middle of the semester of a part time job she did get, and so on. Her life is fraught with failure and disappointment. No one seems to treat her "fairly." Her plans just don't seem to work out even though she "did and said all the right things." The cards (the cat tarot, I'm sure!) are stacked against her. I am not surprised.

With Sherrie sufficing as an example and therefore without citing further examples (of which I have many!), I have to issue this warning: If someone can't function without some sort of psych meds, he/she should never mess around with magick. He/She should not be allowed to take part in group rituals. At least not mine. I know from experience that these people will attract chaos and make magick go really wrong. I'm sure that sounds unfair, but it is a matter of safety for all. Since I believe that many cases of mental illness are due to supernatural attachments or influences, I will not allow such people into my sphere.

Neither is a necromancer open to taking on apprentices, and certainly not those who assume they deserve elite membership just for showing up. That I am a teacher of English doesn't make automatically obligate me to be a teacher of anything else. Besides, witchcraft itself isn't necessarily a closed system. There are many books available for solitary practice. Many Wiccans are willing to train novices, and many neo pagan covens are welcoming to anyone who is respectful and dedicated to learning (even the mentally ill). The New Age community offers unconditional acceptance to most anyone (*Namaste*, and all that), but I do not. People who insist on intruding are unwelcome. There is no open enrollment. Trespassers (or dabblers) might be eaten, a friend of mine quipped. No, seriously. It is really important to believe what we say. It is in one's best interest.

One of my favorite allegories to demonstrate this truth is a very short tale, I think from the Brothers Grimm.

> It is about a haughty little girl who defies her parents and goes into the woods to visit the old witch who lives there because she wants to see all the marvelous things she'd heard the witch had in her cabin. When she arrives, she peers in the window and sees the witch with her head all aflame, and three personages on the doorstep.

Still, she knocks on the door. The witch lets her in and asks her what she wants. The girl says she wants to see all the amazing things the witch can do.

The witch asks the girl what she witnessed outside. The girl says she saw a black man, a gray man, and a red man. These were a collier, a huntsman, and a butcher, the witch tells the girl. Then the girl says she had also seen her, the witch, with her head all aflame. The witch is delighted by this, and informs the girl that she had seen her true witch form and that she has been waiting for her for quite some time. The girl is still smiling smugly when the witch turns her into a block of wood and throws it into the fireplace, happy that now the fire will finally burn brightly.

This little story illustrates my perspective on the "lookie-loos," the "what-about-me?'s," the "anyone-should-be-able-to-do-whatever-he-or-she-wants-to's," the "oh-that's-cool-I-want-it-too's," the "I-think-this-looks-entertaining's." All those who should tread elsewhere.

Sherrie, of course, missed the meaning entirely when I gave her a copy to read. "The fire was burning brightly because the girl was changed into an enlightened being due to the knowledge she gained," Sherrie gleamed proudly. No, Sherrie, the fire burned brightly because a punishment had been meted out. The girl was dead because of her unwarranted sense of entitlement and stupidity, and the fire's brightness was a celebration of her removal from the world, of justice being served. Greedy for all the amazing things . . . she got her just deserts.

Now, just to be clear, I have never done anything deliberately to Sherrie. However, I am positive my entities did and will continue to make sure she never escapes her mediocrity. Or Sherrie will just ruin her own life. And I'll just have to get over being offended that she thought she could just come in and take what isn't hers.

It is good that certain powers cannot be taught or simply bequeathed to someone. One, in particular, that I have is the ability to make living dolls. It is due to my being a necromancer. not a witch. All right, maybe the Venn diagrams overlap a little. It's not exactly what it sounds like. It means that I can endow someone with certain characteristics or abilities that they wouldn't ordinarily have (not just imagine they are there). Francis was able to do this too. He did it for different reasons. He, like one other necromancer I knew, did it to cultivate devotees. But the amount of energy it takes to marionette a whole set of people at once is incredible.

My reason for making living dolls has always been to fill my loneliness. Plain old humans, non-magickal humans, are woefully inadequate as comrades for me. Whatever my grandmother preset in me with her demon made ordinary, normal relationships impossible. I have always needed a non-human to be a good match for my non-human desire and chemistry. It is my addiction, my hunger. Gargoyles. Dragons. Fay. Shapeshifters. Incarnate aliens. Other necromancers. Demons (if I felt particularly self-destructive). But they are all so rare.

Finding adequate companions is such a challenge. I more often than not have to create them, temporarily endowing a human vessel with my own capabilities. I would house part of myself in the other person until such time as I could no longer sustain the illusion and could not maintain the circle of energy any longer. But I must say I never (well, almost never) chose someone who wasn't willing, whom I didn't warn, who didn't essentially ask for what I delivered. I never preyed on the innocent. I always chose those who had a beacon out already. They often asked for a chance sometimes to step out of their own tedium or dissatisfaction.

Understanding Evil: My Soul Contract

Because there are so few with supernatural gifts available, I would have to bring them into being myself. Literally. The recipients actually become capable of, for a while (never permanently), of exactly what I need them to be capable of. It's not just projection. The men themselves have said, that in my presence, in the time they knew me, they suddenly acquired their psychic capacities, their artistic passion, their sexual endurance, their ability to power up a spell. Sometimes, however, it got to be too much, and they would turn on me.

The problem is that people sometimes don't believe me when I say I will do whatever I say it is I say will do, or they don't understand what they are asking for when they ask me to help them become whatever it is they want me to help them become. It's the classic story of the genie in the bottle who grants the exact wishes a person makes, much to his/her dismay. The proverbial "Be careful of what you wish for" certainly applies in my world. Once in, things get kind of tangled up. Said one of my magickal partners, my beautiful young would-be shaman, "I can't get away from you. I can't say *no* to you. I feel helpless." When he tried to leave, he said everything lost color. Eventually, he adjusted, and we did some magnificent work together, work that he would not have been able to do without my enhancement of him. At some point, the enhancement ran out. Eventually, I had to let him go. Then I grieved terribly, for I was alone again.

Necromancy – or truly, whatever the accurate name for what I am is – does not make for a happy life. I've thought about my own purpose in my family this life, and I've decided that the true meaning of my existence and of my choices in this incarnation, has been to conclude my family's procreation of and employment of necromancy. It ends with me. I have no children. I never joined the coven/cabal. All the members are dead. The legacy will be buried here in the soil of this new land, far from the

European origins. My choosing not to have children also allowed me to protect myself from anyone's (namely my terrible mother in this life!) taking them from me (physically or psychologically), as had happened in my past life.

This life is, I hope, my last one on this plane of cause and effect. It is my chance to sever all astral ties once and for all, and to have my last experience of interacting with the energies here, a last hoorah, so to speak. I am also concluding past associations created by my being a necromancer (or having been used by necromancers) in other lives. I'm not talking about karma – the like-for-like kind of exchange. Nor threefold retribution – that's a Wiccan tenet that I don't believe in at all. It is, instead, about seeing things for what they really are and just ceasing to participate.

A psychologist (or perhaps a poet) would interpret my revelation as an exploration of an archetype, namely the Shadow. I have no real argument with that approach, as long as we allow it otherworldly application. Also, as long as it isn't used as a moral evaluation. That neo-pagan couple (See essay "Join Us") who tried to use my abilities for their own end ironically always scolded me for my not controlling my Shadow. They equated Shadow with sin. In other words, they hadn't dispensed with their Christian upbringing, just changed the nomenclature. They still saw unconventionality as sin; they wanted to impose rules and judgement on free souls and on natural processes. Everything I said to them, I'm sure, sounded absolutely heretical.

Everyone has a Shadow. My Shadow is the only thing that has kept me alive. There's a peculiar aspect to mine, though. The other side of the coin, so to speak. Something about it causes other people's Shadows to rise up in order to harm me or disempower me, in ways that go beyond what people normally do to one another. And just as I amplify people's innate psychic abilities when they are around me, I am an amplifier in this matter as well. For me, it has meant that whatever evil another person's Shadow is most capable of, he/she will inflict it on me, manifold, and without restraint or cessation.

There is also an element of entrapment in how I operate, how my Shadow operates. I would let people trespass and trespass until they got to the point of no return, until the violations could not be retracted. I won't react right away. So once someone else's Shadow is activated, and he/she starts on me, there doesn't seem to be an off switch, no realization that what he/she is being done is unacceptable. The person just keeps going and going, no matter the effect on me. It is as if I were designed to be the vessel of their karmic undoing, the vehicle for setting them up so that my entities can take vengeance.

I don't try to set people up or trick them into doing the worst they're capable of. I'm like a perverse, reverse mirror. I reflect their true nature back to them, if they're willing to look. And I just give them time to hopefully become aware of what they're doing, to monitor themselves. When I finally realize that they're not going to stop themselves, then I fire away. Or make a doll. Or deliberately set my spirit allies loose.

My Shadow inspires people into committing all kinds of atrocities. This is where human and supernatural collide. I always run into people who live by all kinds of lies, personal, metaphysical, spiritual, religious, intellectual, social, familial, psychological, and more. Somehow, they always think I should too. People have sought to "convert" me to alternate ways of thinking by force, by keeping me against my will and subjecting me to relentless intervention (brainwashing). My former friend who brought the dolls into my house is just one of many, as is my "wolf" friend who interceded at that time, and who tried to cage me in other ways. My mother, my second husband, his father, Karen (my old mentor), two former brothers-in-law, a former supervisor, a colleague, and others. No one seems to be happy just to let me believe what I want to believe.

During my stay in the desert Southwest, a man with whom I'd tried to begin a relationship kept me prisoner in my own apartment for two days demanding I justify why I had deliberately tempted Death when I put myself into the path of a lovely young vampire he and I both knew. I had no answer for him but that it was in my nature. He didn't want to accept this; there had to be a hidden self-destructive motive, and he was going to get me to confess it. He unplugged my phone and put it outside the door. He stood in my apartment, asking the same questions over and over and over. Why had I risked my safety? How could he ever trust someone who would be drawn to evil like that? What he didn't want to understand was that the vampire posed no real danger to me.

The confrontation didn't end until an another acquaintance happened to stop by. By that time, I'd been awake for thirty hours and was physically ill. My vampire couldn't possibly have caused me as much destruction as this "human." Nothing had changed, however, in how I viewed the world. Before I left the Southwest, though, I heard that the man had been arrested for breaking in somewhere and was facing prison time. The irony.

Another terrible betrayal concluded a very important friendship. Marge and I had known several years of intense, intimate friendship. We were like sisters. She knew my extremes, my family issues, my dance with Death. After finishing her bachelor's degree, she began a master's program in psychology, and she almost finished it. At that time, I was just back from my time in the Southwest. I was destitute and lonely, but not without hope. I had applied for a full-time teaching position at the university and expected to hear back on that in a day or two, but in the meantime, I did some housecleaning for money.

The afternoon that changed everything, I had had an accident. The ladder on which I had been standing to clean the light fixture on the ceiling broke under me. One rung gave out, and when I fell to the next, it did too, and the next, until I my feet hit the floor and I fell backwards, hitting the corner of the counter with my body. I severely bruised my legs and cracked at least one rib. Without any health insurance, I simply did what I always did under circumstances like this: I drank to kill the pain.

Marge came over that afternoon and found me pretty well self-medicated. From her now "educated" perspective, I was posing a danger to myself, so she decided to call for an ambulance to take me away for a 72-hour hold. Just like that. She was going to have me imprisoned, put into the psych system because now she had the authority to do so, and she was going to practice what she had been learning in her classes! My behavior was unacceptable, and it was her duty to make sure I was saved from myself. Her Shadow loved the power she thought to wield.

Again, I begged and begged that she not do that. "I'll run," I told her. She said the police would find me. I was terrified. Finally, we agreed to two stipulations in order for her not to make that phone call. I had to call, with her as witness, to make an appointment with a counselor of her choosing AND I had to write and sign a note absolving her of any culpability for my actions. The note said that she had done all that was required of her in her capacity as a professional to assure my well-being, and that I would not hold her responsible for anything I might do. Then she left my apartment, and I fled it as well, for I didn't trust her not to make that phone call after all.

I went bar to bar, looking for anyone I knew who might take me home that night. There was no one, though. It was summer break. Finally, at nearly 2AM, I found myself at the coffee shop that was closing. The girl who worked there gave me a free coffee and said I could stay in the courtyard as long as I wanted. As I stood there, of all absurdities, it began to rain. But then, out of the shadowy gazebo, a figure emerged. That was how I met my beautiful young would-be shaman. He came home with me that night, with the promise that he wouldn't let anyone take me anywhere. He would be in my life for nearly two years, Marge never again.

The next day, the VERY NEXT DAY, I received the phone call that told me I had the full time job. If I had been locked up, I never would have received it. I would, instead, have been unable to pay my rent, would have lost my cats, would have been saddled with the hundreds of dollars the 72-hour hold would have cost, and in short, would have had my life ended right before my eyes. My family would have irrevocably disowned me.

So, I wrote Marge a long good-bye letter, letting her know all of these truths, but mostly, pointing my wrath at her hubris, at the right she thought she had to abridge my sovereignty, to intercede in my destiny. As I wrote, I was shaking with outrage and terror and sorrow at what had almost happened to me. That idea of doing something for someone's own good is the source of a great deal of human evil. No one really knows what is in someone else's heart or what route someone else's fate should take. (Note: There is no hypocrisy here – when I act magickally against someone, I do so in self-defense. I do nothing for someone's "own good" and never for the "greater good").

The letter had its effect though I would not know about it for a long time. Marge quit the psychology program, switched to sociology, and became a social worker. It was years before I spoke to her again. In between, she sent me a note accusing me (and mine) of causing the town she lived in to be flooded, and accusing me (and mine) of calling animal control, who came and took several of her pets away, and accusing me (and mine) of causing the foreclosure on her house. Holy shit! My entities had clearly been busy!

I had lost, in Marge, one of the most important friendships I had ever known. The grief was unbearable, is still sharp and awful. I simply could not fathom that she turned on me! That whatever it was about me that tweaked the reptilian part of people's brains had tweaked hers as well! I had trusted her! I had loved her! But for me, there was to be no safe quarter. I know now that this is the price of being a necromancer, with my free-wheeling Shadow, while at that time I didn't know that. I couldn't yet connect cause to effect.

Besides Marge, there was also another psych "professional" who used threats to my freedom to manipulate me. I'm not quite sure how I ended up seeing her. But I was paying her by the visit. When I told her truthfully that I didn't have the money for the next session, she said if I didn't find a way to get the money, she would see it as a sign that I was not willing to save my own life and she would, therefore, have me committed. Her Shadow favored extortion.

That was during the time I was working as an art model. I figured I would use the pay from the one gig I had between this visit and the next to pay for it, forgoing groceries and gasoline and anything else. But the modeling gig was cancelled because the teacher was sick. I went into hysterics at the studio. One of the women who was in the class took pity on me and wrote me a check for the psych session herself. When I went back to that psychologist, I put on the greatest pretense of being fine that anyone ever put on, and I never went back to her again. Then I moved, not providing a forwarding address. I never found out what happened to her, but I sure hope my entities clobbered her.

People don't generally own up to what they've done to me even when they clearly know the extent of the damage and where blame belongs. It took Marge several years for her to reveal to me why she stopped pursuing her master's in psychology in exchange for one in sociology. She understood her trespass, she said. She decided she couldn't responsibly handle wielding that kind of authority over other people. As a social worker, though, she did anyway; even though the circumstances were different, it still meant power over others.

Sherrie still has no clue about the nature of her trespass. She coveted what was never hers to own. She wanted the power of the necromancer, *my* power, as if it were a shiny bauble to be hers for the taking. Marge wanted authority and power over other people's destinies (for she had little over her own) and saw me and my situation as a means to wield it. Sherrie wanted status and privilege she neither earned nor had the ability *to* earn. Her Shadow was greedy. Marge wanted to assert some superiority over me. I do not think if I hadn't been a necromancer, if I hadn't led the kind of life I did, these women wouldn't have been tempted to push the boundaries with me.

But I never had to make dolls of either of them. They were marked by their own transgressions just as surely as if they'd branded themselves on the forehead, as have many people who hurt me found themselves labeled. I reserved my dollmaking for the rare times I knew no one was listening to my appeals for justice or the urgency left me no other choice. My creations were born of deepest agonies, when no deity, no elemental, no dragon, no denizen of the world beyond this one would help me.

I've read one mythology that suggests the necromancer is an entity born of inconsolable grief or a power born of terrible loss. Perhaps. I know that I was born grieving – for a loss in the previous life. In that life, I had lost my two children to an evil man. He may have been their father or my father, but either way, he took my children from me, and I never saw them again. I ended my life – *that* life – and couldn't make myself return to this plane until the circumstances were right. I waited a long, long time to reincarnate, more than two hundred years. The wound that kept me away is maybe due *to* as well as responsible *for* my nature as a necromancer. According to the mythology, the necromancer remains a necromancer until the grief is resolved, one way or another. I am still holding out on whether or not to believe this.

A necromancer might also be the host for another spirit. There are special types of spirits that can/may/must live inside the other personality and manifests when necessary, aides the carrier soul in its navigation of this plane. It is like a sentient weapon. In junior high school, a group of girls ambushed me in the park. Earlier that day, I had defied them by rescuing a kitten they kept putting in a dumpster. They put it in; I got it out. They put it in; I got it out. Eventually, the kitten got away and successfully hid from them. Well, they were not going to let me get away with disrespecting them in such a manner.

When they surrounded me, they brandished knives, were threatening to cut my long hair and my face. I felt something in me come to life: my sword, as I generally refer to it, though it has a name, which I don't generally share. I was ready. But they suddenly scattered. My appearance must have changed remarkably, for all of a sudden, they were shouting, "Mal ojo!" and running away from me. I hadn't said a word. Once they were gone, I felt something inside of me deflate, fold up, resheath, quiet down. It was the first time I had felt it rise up like that. I've got to say, it was astounding. I'm smiling as I'm saying this here.

I believe that it is this additional entity that has prevented any of the demons that have wished me harm from accomplishing that feat. Unlike in all the TV series of paranormal shows, I have never been scratched – those infamous three-part scratches that supposedly represent a challenge to the Holy Trinity. It's possible also that because I do not believe in the Holy Trinity – no Jesus for me – that I haven't been touched. But I am more sure that it is due to my passenger or to my status as a necromancer. Not suitable prey. Nor suitable home. I have also never been possessed, despite my intimacy with otherworldly entities. Perhaps that is because there is only so much room, and I have no vacancy.

What I have not mentioned in this whole discussion, though, is the beauty, the intense, unearthly, breathtaking beauty I've experienced in my life, that I would never have known had I not been a necromancer, not been a witch. It is fully the reward for all the trouble. The other planes are real. The other beings are real. The business of necromancy is real too, as real as any religious delusion, as real as any nightmare, as real as any theatrical presentation, as real as prayer and ecstasy or the intense airspace over a cemetery.

I bring that other world here to this one, both by design and by accident. But it *is* as real as it seems if only for the time a person is in my presence. It *is* real until it slips back into the ether. For just a while, ordinary practices become amplified. Psychic abilities and perceptions become heightened. Entities might manifest. One might feel light-headed or spooked for no apparent reason when certain topics are broached in conversation. Because the necromancer changes the atmosphere. And that's the telltale sign.

Understanding Evil: My Soul Contract

Say My Name

Unless a practitioner of the occult works in complete isolation, there will be a time when another person's actions will change the course of his/her life. To what degree that change occurs depends on how much the other person means to the practitioner. In my case, he meant everything. Through our interaction with what we came to call the demon in the book in the box (the DBB), I came to understand how (how very familiar the dilemma felt!), in other lives, I had managed to become entangled in dramas that irrevocably altered my destiny in those lives and my fate in those that followed. I learned exactly how it happens, what one must trade in order to prevent catastrophic loss, and why the choice is not a choice at all. In my case, in this life, it happened when novice met demonic interloper, and I found myself exactly in the middle.

I had only known Riley for a few months. Motivated by one of my rare but irresistible life-changing compulsions (the voice that speaks to me at critical times), I found myself "sent" to one of those pagan clubs that forms at universities. It was, as one might suspect, a haven for all sorts of lost souls. They were the typical collection of misfits who were looking for identity or power or community that they couldn't find otherwise in their lives. Most were taking refuge from or looking for an alternative to religions that had rejected them or that they had rejected. Its members also overlapped with the GBLT club members. Riley was in both. Fate, the Goddess, chance, something, made absolute certain I would get together with him.

The club had already met a few times before I joined them. After the impulse hit me, I went to the group's usual meeting place, but they were done for the semester. The next semester began, and I had no idea when or where to find them, until I literally bumped into the leader of the group in the grocery store. The force behind the voice that prompted me to find these young people clearly saw fit to back up its intentions. The voice, when it comes, comes without warning, and I am unable to resist. The commands often make no sense at the time, and sometimes they are incredibly inconvenient. Like being in my mid-forties, having just landed a tenured teaching position at the community college, and finding myself compelled to join a group of questionables who were less than half my age.

But here I was. I was often embarrassed by these kids' naïve discussions, their absolute certainty about things that they knew nothing about, their petty power plays. Still, after a few weekly get-togethers and all the drama that one might imagine could ensue from such activities, Riley and I bonded. Some of the group's events were intense: an amazing costumed Samhain, an incredible, out-of-this-world, three-day retreat in the mountains for Ostara, a fantastically spectacular Queer Prom. We made May wine and extravagant meals. We sought out metaphysical bookstores and spent hours in them.

Within half a year, Riley and I were fully committed magickal partners and were, at least for all intents and purposes, a couple as well. A middle-aged (though I didn't look it) English instructor and a young gay man, twenty years younger than I. For me, that was not unusual. Riley was not the first gay boyfriend I had had in my life, and I've always gone for younger men. Riley fit both criteria.

Riley's motivation was to find out for sure if there was a world beyond this one, if magick was real. He had joined the pagan club because he was looking for a teacher, under the impression that becoming a witch was a step-by-step-ala-Hogwarts kind of process, but that's not how things work in my reality, not then, not ever. We simply began. I took him to sacred places, collected magickal supplies; told him the story of my life in elaborate detail; in short, I "threw him into the deep end." My approach was learn-by-doing. Maybe, I should have gone a bit slower. But I didn't think there was time. I filled his senses, which were to a great extent empty. I don't know how that happens, but that's how it was.

For me, this was the opportunity to try it all out, try it all on, again. I had taken apart my magickal fortress/set up when I left Robin, my second husband, years earlier and never thought I would supply myself again. Yet I resurrected it once more, this time for the last albeit short time, though I didn't know that then. I got to bring it all back to life one more time, to look at each aspect again like a photo in an album one final time before letting go of it forever. I collected candles, mirrors, incense, sage and cedar, oils, wreaths, storage containers, doll-making materials, tarot cards, books and books, skeleton replicas, gargoyles, stuffed animals, knives, a fire pit and hurricane lamps for outdoor ritual, sculptures for the backyard, wines, woodruff, ceremonial glassware, and, and, and. It was an explosion of self-indulgence, an absolute extravagance. And I was able, through it and Riley's perception, to relive, re-experience all my past magickal practices and endeavors one more time, to see them through his eyes, his emotions. It gave me a chance to reevaluate everything and also to fully understand the "staged" nature of it all.

I also recalled my previous otherworldly associates into service, specifically my gargoyle. Two decades earlier, when I returned from my time in the Desert Southwest, I purchased a foam gargoyle to house an entity that I became aware was attached to me. As soon as I provided him a home, I also purchased one of the Halloween skeleton props to house another entity that clung to me as well. I sort of played matchmaker for the two. I am fairly certain that I had chosen well. Anyway, when I ran from Robin, my horribly abusive second husband (See essay "Promise Me"), I dismissed the entities and gave away the vessels so that Robin couldn't call them back or abuse them. The separation was agonizing, but I had to do it to protect them. I couldn't take them with me in my flight for my life.

Now, with Riley, at the shop where the annual "haunted house" that we attended was held every year, I spotted another such prop, another faux granite foam gargoyle. I asked Riley if he wanted me to bring my entities back, telling him also that if I did, and something happened to me, they would be his to keep. After a bit of a shock, he said, yes. I considered it a promise, so I purchased the item and took it home. Over the next two years, I bought more and more vessels, building up my little supernatural "army" as I had done before and before in this and other lives. Once again, I brought in the bride spirit to be with my gargoyle, plus guardians of all kinds, and many, many animal spirits.

The gargoyle and I knew each other quite well. He had told me his name. He used the prop as a resting place, but was never confined to it. He was much bigger than the foam vessel and much more beautiful (well ... to me, anyway). I often fantasized that he would someday take over the body of a flesh and blood man on this plane so that we could be lovers. On occasion, he would go on missions to other planes for me or with me. I talked to him constantly, shared whatever alcohol I was consuming with him. Riley avoided interacting with him, though, for the presence of the creature was unnerving, and he did witness the gargoyle leaving the vessel and moving around my house. But it's not as if I didn't warn him ....

On our first Samhain, and as an aspect of developing the portal aspect of my circle in my backyard, I asked Riley to help me split apart a pair of smoky quartz crystals. (See essay "Promise Me") It was given to me by a Native American student some years ago when I had an enormous falling out with my mother, after which came one of the two times she and I didn't speak for a year. My student said I looked like I needed it. I kept it with me at first, and once my mother let me into her house again, I put it on a shelf in her living room. It gathered her energy for several years before I retrieved it for this purpose: to sever my grief over not being able to ever be anything but inadequate in her eyes – instead, in her words, a whore, a delinquent, a failure, a liar. The stone had absorbed and contained my grief over my mother's refusal to ever love me unconditionally, to free me from needing her love, to stop my trying still to pointlessly win her approval. It held in its molecules the outrage I felt at my mother's betrayal of me.

Riley helped me break it. I chose the night when the Dead roam and the Veil is thin. In the dark, in my backyard, I tried to split it with a chisel and hammer, but didn't have the strength. He did. I kept my hands over his as he smashed the hammer down. The crystals separated with such a loud crack and blinding light it was as if an explosion had occurred. The entire backyard lit up as if by lightning strike. My grief rushed out of me so suddenly I couldn't stand up. Riley held me as I cried and cried and cried. I felt protected in his embrace. Our connection to one another soon called attention to us.

I should have recognized that a demon (and a particular one at that) was already after us because of two very strange things that happened to me and Riley. One occurred as we were walking the half mile trek around the lake in a park. We often walked together, and symbolic of our compatibility on so many levels, our strides match one another's exactly even though Riley is much taller than I. It was a beautiful evening, and we were on round two of the circular path with our legs moving in unison when a woman came up behind us and all but growled at us in an uncharacteristically low voice, "Could you even try to be any cuter?" We turned to look at her, but she kept on walking in her little pink running outfit and water bottle in hand, as if she had never spoken to us. She gave no indication that she had acknowledged us.

The other "touch-n-go" happened at a sporting goods store where Riley was buying hiking boots for the upcoming Ostara retreat. With boxes stacked beside him, he put on one pair, then another, while I found a restroom. I happened to be wearing a baggy, but very red sweater. When I returned, I sat down beside him on the little bench. A saleswoman came up to us, and from behind us, in a voice that wasn't hers, said, "I see you have grown an appendage in red," and then walked away, later coming over to us as if for the first time, "Do you need any help?" Riley chose his boots quickly, and we left as fast as we could. "WTF?"

Then came our first Beltane ritual with the members of the pagan club. We chose to hold it out on the plains, an open space in the grasslands, out under the stars, in spite of the incredibly powerful and gusty wind. Among the participants was Jack, my incarnate dragon friend. I asked him to come with us as he knew most of the members, and I knew I would need him. The wind howled, and yet somehow the men managed to get the tent set up despite its best efforts to fly off to Oz. The ceremonial aspects focused on the May baskets we all made to hold our greatest desires. The tent nearly shredded around us. The pinnacle of the ritual was the enactment of the Goddess (me) putting the old God (Riley) down and Her waking the new God. I always did that at Beltane and its reverse at Samhain, not at the traditional Midsummer and Yule.

But something this time felt, the best I could explain it, wobbly. Still, we finished the ritual with joy and wonder. The wind never slowed for a moment. On the way home, Jack revealed to me that an entity had tried to force its way into our circle. Its goal was to get into Riley, he told me. Jack said he stopped it. That night, on the way home, I told Riley about it, just as conversation. The next day, I met Riley in the coffee shop, and he told me something that nearly stopped my heart.

Riley had taken it upon himself to issue a challenge to the entity. He was furious at it for thinking it had the right to use him, to interfere with his life. So, he challenged it, said he would write its story and would find its name by doing so. Of course, because such a thing works in the movies or in popular fiction, it would naturally work for him. He was going to trap it in the story he would write. I thought for a moment that the floor was going to slide out from under me. *What had he done? Oh, no!*

And so began the fight with the DBB (the demon in the book in the box). It would take a year and a half (or was it two and a half years?) before the battle was finally concluded. In that time, the entity spoiled the romance, squelched what was beginning to blossom between me and Riley in spite of his being gay. I was faced with a decision: send Riley on his way for his hubris or help him fight the entity. My heart shattered. I knew, after all I had been through in my life, that I was about to forfeit whatever future I might have thought I would have if I took on this challenge. If I didn't, I would no longer have Riley in my life, and would, I was absolutely certain, be utterly alone (I am still convinced that is true), but more than that, if I didn't help him, this foolishness would be the end of Riley.

So, I chose. I did not want to be without Riley. I could not face being alone. There was no chance for me to meet anyone else. My mother had had her heart attack and refused to drive anymore. My Saturdays were forfeit indefinitely as was at least an hour each evening. I was subject to the whims of her personality disorder and viciousness without any chance for a reprieve. My job involved endless grading – the English teacher's homework!

With the exception of the university, the town had a population of conservative, ignorant, belligerent, meat-eating, gun-toting, Bible-thumping, country-music-loving yahoos. I was living in a place where finding someone to even consider as a partner was impossible. That part of my life was clearly over. I tried the online dating venue – what a disaster! I am an alien creature, and most of the men who contacted me were psychos or pigs. That about covers it. But here was Riley, and he was civilized, beautiful, and we had begun to create a mutual and powerful chemistry that was somehow bypassing the barrier of his being gay and my not being a man (the illusion I had been able to weave to bridge the gap had fallen utterly apart.).

Soon enough, my warning came. Sometime after the Summer Solstice, I woke up in the middle of the night with the black-eyed demon, my immortal harbinger of doom, lying beside me in bed. It was twilight, just before sunrise, so I thought maybe I was still dreaming. I blinked and rolled over onto my elbow to truly see him. No matter what I did, he did not vanish. He lay on his back with his head turned toward me and stared at me with his empty eyes. I reached out to touch the cold hologram that he was and pulled my hand back. It had no effect on him. I didn't know what to say. He didn't speak either. But he remained with me nearly an hour, until the first sun rays of the day became visible outside.

So, when Riley's new roommate in the student housing turned out to be suspiciously delusional, I knew what was happening. From day one, Daisy acted as though she "owned" Riley, that her rights to him preceded mine, as though she had found him first, and *I* was the interloper. "I just don't have space for you in my head yet," she said to me on our *first* meeting. In her eyes was a light that to me signaled demonic entity, which I immediately understood was the demon from the Beltane on the plains. It was letting me know it was aware of me. In the depths of her eyes was an unearthly blue light. I had seen it before . . . yes, there it was! The black-eyed demon had come to warn me (and to gloat) about the blue-eyed demon, who was about to ravage my life. Daisy's eyes were not blue, but the light that came through was.

Daisy's actions were just like from a movie script, where comes in from out of nowhere and just moves into someone's life and just takes over. I'm not sure what she thought Riley was. A pet, a buddy, a patient? Daisy insisted that she was going to make Riley become a hugger – something entirely out of character for him. She constantly ambushed him, throwing her arms around him, and with her substantial weight to anchor her, trapped him in embraces whenever she could. She prepared food for him even though he asked her not to, even when she knew he had plans to go eat with me, and then acted hurt when he didn't eat it.

Sometimes, she left the windows open – at ground level – a temptation for thieves. She wanted keys to Riley's movie cabinets so they could share "our" entertainment, as she put it, laying claim to Riley's collections. This whole situation was really wrong, way off. Therefore, when she left her stash of medications on the breakfast counter, I took note of them: an assortment of anti-depressants and anti-psychotics. I was right.

I could see that Daisy (and the demon in her, using her as a convenient vessel) was setting Riley up for a false accusation of some sort. I *knew* it was in her plan to make him completely subservient to her or to crush him if that couldn't be accomplished. I recognized that method of operation from having been similarly victimized in my own life. I also knew that my fears of losing him (for instance, if charges . . . say . . . of attempted rape, maybe, were made against him) were not unfounded. I knew she was perfectly capable of making up something that didn't happen if she didn't get what she wanted. Daisy had all the markings of just such a confabulator. I couldn't detect even the slightest hint of conscience, just plenty of delusion.

But my attempt to prevent such a thing from happening went nowhere. I tried to report my concerns about the girl, Daisy, to the mental health center at the university and only managed to get into a fight with the director there. The counselor was no help because I clearly didn't approach the situation from the right angle. Not that there was a right angle. I had hoped to proactively start a paper trail on Daisy so that if something happened, information already existed that could help Riley. When I tried to report her, I found out that unless she actually harmed Riley or herself (in which case I should call the police), the only thing mental health reporting system would allow me to do was voice my concerns for *the girl's* well-being!, and then someone would come do a welfare check on *her*!

Well, I didn't give a damn about the girl, and I could not get through to the counselor that it was Riley who was in danger from this psycho bitch. When himself Riley went into the counseling office and expressed his concerns, they offered to enroll *him* in a class to teach people how to get along with each other better! Riley was polite and civilized and needed no such instruction. I was furious! No matter how we attempted to put up warning beacons, our efforts were thwarted. The demon's glamour held. And Daisy continued her gas-lighting.

So, with no other recourse, I helped Riley move to another apartment. All his furniture and belongings. He and I, my car, and two fights of steps. Physically, the move drained me, weakened me. But after that, we spent more and more time together. Riley had already begun to work on the book at my house, letting himself in with the key I had given him. His presence led to my cooking dinner for us or my taking him out to eat. The handmade book (he made even the book itself) into which he was writing the story of the demon stayed at my house.

The story began with Riley's meeting me, but the first lines were not about the demon, but how angry he was with me, expressing that he was "not a doll." What a thing to say! I still think of that with a deep sorrow because I was indeed "making him" as one would a doll because he had *asked* me to "make him" (adept, my partner, a witch, whatever), and now he was indignant about what I was doing, treating it as though I were engaging in something immoral. I had invested a great deal of myself in peeling back the Veil for him, and here I had been labeled a villain for it! It was the first of the sorrows to come.

The goal of the book was to discover the demon's name. To control a demon, one must have its name. Even the Catholics or Evangelicals or you-name-'em know that. As if it were that simple! Riley believed that the magick of writing the event out in detail would elicit, as the story closed, the demon's name. In fact, the last lines in the book were intended to be the demon's name and the words of a binding, trapping the demon in the book. In the end, it worked, well, mostly. The demon did take an interest in the story and stayed nearby as the book developed. It was patient.

Another Samhain came and went. There were more shenanigans with the pagan club people. Eventually, the group disbanded. One of the officers stole money; others graduated; Riley and I lost interest. There was another Queer Prom, for which costuming was again required. It took quite a bit of time and effort. Also, I was busy at work. Riley had a few dates with this young man and then that one. But Riley and I were together most of the time when he wasn't working, for he came over to my house to write in that book, and to eat, and to watch *Buffy the Vampire Slayer* and *Angel* and other TV series that I bought as fast as I could, anything to keep Riley with me. My fear of abandonment ruled me.

And I assumed, as we headed for spring, that Riley and I would have another Beltane ritual together. I actually expected it up until the day that preceded it. We went to a party we had agreed to attend that day, and Riley asked that we drive separately because ... because ... he had a date with a man he'd met online and had been communicating with for some weeks without telling me. There I sat at Beltane by myself abandoned and ashamed.

This young man turned out to be the same guy who had come into the writing center at the college where I worked three years earlier. He had a camera in hand and said that he was taking pictures for the school paper. I didn't believe him, but didn't see a problem with his taking a photo of me. He promised that he'd bring me a print of it when he had the film developed. A few days later, he did just that. Then, he admitted there was no article for the paper. He just thought I looked interesting. He also asked if I had ever read a book about local Satanism, by apparently, his father. No, I said. "Oh, OK," he winked – he actually winked! – and left me holding the black and white photo of myself wondering, WTF?

Riley's relationship with Justin (whose last name neither Riley, nor I can remember anymore!) lasted two or three months. Riley stood me up a couple of times. Midsummer passed without acknowledgement. During those months, two of my three old Siamese cats succumbed to kidney failure and had to be put down. I believe they were unable to bear or heal my sorrow. Riley did not go with me to the vet, did not come to say good bye to them. Their absence rent my psyche. I was stunned to my core.

In that time, as well, Riley's lease ran out again, and he chose to move to an apartment close to mine. We "cleansed" and protected the apartment before he move in. The first thing he took over to the new place was the book in the box (by now it was completed), and he put it in the storage on his porch. Just as we got that all settled, Justin dropped in. He walked right through the apartment, opened the patio door, went right to the outdoor closet, opened that door, and was about to grab the box before Riley stopped him. "What's in there?" Justin demanded. "Some stuff my mom sent up here," Riley answered. Justin still wanted to investigate, and Riley had to physically stop him. The confrontation was brief but very strange. Justin accused Riley of keeping secrets from him (and he was). Riley knew the demon was at work.

There was still the physical move to accomplish. Again, I helped him. Still the two flights of stairs. But this time, it was summer and hot. I agreed to help for one day of the move, and Justin was supposed to help on another day, but Justin came on the day I was there too. Riley had meant to keep us from crossing paths too often. Now here was Justin watching me suspiciously. The move accomplished, the two had a couple of more dates. The physical container for the DDB stayed in the shed, but not all the energy. Some vague conflict between Riley and Justin had begun. Truthfully, I don't remember what it was about. I just remember feeling erased, reckless.

Then, one day, Riley spent the better part of an afternoon at the laundromat. He wanted to wash a lot of his stuff before putting it away in his new place. He had no internet on his phone at that time, was nowhere near a computer, just doing laundry and listening to music. But in those hours, Justin had a meltdown on Facebook, freaking out that Riley wasn't responding to his postings, and complaining that he too had "witches in his family" (in reference to me and my pentacle and the fact that Riley compartmentalized aspects of his life), and after a few more outrageous exchanges, the relationship was over.

The last of my three Siamese died. I considered giving up on

Riley many times. But I couldn't, not till the DBB was gone. I couldn't risk our not finishing what we had started. The book might be done, but what we had was a very pissed off entity that couldn't go far, but could still reach out from its container to cause havoc. The exact sequence of events in those months is still very confusing. I am sure that no matter how I tell the story, the events might be all out of order, but I cannot put them together correctly, a lingering effect still of the demon.

Some aspects of our life were mundane. Riley attempted dating another couple of men, each attempt marred by some bizarre turn or outcome. I experienced some problems at my job that kept me occupied. Riley and I had to do a number of repairs in the house to "kitten proof" it for the new little precious monsters (Silver and Trixie) I had adopted after my Siamese were gone. I covered many of Riley's expenses in those days as well as in years to come.

But much of Riley's and my time together was amazing and fulfilling. Riley and I attended my brother's wedding as a couple, attended my 30 year reunion as a couple, took a ten day journey across the country together to see a friend of mine. We put in many hours of work perfecting the stones and gravel and brick boundaries of my magickal circle in the backyard. It was of sufficient size to be visible from space – in satellite images on the Internet!

However, the most significant aspect of that time was that Riley and I celebrated the Sabbats the way I always wanted to with a partner. Gay or no, Riley was young and determined still to experience the world I knew as a witch, and that way included sexual union of male and female energies, manifesting the divine in the flesh. For one turn of the wheel of the year, at each Sabbat (except the Samhain we burned the demon), we indulged in the most elaborate celebrations, ritual, food, wine, evocation, and spellwork. And sex. I had been through many, many men in my life, but I had never experienced sex with such simple purity; it was sacred in the true definition of the word. We sanctified my circle together under the open sky at the Summer Solstice. After this particular turn of the wheel, there was no more physical intimacy between us, and because of issues with my own health, there is a good chance that I'll never have another lover at all, so in spite of all the trauma caused by the DBB and other entities, I am grateful to Riley beyond measure. If the last lover I would have in this life is Riley, that is OK.

It began with Beltane. We made the ceremony and the evening so completely elaborate that I am certain we were both transported to another plane. Incense, candles, oils, music, costumes, wine. Riley and I wore masks he made. I had had my entire body decorated with patterns of henna. We made love on a special fake fur Beltane rug. It was the first Beltane where I was not the dark Mother or Crone who put down the old god. In this one, I allowed myself to be the Maiden for the first time in my life to unite with the God. All my other Beltanes, I was not the Maiden. The night was a journey into the myth, into the divine.

What I did not know is that Riley had not in our ceremony committed himself to serving as the vessel for the God as I had committed myself as the vessel for the Goddess. His commitment was only to me, not Her. He let me believe what I wanted to, I guess. I didn't find out until months later. But what I did know is that the next day, Riley told me about the coincidence of his having received a couple of emails from a man he'd been communicating online the night before the ceremony. He almost did it again! We still had a year to go! Why can't anything remain unmarred, unsullied? Besides the DBB still hadn't been dealt with! I was too stunned to say anything about it, and soon something interrupted the conversation. Then he happily ran off to work. I thought I had been ripped in two. My fury was a mix of murderous jealousy and the sense that what I thought was sacred had been somehow desecrated. Couldn't he have waited a few days to tell me?

That night, I took action. For if I hadn't, I knew my very integrity was at risk. I felt dishonored; the Goddess felt dishonored through me. I could feel Her rage. I didn't even know all of the reasons for it at that time. The next day, Riley brought up the topic of the online guy again, but I didn't let him finish speaking. This was unbearable! Instantaneously, the sword-spirit that I carry in my core rose up and snarled at him, "I will never allow myself to feel like that again."

Then, I told him of what I had done the night before. I watched him absolutely recoil and leave my house. "I need to think," he said. I didn't know if I was going to see him again. I knew I might have blown up everything we had formed together with my ritual the night before, but it didn't matter. This was the last time I would ever be betrayed at Beltane (The previous time I felt this kind of pain, it toppled a tree over onto the house I was living in!). My Goddess fury was very old and sacred!

What I had done the night he told me of his communication was call up all of my power into one cacophonous burst of transformation. I made a fire in my fire pit in the backyard. In the pouring spring rain! It was an enormous fire, fueled by enough Ever Clear to have burned down the whole neighborhood had it not been raining. The flames were three or four feet high. I drank Slivovitz (plum brandy from my family's "home country") as I danced around the fire, and then I danced in my circle, spinning around and around, until, I suddenly realized I had levitated, actually levitated, a few inches off the ground, still spinning, still spitting out my pain and fury to the elements, the Goddess, the night.

I levitated! My body lost its physicality for a little while. I was filled with electricity and burning from the inside out. The rain steamed off my body. For a few hours, I felt invincible. The effect was fundamental.

I still feel the sensation in my bones when I think back on it, the sense of the physical restrictions dissolving, and I, who or what I am transforming into ... what? I have no words for it.

Among the many items I burned that night was an email I'd printed from Riley the previous summer. It represented another tangent of my pain. In it, I had written him while slightly intoxicated, to voice my dismay over a stupid sexual encounter I'd had with someone from a writers' group I was part of at that time. Riley had responded to that email, with just one curt line stating that he didn't appreciate receiving drunken messages like that, that he deserved more respect than that. It was a slap. We were not intimate at the time, and we both were exchanging similar discussions. That's how I heard about some of his encounters.

All of a sudden, such communication was unacceptable, with no warning, arbitrarily shut down. Oddly enough, when I brought up that email a year or two later, he didn't seem to remember writing it! As he still doesn't. As he still doesn't remember certain cruel and cutting things he said to me during that time – about my being too old for him to consider having a relationship with, about my perfume smelling like an old lady's. Can I attribute this to the demon? Were these incidents moments of possession? I think so because of the not remembering. That is a sign to me – specific holes in memory.

The permanent effect on me was that I could no longer express myself naturally in emails from then on. I would censor them of all but the most benign and/or ordinary information. In effect, he had silenced me, eliminating one important way for me to interact with him. We could talk in person or on the phone, but I was no longer comfortable writing. Writing! Writing has been the only means by which I have been able to say what I want to say without the demons interfering in people's interpretation of what I say. So, among the other items for my spell, I burned that email, symbolic that it was, in the bonfire in which I transformed my outrage at having been dismissed after Beltane into liberation from that pain.

What the effect on me still of that night is, the intent, the levitation, any of it, I don't know. Perhaps I had cursed myself in the process too. It took a week before we spoke. In that time, apparently, Riley decided that the new man he was communicating with was not that interesting after all, and so he'd broken off contact with him. We slowly reestablished our routines. Over all of this, though, the DBB loomed over us. No matter what was happening to us, between us, we had to do away with it.

The plan was to burn it on the next Samhain, but what to do with it in the meantime? Well, temporarily, the solution was to get a bigger box, fill it with salt, and put the smaller box inside of it. The total container probably weighed eighty pounds by the time we were done, and it still stayed in the outdoor storage on the porch. The salt muted some of the buzz that kept emanating from the thing. We needed to come up with a plan. Burn it, of course . . . and then what? Do what with the ashes? We had to think. Bit by bit, we came up with a method of disposing of the DBB.

By the time Samhain arrived, we were strung out, many of our lives' activities having experienced difficulties or absolute sabotage. We were demoralized and sometimes not getting along. My own physical health was deteriorating (some of the effects permanent). Riley's too. The planning and preparing were exhausting.

Then we did it. We cast a double circle. With lots of wood and probably two pints of lighter fluid and hours and hours later, everything was finally turned to ashes, which we stirred into freshly mixed concrete, which we poured into a dozen small plastic containers, which we drove back out to the plains where we "first picked up" the entity and dumped them miles apart, one here, one there, along the road, and then found a trash bin (without security cameras) to dispose of everything else. I could barely walk from the trauma and terror of the whole procedure. I was soul-sick. It had fought us very hard.

But I know the demon's name. I had to know it. As the fire burned, I asked Riley to write one letter at a time on a piece of paper, show me the paper, and then put it in the fire. But I could not follow it, could not keep track of the revealed letters to spell it out in my mind (the demon fought so hard!), and he finally had to write the whole thing out and then quickly throw it into the flames. I will never tell it to anyone, for to do so might set it free. Riley and I will never say the name out loud. It will continue to be that-which-will-not-be-named (Ha!), other than, of course, the DBB.

The name, however, of the entity, told me a great deal. It was a German name, and it had significant meaning. I am, therefore, absolutely certain that it was not a random supernatural passerby we encountered out there in the planes. It was one that had followed me in order to look for an opening, and even though the ritual was protected, Riley, once away from the security of the circle, was not.

I should never have told him what Jack had told me. It never occurred to me that Riley would poke a stick at it, would invite this sort of trouble himself. I am still flabbergasted at how, in one ill-thought out moment, Riley had changed the course of his and my history irrevocably. But as a result of it all, I finally had the name of an entity that had haunted me ... for how many lifetimes? And for the time being, it was trapped.

There was so much damage, though. The circle of grass under my firepit never grew back. The following season, I decided to have that chunk of grass removed and replaced by rocks. The light-hearted times Riley and I had had were becoming fewer. We both were having financial troubles, arguments with friends.

Mostly, however, what haunted me was something else. What I could not reconcile in my heart was that Riley and I had destroyed an entity (well, at least for the rest of our lifetime). We had killed someone/something. It was like in the movies, when a character explains that it is not easy to kill someone, that it changes a person. Even if the murder can be justified hundreds of ways, it is still final. Even if the murder victim brought on the consequences himself/herself, he/she can never right them once he/she is gone. If someone is destructive in our lives, we generally don't have the privilege of just doing away with him/her. And if we did, his/her chance at redemption would be lost.

As Riley and I were destroying the demon, therefore, I apologized to it. It's not that we could have *not* done what we did. Once the challenge was made, we had no choice. But I did want it to know that I was fully aware of what was going on. Riley wouldn't do it, wouldn't feel it, wouldn't say it, wouldn't admit that we, even though we had to do what we did, still did a terrible thing. If the entity ever escapes (eventually, centuries maybe from now, it will), it will come after him, not me. I know that. That makes me sad too.

After the vanquishing was accomplished, I also thought Riley and I could recover, maybe restore our relationship to something more joyful again, more innocent. But the next year and a half were fraught with troubles. They began already with plans for the upcoming Winter Solstice. Riley and I were planning to go to a Cirque de Soleil performance and then have our ritual and union. But his coworkers, led by a narcissistic, ignorant, bully of a girl, decided that going to a place where the beer bongs were three feet long was where he was going instead, an activity that was not supposed to include me. I was simply dismissed, demoted. I knew this girl from all the trouble she had caused other teachers at the community college with her lies and her manipulation and was just horrified. Did I imagine the relationship I had with him?

And what about our plans? I watched him stand there, wavering, and realized that even though I had just sacrificed my health to help rid him of a powerful enemy, spent thousands of dollars assuring his survival as he was completing the DBB task, given up important time with my friends, forfeit any opportunity to have a life separate from him anymore, that I was inconsequential when my value was pitted against this master manipulator. As petty as it sounds, I had thought we were a couple, unconventional, perhaps, but a couple, nonetheless, and suddenly I felt disposable. Was this still the demon lurking about? Did the demon have associates? Were there still lingering thoughtforms created by the demon doing their thing till they fizzled out? I don't know, but I was devastated.

In the end, due to circumstances beyond our control, we did not go to the show, nor did Riley go to that bar. We had our Solstice. The one turn of the wheel I wanted more than anything to complete with him was almost over. By Imbolg, Riley's commitment to the Goddess (whom I was serving then) and to the magickal world had almost ended. Imbolg was strained, and it was the last of our Sabbats. Riley's interest in the magickal world had run out. As if it were just a game he could stop playing. Well, and then I guess he did. And this sacred soul-path of mine had been nothing but a jaunt into self-indulgence. The beauty had been spoiled by the DBB. There was no reset.

Shortly after the last of our Sabbats came an episode involving another of the human carriers of evil I had encountered in the few years prior to meeting Riley. This boy, Terry, had been a student of mine a few years earlier, then a ninth grader in the rural high school where I taught for one year. He was a sociopath whose true danger hadn't manifested yet because he was still so young. But at that time, I became aware that he was devious. He admitted to changing his grades in the school's database; he plagiarized material from the internet; he would "borrow" other students' phones and purchase applications on them before slipping the phones back into the owner's bags or pockets, but not before keeping track of other information on those phones for the purpose of extortion; he found out where I and my family members lived, and seemed to know what my brother did for a living and recreation, and so on.

This fascination wasn't natural for a fourteen-year-old boy! I was very glad Terry lived so far out in the farm country and wasn't old enough to drive yet. He was unnerving, intimidating despite his physical meekness. I never "told on" him because I was afraid he'd use information he might manufacture on me to retaliate. I was very happy to be rid of him when I quit teaching at that school and went back to teaching adults.

Then suddenly, after Imbolg, here he was in my office at the college. He had enrolled in some classes so he could, as he put it, "explore some options and kill time." He had stopped in just to say hi. I completely freaked out. I told Riley about Terry, about how I could just feel Terry spinning a web to catch me in, that he had the capacity to steal my identity or cost me my job, or harm me some other way. He wanted to toy with me. I was terrified.

The next time Terry dropped by, he let me know he got a job at the same retail place as Riley. He also informed me that his coworkers had seen Riley and me holding hands while we were shopping. He tried to pry information out of me about my relationship with Riley. I gave him nothing. I knew that as a professor at the college, my reputation had to be protected, and this kid could destroy it just like that with a lie! He would do it for fun.

The next time he came by was to tell me he had made "friends" with Riley online and that the two of them had been communicating.

"You don't mind, do you?" Terry asked me. My head was reeling. "What are you looking for?" I asked Terry. "I don't know. Maybe. I figured I could try it out," he answered, "it" being sex with a man. Then, he realized by the look on my face that I knew nothing about the connection he and Riley had made and smirked his victory. His goal clearly was not Riley's affection, but my mortification. I almost vomited. Another demon had found another route in. It didn't have a green light in its eyes or a blue light. It had no light. A compatriot, maybe, of the DBB? One of many others that exist?

Eventually, Terry disappeared entirely, but not before he dismembered my trust in Riley. "How could you do that?" I asked Riley. "I just want someone to feed on," he answered, "Just something." "But why him?" "He was available." I just about stopped breathing. My safety was secondary to this self-indulgence. He could have picked anyone else, and I would have been all right with it. But he chose Terry. And Terry chose us to destroy just because he could.

Feeding. That's another facet to me and Riley. Up until the destruction of the DBB, Riley and I engaged in a regular energy exchange. (any reiki master would know – though possibly not approve of – what I am referring to.) I have always run on a deficit of life energy, but didn't understand the mechanism until my encounter with a certain vampire boy in the Southwest. That boy took the interaction beyond the electrical/physical level, and while I'm not inclined to explain it here, I have to say that afterward, I was changed. Something in my core was profoundly altered. But it was, to me, a familiar, even natural event.

I was still young and still had my beauty, so I had lots of young men in my "stable," and it was easy to keep myself "fed." I could just help myself to their abundant life energy. They were never harmed and, most of the time, were never even the wiser. If there were no young men around, but I had other influences of beauty or excitement, I could regenerate. At this point, however, it had been a long while since I had a "stable," and I no longer had the freedom I had had in the past to go out and "hunt." My other "influences" were extremely limited because of where I lived and where I worked. But I found I could feed off Riley.

At first, he enjoyed it, the illicit nature of it. We made a game of it. Standing in my circle at full moon, I would hold onto him, and through specifically choreographed physical contact, would draw energy from him until I was fully recharged. He said my eyes would glow and look absolutely reptilian afterward. He would feel dizzy and thrilled. It was part of our relationship, a part of our special chemistry, a commitment, at least as I saw it. Then all of a sudden, it wasn't.

After the destruction of the DBB, Riley refused to let me feed. In fact, he suddenly said it caused him to feel ill and tired – and (because that's the way it happens on television!) it was turning *him* into a vampire. I tried to tell him that's not how it works, that it's not contagious like that, that I am not now the same kind of creature as the one that had changed me, but he stuck with the idea. I became afraid to hug him because sometimes I would accidently "plug into" him for a moment or two, and he would notice, push me away, and reprimand me with a reproachful look. Essentially, not only did he break the unspoken promise to me that this would be part of our relationship, he shamed me for my need. Not only was I deprived of a source of what I needed to really live, I found myself in a committed situation to him where I remained unfed, and to make it worse, felt humiliated by my hunger.

He has long forgotten about our activity of energy exchange. To him, like many other activities, it was something he could just turn off when he chose. To me, it was a promise implicit in the formation of our relationship that I assumed would continue as long as we continued, certainly not with the sort of frequency or intensity as at the beginning, but always, at least occasionally. It was essentially to me the substitute for sexual contact with him. His being gay is not exactly negotiable (with the exception of our few encounters during ritual). His refusal has left me vulnerable ever since. Because I am no longer capable of flight or fight, I live with the deficit that every day takes a toll on my will and my health and my self-esteem. I don't mention it to him. But I know the deficit will be a component in how my life concludes.

Terry's influence and Riley's shutting me down weren't the only troubles I had to face. I will, in retrospect, blame all of it on the aftereffects of the DBB, because I don't want to consider that it could have been anything else. But then, it was just annihilating. Riley had to prove his viability as a student because he was on academic probation. He lost some of his financial aid, so his mother cosigned on a loan for one semester (the one after having to move away from Daisy), and I for another one, after he spent his energy, time, and money on participating in a drag show at the university, and the wild lifestyle of the drag show atmosphere contributed to the unstable mindset Riley was exhibiting. Riley's success in college was evaporating.

About three or four times, I found Riley just sitting in the dark, unwilling to speak or move. For instance, when my water heater broke and was flooding my hallway, he just sat on my sofa immobile, uncommunicative, while I scrambled to stop the water, call a plumber, let the plumber in to do his work and out when he was finished, while Riley remained mute and motionless. Plans fell apart. I found him at his apartment the same way one day, and realized our dinner date was off. He didn't call me for days.

It became a crapshoot whether we would go through with something or not, even the creation of scrying mirrors that we both decided were important to our connection (pair of black mirrors, bound together magickally, one in his home, and one in mine). I tried to plan my schedule of grading and such around days he had off just to spend them myself sometimes. This was not how I wanted to live.

At home, in my backyard circle, in those days, I begged my entities to take Riley from me. I received, in return, an audible, "No." Eventually, I would know why, for my life, the quality of my life, was soon to be forever compromised, and I would need him.

But not everything was terrible. Both before and after the DBB incident, we created our habits as a couple. Some of the activities we began as seasonal traditions were the nicest I've ever known. At Beltane, we went to the hot sulfur springs in the mountains. Every fall, we went to a specific elaborate haunted house and took a run through the enormous local corn maze. On my birthday, we went to the art museum. On his, we went to the zoo. These beautiful, bonding activities made up for the unsettling events and even gave me the illusion of home for a while. They provided a framework for consistency and togetherness.

Then came my diagnosis. I was going to have to undergo orthognathic surgery. In essence, my entire face was going to have to be broken and rearranged. If I didn't do it, my lower jaw would keep retreating until my already narrow air passage would be completely cut off. My sleep apnea was extremely dangerous. I couldn't do anything aerobic (another reason the last of our Sabbats had become unmanageable). I was suffering from oxygen deprivation and no longer thinking correctly. When I had bronchitis, I almost died, because there was no way air could get into my lungs. So, that was it.

It was going to be a long process. A year with braces, then the surgery. Months of recovery, braces a little while longer. The surgery happened in a hospital on the West Coast. We were over a thousand miles away. And I don't fly (I wouldn't have been permitted to after the surgery anyway). I would have to stay in the West Coast for two weeks after the surgery with 24-hour supervision. I realized then how absolutely alone I was.

Everyone I knew had lives to lead that would not allow them to travel with me. I have no children. My brother and his wife were not prepared to be there for me. My mother was in need of a caretaker herself. The only of my colleagues who might have had the time was a drunk and not to be trusted. There was only Riley. Then I understood why the Goddess and spirit allies would not allow me to let go of him.

Riley took care of me the entire summer of the surgery. The night before we left for the West Coast, I came down with a terrible cold or something. I was shaking uncontrollably from fever, too weak to do anything. Riley literally carried me and my luggage onto the bus. He managed the bus and train exchanges, the shuttle ride. Once at the location, he did all the driving; he took charge of my medication (I was in and out of consciousness for days); he communicated for me with people back home. When I was able to move around a bit, we walked the pier by the ocean every day and stayed on the beach breathing the healing salt air for hours till the sun set. Then, he got us home.

Because of the swelling in my head, I was nearly deaf for the entire summer, and unable to be steady enough to drive. Riley took me to all my appointments and to do my shopping. As part of my recovery, I was supposed to walk to keep my lungs clear and improve circulation. Riley mapped out a route of exactly two miles in my neighborhood so that I wouldn't have to risk crossing a major street, being as I was unable to hear approaching cars, or risk losing balance to hurry across. He walked it with me several times until I was sure I could walk it myself without getting confused. I remember the first time I set out on my own, I cried because I was so afraid. It was the first time I ventured out without his being right there holding my hand – literally. He never, in this entire venture, let go of my hand.

Immediately upon our return from the West Coast, I experienced what was maybe the loss that finally tipped the mechanism in my heart: the loss of my favorite cat to kidney failure, my three-year-old silver and black tabby, Silver. I will never get over losing him. It was the first of the dominoes to topple, followed by another, and another, and another. The death of the cat ended my relationship with the Goddess. (See essay "Wield My Sword") It was time, anyway, for my contract with Her to be over. But the loss of Her presence was palpable.

I would not be alive without Riley. But what now? He was not able to continue school without paying back loans that had borne no fruit. His job at the retail store was in jeopardy because he was always late and had taken so many days off, both to take care of me and to come to the Northwest to visit his father a few months later. He had no more intention to stay in the town we lived. And that would leave me there, without him. When he returned from visiting his father, he lost his job. So, he enlisted in the Navy, and prepared to leave for good. The year that followed was surreal.

My mother collapsed in her home and had to be put in a nursing home (where she thrived for five more years!), but that meant my having to empty her house. Going through every scrap and morsel of her belongings soaked me in melancholy PTSD for months. Riley put his stuff in storage and left for boot camp. After all we had created together, he left me! I cried the entire sixty miles home from dropping him off that last time.

Once home, I set my gargoyle free as well as the other entities and filled garbage bag after garbage bag with the vessels and donated them to a thrift store. Riley would no longer keep his promise to be the caretaker of my entities. In short, everyone and everything I had been associating was gone, by my own doing or the universe's. The symbiosis was broken as was my heart. A colleague told me months later that it seemed to her as if I had stopped breathing.

The elements too themselves turned on me. A hailstorm destroyed the sanctity of my backyard and magick circle – and roof. Tornados came so close several times that I actually took my petrified cats into the crawlspace twice to wait out our possible deaths! A small earthquake cracked the cement in my driveway, garage floor, and back patio.

My job disintegrated right before my eyes. At the college, the curriculum I had designed was going to be replaced by a new program initiated by the state. The department for which I taught was going to be subsumed by the regular English Department, and my job would no longer be what I loved, what I believed in. Finally, the chair of the English department tried to lay claim to the grammar book I had been writing for years, beginning long before my employment at the college. With the intervention of a lawyer, I was able to able to secure the rights and get it published on my own, but what a fight! My department chair retired. My fellow full-time teacher left for the Northwest.

I was alone in my work and at home. So, I quit my job and began packing to join Riley where he had requested being stationed. It is here, in the Northwest, that I am writing these words. Riley and I will live together until I am dead; that's the deal. He's made the commitment to me, and I to him. I don't trust the universe, but I have to believe in Riley. And so mote it be.

The move out here was absolute chaos. All the remaining demons converged to make it nearly impossible. By the time the house selling and house buying (a trip out here and back by myself by car) were accomplished, and another cat became ill with kidney failure (but this one lived!), and the moving truck had broken down, and we had do find a different driver, and so on and so on, I just about crawled into my new house.

And then, no more than five weeks here, we were involved in a roll-over car accident, which, because I was the only one not wearing a seatbelt, incapacitated me for several months. The ship to which Riley was assigned was to go into dry-dock in a port about 45 minutes from my – a commute easily manageable. About three months after we got here, the Navy changed its mind – the ship went a three-and-a-half-hour commute by ferry and bus away. I spent three years mostly alone, sometimes for weeks at a time. I did get a job nearly a year after the accident, so that helped with the isolation, but my loneliness is still the most oppressive force I have ever known. Once out of the Navy, Riley finished an associate's degree at the community college down the street, but then transferred to a university far enough away for him to have him live in the dorms. He comes up on weekends and holidays, just like the time in the Navy.

So this is it. I have a job, but it doesn't pay enough. Better jobs would require a lengthy commute or move. But I haven't the strength or the resources or the will to do anything more than wait for Riley to school and then get a job and go with him wherever he goes. I am in a holding pattern, with no idea how it will turn out, and almost no control over how it will turn out. If he doesn't finish school, I'm not sure I can continue. As of right now, the outcome is to a degree uncertain. On top of the anxiety from that, I keep incurring injuries that are depriving me of mobility incrementally, substantially, and I'm afraid permanently.

Still, and for now, and generally, Riley and I make good companions. We did finally see a Cirque de Soleil here in the Northwest. Riley spent a lot of money on really good tickets. No one had ever done something like that for me. Ever. Maybe things will be all right, I have to tell myself, but nothing is as it would be if Riley hadn't challenged the demon.

And that brings me back to a few caveats worth mentioning here. If someone takes on an apprentice, conventional thinking is that he/she is responsible for whatever that apprentice gets into or initiates. I don't know that I particularly buy into that, but most people do and so have ensuing expectations. We are also expected to stand up for our friends. Taking on someone else's fight, though, means relinquishing one's independent destiny to a new shared one.

None of this, however, is to say that one should never take on another's battle. Neither am I advocating the opposite – martyrdom. When I have taken on a protection or rescue operation, I've done so only when the cost of not doing so was greater than of doing it. Other than that, that idea that the cost or the success or the scope of these situations is negotiable is outright illusory. In for a dime, in for a dollar – or ten.

I could hardly believe it when I found myself in the position I did when I chose to help with the DBB. Most of my life, I've avoided any request to be someone's ghost buster or exorcist. I've had enough to do for myself. But with Riley, I couldn't just sit around and wait to see how he fared on his own. It might be argued that I was too codependent to allow it, to let him have his independence or his learning experience. The argument might be correct.

But as soon as I saw the first effects, in the form of Daisy, come into being, I found it utterly impossible to not take action. Riley should have learned from my stories not to do what he did. Having him sleep in the bed he made might have taught him a valuable lesson (as the ludicrous parenting guidelines say) – or cost him his freedom and future and maybe his life. But I could not gamble on the outcome. I had to assert some control over it.

Understanding Evil: My Soul Contract

Yet, it is more than that. Sometimes, we all need rescue from the stupidity we engage in. This time, it was my turn to do the rescuing, to be a martyr. Also, it's not just that I loved Riley and didn't want to lose him. He was worth saving. Maybe I've earned my own redemption this way. But then again, I don't know that I totally buy into this notion either.

But I *am* certain that this very scenario occurred to me in at least one other life, and this was a chance to put it all into perspective. It felt so familiar. Perhaps one or more of the entities that have been so angry with me in this life were enemies created in exactly this fashion in the distant past. Would I ever take on someone else's battle again? No. Not that I even could anymore. This one used up all my strength.

Once the gauntlet is thrown, there is no backing down until the mission is completed. If one challenges an entity, one gets its attention. It may take a little while for the reaction, but it will come. Just because the effects are not blatant or immediate, one cannot assume there are no effects. There will be, and they will be cumulative AND long term. I could not endure such a struggle again. I would have to walk away. Only walk away, to me, at this stage in this incarnation, would mean to end my life and thereby avoid both consequences of engaging and of not engaging simultaneously.

I think the greater caveat in these circumstances is for the person who creates the situation in the first place. A person's actions have indelible, unavoidable effects on others. If one sets loose a monster, one causes reactions and imperils others. Herein may lie the greater accountability. Who knows? Either way, someone must deal with the monster.

Then there is the matter of the demon itself. As I said, I'm absolutely sure that it was one I have known all my life. The look in the eyes was so familiar, as was the way it operated. Unlike the demon from my family that had a green light to its eyes, this one had a blue light. It was the same entity that disturbed my classroom when I taught high school (where Terry took an interest in me). It was the same entity that took over a friend of mine when I was still married to Gavin, my first husband, decades ago.

The way it acted once it got into Daisy was incredibly similar to the way it's behaved when it took over other people I have known. It was the same pattern. They would, like Daisy, suddenly (and I do mean suddenly!) appear and try to usurp my position in a relationship. They would, like Daisy, simply dismiss me as irrelevant. They would, like Daisy, simply help themselves to whatever plans I had with the other person. They would do it with such authority that I would find myself abruptly and rudely pitched out the door with no recourse, like a bum tossed out into the back alley, or a party crasher sent packing.

I have had this happen to me over and over in my life, the first incidents that I recall happening in junior high. It is statistically impossible for these incidents to be coincidental. Each time the interloper would follow the same damn script! "He's going to be mine, you know." "He doesn't really need you, you know." "You've never been a good fit for him." "You don't mind if I take him for a while, do you?" "Too bad you can't keep him." "He's going with me." "He'll be happier with me." "If only you knew him as well as I do." In other words, "I want what you have and will simply take it." People actually said these things to me!

The "he's" were different people at various times in my life, but in each case, the "he" really meant something to me. In a couple of the cases, I had known the "he" for a long time when the trespasser abruptly entered the picture. It's just been absurd. It's just been evil. This last round, though, became truly horrific because the "he" was Riley, and he challenged the demon, and the demon was compelled to fight back.

Understanding Evil: My Soul Contract

As for Riley, I am committed to the end, either because of the DBB or in spite of the DBB. The alternative is unthinkable. I will never find another mate with whom I can share a home. I will never find another mate whose tastes are so compatible with mine. I will never find another mate, period. My beauty is gone. My face is crooked since the surgery, and nerve damage makes the lower half unwieldly sometimes. My beauty is gone. The accident left my neck and shoulder visibly damaged. My beauty is gone. I am also getting old, with all the maladies that that implies. And I've given up my entities and my magickal practices. (See essay "Wield my Sword") I can no longer sustain them. There is nothing left.

All relationships have their crests and troughs. It's just that everything in my life is just more extreme than most. I also think that through Riley I was able to re-experience many things one more time, perhaps to see if I understood them better now. I think I did. I've been clearing the deck of unfinished business. When all the physically crippling "down-the-roads" finally hit, I intend to exit this plane. In the meantime, I'm trying to shed as much figurative baggage as possible, and that especially means demons.

As far the obvious implication in this narrative, that looming, nagging question about whether this is the best or the right relationship for me, I can only say that I am making no more decisions. I have put enough forces into action over the past few years and over my entire life time that I am just going to wait and see how they all pan out. I have enough entities around me still that have agendas to work out with each other, with me, with people in my life, so it would be pointless for me to make any more choices, to voice any more preferences.

Riley has promised to stay with me until the end of my life. I must believe in that promise. I have to trust that what we have – our home – is not just something that can be dismissed on a whim. He is learning to consider the effects of his actions on other people. I know, however, that he has little experience yet with sacrifice, and only a limited capacity for self-discipline, and that worries me.

What if I had known all that would happen after Riley challenged the demon and I agreed to help him see that challenge through? Would I have gone through with it? I don't know. Really, truly, I don't know. People at that time were giving me the tough love lecture … but it's never that simple. I would have been punished too if he would have lost the fight. Sometimes, it's necessary to make a sacrifice in order to keep the person in one's life. It's the same principle that operates with the act of forgiveness. At some point, one has to decide what is worth more – the relationship or the need for restitution or apology? One can't always have both.

Understanding Evil: My Soul Contract

Wield My Sword

My relationship with the Goddess ended because of a cat. How strange it sounds to say that. My decision was not petty, nor capricious. The contract was just over, done. We had both honored it for over a quarter of a century. Then, suddenly, the partnership concluded. My heart closed, and I was suddenly free. And as stunned as I was when I withdrew my affiliation, I did realize that nothing is forever. Not even this. There is no forever. Before we parted ways, though, She and I covered a lot of territory.

What happened to me was nothing new. When someone is engaged in spiritual battles, at some point, it might become necessary to resort to extraordinary means, if not ironic or contradictory ones. As a result, in the course of my life, I often found myself with some strange bedfellows, enlisting certain entities to fight other entities. Fighting fire with fire. Calling on a deity. The thing to know here, though, is that deities, like demons, have their own agendas, their own rules, their own allegiances. They can be trusted, if at all, only so far. Still I chose Her, the Goddess, to align myself with.

The Goddess was, to me, not the female equivalent to the Christian god. I did not see her as an omniscient, omnipotent being. To me, she was the many-faceted manifestation of the Earth's soul, which couldn't be anything but female and aligned with women and their power. The feminine trinity was not, to me, the counterpart to the patriarchal one. It was the trefoil of magickal energies.

My choice was never about the need for a religious structure. Religion is too complicated and too tedious. I don't have it in me to worship anyway. I find blind faith physically, psychologically, psychically impossible to tolerate. All the Western religions were clearly out of the question. Even the Eastern ones were not reasonable for me.

My interaction with the Goddess was, instead, an alliance. My soul partnered with Her for an agreed-upon purpose/exchange. I asked Her to help me understand the demons that were coming for me at every turn so that I could be free of them. I offered to be Her representative in whatever capacity might be required. I would metaphorically wield Her sword. Those were the terms, without clear definition, but terms nonetheless. The cost to me was great, on Her behalf and on behalf of my own quest. But I knew the demons would keep coming, and until I understood them, I knew I would continue to be a victim. While it might be good to have the favor of another demon, it might be even better to have the favor of a deity. So, I chose. Needless to say, it didn't turn out quite like I thought. Still, I believe it was the right choice.

But before I chose Her, the stage had to be set. My mundane life up till then (and certainly after) had been a steady stream of outrages mostly perpetuated by my mother. At the time of this writing, I am in my mid-fifties, and only five years ago, my mother was finally and officially diagnosed as having borderline personality disorder with narcissistic and sociopathic tendencies. In the nursing home where she finally died (in her early nineties), the staff figured out to never deal with her one at a time, but to go into her room in pairs lest she make an accusation of one sort or another. She knew what she was doing, what trouble she caused, but simply didn't care. Never did. Photos of her at any age, at two or ninety, show an expression in the eyes completely bereft of compassion or mercy. The lack is utter and unfathomable. For all intents and purposes, she was literally and figuratively my primary demon.

A clinical definition of borderline personality disorder (with narcissistic and sociopathic tendencies) cannot possible paint an adequate portrait of the actual situation. For me, as a child, it meant a terrible paradigm in which I was always at the mercy of my mother's arbitrary tyranny. There was no safe quarter. My mother's insanity became my prison. I was never the owner of my own life story, was never permitted to choose even the characters for that story. My mother isolated me from friends and other family. Any attempt to reach out to someone else was treated as a betrayal.

    I grew up with the constant threat of unconscionable extortion, false accusation of both absurdities and atrocities, unable to defend myself. The child I was didn't dare make mistakes, for mistakes were signs flawed character or disobedience. I could never figure out why no one believed me when I tried to describe what happened to me. Typical of a borderline parent, my mother had the ability to put on a disguise for outsiders or to fabricate elaborate counter charges for others to be convinced that I was lying. She could gaslight like a demon! Childhood was a nightmare from which there was no waking. Experts call children of borderlines like us (me and my brother) survivors.

    In order to cope, I chose a secret existence. It revolved around books and books and books. I wrote poetry. I talked to ghosts and to elementals, the Death Angel and the Dead, because it was natural for me to do so. I took comfort in willing my soul out of my body, down into the earth and up into the sky. Later, once I had my driver's license and some opportunities to venture out on my own, I ditched classes in order to go to the university to listen to the poets and political speakers. I left at lunch to go to the hospital cafeteria for cups of coffee I couldn't get at the school. I did anything I could to ease the pain of just being alive. I took over-the-counter pain killers, speed, travel-sickness pills, anything that would alter what I was feeling. I stole alcohol from my father, and later, I had my future husband purchase it. I lost myself in sex. Every time I turned around and faced another outrage, I found a new way to relieve my torment.

For me, there were several significant episodes that scarred me so deeply I will never recover. But it was my first wedding that stands as the symbolic epitome of the mother pain that formed my consciousness. What a composite it was of failure and broken hope that set the tone for the rest of my life.

Gavin and I met in high school. My heart, at that time (and still is to this day), was devoted to another boy, an artist, Bjorn. For reasons internal to our relationship, a future for Bjorn and me might never have manifested anyway, but the external reasons made it utterly impossible. My mother had coerced my father into threatening to shoot Bjorn if he ever came near me. My mother had telephoned Bjorn's mother to scream at her for raising her children to go out to destroy other people's families. He and I stole moments, but I was still in high school, and no matter how I tried to spend time with Bjorn, I was powerless against the juggernaut that was my mother. She had spies and tentacles and unimaginable brute force.

Then, there was Gavin. He somehow got through the barrier, and he was kind. I didn't know then that he and I were not really ever going to be compatible. We had no common interests, but quite honestly, I had never fully figured mine out by that time. I had never been allowed the freedom just to *be*, to develop my tastes and talents as they would naturally suit me, to become my own person. There had never been opportunity for me to do that. It's impossible to evolve in a cage. So, when Gavin pursued me, I gravitated toward him immediately. He was handsome (we began a sexual relationship immediately), and he had a vehicle (in which we went off-roading quite often), and he had his own identity and job.

We graduated high school. Two weeks later, we were engaged. My parents wanted me to go to college, but Gavin did not have college plans. The compromise was the community college. My parents had money for my education, left me by my maternal grandmother, and so off to community college, I went. I was still living at home, and then ... and then ... the event we came to call the Old Hospital incident happened (See the essay "Come to Me").

My brother, Rudyard, one of his friends, I, and a man named Winston, whom I met in college (and who housed the black-eyed demon that prompted the entire episode), embarked on a foolhardy mission to free residual ghosts from the Old Hospital in the old part of town. We ended up walking right into the middle of a Satanic worship session instead, and all kinds of chaos and mayhem ensued. Afterward, I could no longer live at home.

Gavin helped me find an apartment a few blocks away from my parents. In the middle of the night, after another terrible, terrible fight with my mother, I simply left. I regret not taking Rudyard with me though I don't know if it would have even been possible. My father demanded I turn over keys to my room (at the small motel my family owned and where we lived) and to the car I shared with my brother. I had been ejected from the family. In that new apartment, the black-eyed demon (again, see the essay "Come to Me") found me again, raped me, and took a piece of my soul. Then, to not be by myself, I took in a roommate, who instigated trouble for me anywhere she could, spreading lies and rumors of drug use and prostitution. So, she had to go. Then, I was alone.

It seemed that Gavin should move in with me. But my mother said that if I live with a man without marrying him, she would withhold any tuition money. So, Gavin and I set a date. My mother said that she would not help me with a wedding just so I can gratify my animal appetite. So, we began planning it ourselves. I chose and reserved a place in the mountains. I also chose a pattern for a dress and tried to sew it myself.

That didn't go well at all.

One day, as I struggled at the sewing machine that Gavin had bought me, ripping seams that had gone wrong, sobbing uncontrollably, I was visited by an incredible light and was spoken to by a supernatural voice. "I am here with you." It was that voice I would hear only a few rare times in my life, and that each time, instigated a major change in my destiny. Karen, the psychic who was staying at the motel and who had me completely in her grasp, said it was Jesus talking to me. I knew it wasn't, although I could not name the speaker. It was the first time I ever heard the voice, but not the last. And I put away the dress.

Finally, my mother said she'd pay for a wedding as long as only immediate family, plus Karen (the psychic who had installed herself into our family) (See essay "Trust Me") and her husband were invited. No aunts, uncles, or cousins. No friends (not that I had any anyway). She said that she didn't want me to have a hippie ceremony that would embarrass her. We reserved a weekend at a small wedding chapel. We bought a dress (a country-sort of prom dress – not a real wedding dress), a lacy floppy hat. Gavin bought a beige polyester suit.

My mother and I went to the chapel one afternoon a few weeks prior to map out what would happen in the short ceremony. On the way there, my mother told me that the only reason my father agreed to my getting married was that Gavin had promised to keep me out of the gutter. Nice. We had our mini rehearsal. The girls whose job it was to facilitate the weddings said the bride usually walks down from there, pointing to one entrance in the back; the groom walks down from over there, pointing to the other entrance; they come together here. Blah, Blah. Was there anything I would want to change? I couldn't think of anything. I looked at my mother. She just shrugged. OK, so all was set.

On the day of the wedding, it was quite warm, and I was terrified and nervous, wondering what I was doing, all the cliché stuff. The ceremony was brief and simple. Afterward, I was supposed to and able to sign the marriage certificate with my new name. Exactly as I was doing that, signing a document with the moniker of my new identity, my mother came up behind me and said, "You just deprived your father of what he wanted most in his life – to walk his daughter down the aisle. I hope you are happy now in your new life." She whirled around and stomped off. I looked at my new signature and nearly fainted.

I never wanted to deliberately hurt my father. She had set me up, whether to hurt me or my father or both of us, I'll never know. When she told me he only agreed to my getting married because it would keep me out of the gutter, I took it as her telling me that he wanted nothing to do with the whole thing, that there was no approval. When the girls had asked if we wanted to change anything, she could have brought it up then. Instead, she waited until that very moment. It was as if she had placed a curse on me.

After the wedding was a dinner, for which the menu had also been limited, but which was acceptable. I drank a bit more wine than I intended, still stunned by what my mother had done, and so got through it. Then, Gavin's parents invited everyone over to their home for coffee and cake and the opening of presents. Gavin and I went with Rudyard in a limo he had rented for us. At Gavin's parents' house, we waited for my mother and father. And waited. Finally, I called them. My mother informed me that because Gavin's parents had not specifically and especially come over to her and my father to thank them for the dinner and to extend the invitation personally, they felt morally offended and would never have anything to do with "those people" ever again. And they did not. Not ever.

Every holiday after that, from Mother's Day, Father's Day, Thanksgiving to Easter and Christmas (these only for the sake of appearances, as there was never, ever, any Jesus story as part of them), I was separated from Gavin's family to have the holiday with my mother. If I didn't submit to my mother's demands, I was told I would no longer be considered a member of my own family. Year after year, I could never host a holiday dinner at my home because my mother refused to be in the same location as Gavin's parents. Even if Gavin and I could have made the marriage work under normal circumstances, under these, we didn't have a prayer. The worst of it was that Gavin's parents were actually really nice.

Then came the other weirdness, the intrusion of Gavin's younger cousin, Greg. I still don't understand fully Gavin's motivation, but he suggested that I teach the boy about sex. Because he was a suitable vessel/receptacle and because the timing was right, the boy became the vessel for the green-eyed demon, my paternal grandmother's demon, and we consummated our relationship exactly during my grandmother's funeral (See essay "Serve Only Me"). What we shared was twisted and intense and destructive, but it served a purpose. My life was outrageously, stupidly agonizing, and the demon had provided me with an outlet for the energy coursing through me.

Soon, Gavin and I had other problems, and I ended up divorcing him. All I really wanted was some time away from him to think, but my mother gave me an ultimatum. She would not finish paying my tuition if I did not divorce Gavin. So I did. And then moved. And moved again. But never stopped seeing him. We weren't finished yet. I also wasn't finished with the demon. The cousin and I still interacted. When I finally remarried Gavin, my mother didn't speak to me for over a year, that is, until she needed Gavin's help moving furniture.

However, when Greg found a girlfriend, I nearly imploded. When my relationship with him ended, I could not let go, and neither could the demon. I all but tortured the boy for leaving me. The demon had given me a way to physically and metaphysically interact with my rage and fear.

Then it was suddenly gone. I was out of my mind. I, also, then found out that the cousin was not the only vessel the demon could inhabit, but it was the only vessel I could mate with while the demon inhabited it. For a long time, the demon followed me from person to person, taunting me, threatening me, saying cryptic things, but never again giving me a chance to unite with it. I found no way to fill the cavern in my psyche, and no way to defend myself against the bullying. No one even remotely adequate came my way. Trying to get help from counselors was utterly futile, even dangerous.

It was then that I made my first supplication to the Goddess. One night, after pacing barefoot up and down the street outside mine and Gavin's home every weekend for weeks, with a drink in hand, too agitated and desperate to do anything else, I knew the situation had to end. I asked Gavin to drive me out to his family's abandoned farmland, away from the city. He did. Out in the hot sand, under the moonlight, I made my request of the Goddess for the chance to learn how the demons operate so that I could be free of them, and then I made love with Gavin on the open ground to seal the deal. It was the first ritual use of sexual energy I ever engaged in, but it took. I could feel Her presence rise up out of the earth.

I felt the binding of the contract fall into place. I offered, in exchange, for the knowledge I requested, to be Her vessel, Her spy, whatever She needed me to be. I would be Her in the flesh, and She would provide me the circumstances and insight and sometimes allies, whatever I might need to comprehend the demons. I made my plea, my offer, and felt Her accept it, but there was no promise or provision of protection. I should have taken note of that.

What is interesting is that I had never heard of the Goddess before I simply went to Her on my knees. Neither my public school education, nor my family's discussions ever mentioned Her. Karen, certainly, with her "Theosophical Christianity," never said a word, yet, to the Goddess, I came. I just knew Her, knew Her from another life, knew Her from my awareness of the other planes.

I was twenty-three and in graduate school. I took out loans and worked as a teaching assistant to pay my way. The fund in my mother's possession had run out (It was reparation money paid to her mother as compensation for the loss of her home and land as a result of the Yalta Conference at the close of WWII). Once I finished my degree, I gave Gavin a choice. If he wanted children, he would have to take me at least one thousand miles away from my mother. We would have to move. I could never bring new souls into this situation. They would never be safe. She would turn them against me, or take them from me, or break their spirit like she'd done mine, or use them as a means to annihilate me. But Gavin said no. I should grow up.

So, I had my tubes tied. I was lucky to live in those few years when women finally and still had the right to make those kinds of decisions about their own bodies for and by themselves. It was the most irrevocably liberating step I had ever taken. And then came Francis (See essay "Believe Me"). My one and only fully consummated afternoon with my fellow graduate student alchemically transmuted me. He caused a metaphysical change in my heart that affected all of my soul bodies. My marriage to Gavin was over in my heart. It was just done.

The realization led to several undertakings that I would never have considered before. Again, they came from my own sense of truth, not from anything I'd been taught or that I'd read. One night, I walked out the front door of my home with Gavin, up the hill several blocks to a park that I had never visited before. It was a full moon night. I stood among the trees, in the cool night, and for the first time in my life, and without forethought, drew down the moon. Something shadowy (my Watcher) lurked in the trees watching me.

Wield My Sword

I was not exactly prepared for the effects, for the good came with the bad. The most unusual was that I became instantaneously and permanently averse to garlic. I tell people I'm allergic because that's partially true, but also because aversion sounds like a choice. But what happens when I ingest garlic is overheating, facial flushing, difficulty breathing, inability to concentrate, and the genuine feeling of poisoning. However, after drawing down the moon, my perception of the world around me was different. I saw things as participant AND spectator, as less "real," less permanent. I was no longer the same person. I felt "evolved" in ways that Karen would never have acknowledged in me.

Soon afterward, I moved to the desert Southwest, having been drawn there by the energy in an old mission along the Mexican Border. Gavin and I, ironically, during one of our summer road trips, had visited the mission on a casual recommendation from Karen, my intrusive mentor, the previous summer. As soon as I entered the place that first time, I was transported to another life, to more than two centuries earlier, when the mission was new, and I was a young Native American woman who then truly believed in Jesus and Mary and the saints. I remember looking around, thinking, "Why are these things arranged like this?" (the pews) and "What am I wearing?" (jeans). The echoes in the building were the same, though. I had been here! So, when I chose to leave Gavin, I moved to this part of the country.

What an odd thing for a witch to do (but then, witchcraft was not my religion), but I think I know now what it was all about. I believe I needed to return to a mindset from another life when I had found comfort in my then Catholic faith. In that other time, it had provided a place for my soul's sorrow and given me strength. So, I chose to revisit it for a while, to get another dose of it when I needed it most. It just seemed right, for being back in the atmosphere and the trappings, I felt at home, at least for a while.

Understanding Evil: My Soul Contract

My first purpose was to petition for divine forgiveness from Mary, the suffering biblical mother. I needed her to be my mother for a while. The missions in the Southwest are built in the shape of a cross. I was told by an old man in the gift shop that each portion had a purpose. The top part (presumably, the path to heaven) is the Jesus part; one half of the crossbeam is the resident saint's; the other half is devoted to Mary. The bottom of the cross is the door, the opening to the mortal world, the earth. I was compelled to sit in the Mary alcove and talk to Her, to deliver my grief and shame to Her. My leaving Gavin had hurt him terribly. I didn't know if he would ever forgive me, and I don't think he really has yet, but he has moved on. I needed to know that forces greater than I would forgive me for hurting him, that I did not owe him the sacrifice of my entire life. The seeds of guilt came from ... where ? ... or when? I needed Her to heal me. And She did. Or whatever listened to me when I spoke to Her did.

My commitment to living in the beautiful Southwest desert ended one night in that very mission. I drove there often. After a particularly traumatizing event involving someone I had met there, I made a late evening dash south to the mission. It was late, but I got in. The repetitious recording for all the tourists was playing in the background, but there were very few people present. I took my customary place in the pews, hoping the peace of the mission would soothe my soul. I needed it to. But as I sat there, I saw my old green-eyed demon, translucent, shimmering, simply float in above the pews, right up to me, where it laughed in my face. (See essay "Serve Only Me")

That was it. Whatever business I had had with Mary, it was over. My temporary return to an old place of solace came to an end. The Mary energy was authentic, but whatever Karen had told me would be beneficial in Christianity had just proved itself impotent, fraudulent, empty. I was done with it, and done with the location. Without the mission as an anchor, it was soon time for me to leave the Southwest and go back home. I had already engaged in a few dangerous enough liaisons. They had changed me.

As a result of them, I came to realize that to fight the supernatural forces in my life, I would have to engage in them as well. I made my decision to aggressively study witchcraft in order to fight witchcraft. I was 29 years old. It was going to be a strange study, for my soul remembered magick from other lives, but it was from long ago, with different language, different paraphernalia. Magick and Goddess represented only partly overlapping categories in my world. I was going to have to learn how to coordinate them. Truthfully, I'm not sure I ever fully did.

At the time I made my decision, I had living with me a young man, one who was out peripherally recruiting for some sort of a coven. I had picked him up at a coffee shop as a buffer between me and the things that were happening to me. Soon, I "let" him "introduce" me to the modern, this-day-and-age vocabulary for what was all too familiar to me. He "taught" me the ways of his coven. It was also Goddess-centered and seemed harmless enough.

But what I shortly learned was that the literature and rhetoric were at best inadequate and diluted, and at worst, deceptive and misleading. This was not what I remembered from my past lives. In some cases, the concepts were essentially Christian, just with a different nomenclature. In other cases, the concepts presented as truth were delusions, psychoses, or propaganda. It did not take me long to realize I was a renegade before I had even begun. Still from that moment on, I began testing out my innate powers according to whatever practice I read about. I learned to "walk among" the assorted contemporary "practitioners" and to "talk the talk." Why not?

Within just a few months, I was back in my home at the edge of the Great Plains, but everything was different. My life suddenly became something wild, without boundaries. My limited income came from working for three years as an art model (which was one of the most fulfilling, beautiful experiences of my life!). Artists, art, freedom, poetry, laughter, color, texture – a sensory banquet. And those years were the most sexually rich of my entire life as well. There had always been a lot of men, but that time was a true bacchanalian celebration. Underlying it all, however, was my search for a magickal partner. I wanted someone with the courage to accompany me on my extreme excursions. It wasn't long before I found David.

Beltane became the primary focus of my efforts. I could, in the process of the Beltane rites, sustain myself. I could feel the presence of the Goddess in me. I *was* Her. But I needed someone who could be the God. David proved capable, at least in the magickal world. With David, I was able to transform myself, find the polarities balanced with him. I learned to become the elements, to *be* flame and wind and earth. He was fearless and free of dogma, free of "training," free of "tradition," free of restrictions.

But the problem with those who can host the God is that, in the mundane world, they are rarely viable. In the end, I could not manage a life with him. He had no education beyond his GED, which, in those days, wasn't nearly as demanding as it is today. He loved his marijuana and his ambitionless lifestyle far too much. To be with him would mean evictions, utility disconnects, transportation snafus, unannounced absences so he could "find himself," instances of street people sitting around the living room when I got home, tomorrows sacrificed for the moment. He simply burned up any stability or security that I tried to create and that I needed so desperately.

It became clear that I could not have my god AND a life partner, certainly not in him, and most likely not in anyone. Men capable of functioning in the real world were too inhibited in the other worlds. I had grieved the loss of many things and people up till then, but having to let him go was one of the most painful things I ever had to do. This was the Goddess tragedy. This was my half of the bargain. It was my offering on the altar to pay for my learning.

Man after man appeared in and then departed from my life, joining me in the real world or the other world, never both. I would love and desire and sometimes reach incredible heights, and then end up empty handed or disappointed, or worse, betrayed. But as long as I could still experience the divine union at Beltane, with *someone*, I stumbled on. It was the only thing that kept me moving forward and prevented me from annihilation. There was no support system for me. My best friend, Marge, at that time had utterly betrayed me and was completely removed from my existence. It was as if she died. I lived on the fringe. My family had turned me out. Getting a foothold on hope was impossible.

But for about a year and a half, I had my Native American magickal partner. I met him the night my friendship with Marge (See essay "Believe Me") ended. He stepped out of the shadow behind the coffee shop in the middle of the night, in the rain no less, to say he'd be my protector. He was so young, also like David uneducated and free of any real world obligations, but psychically powerful. There was no magick he and I couldn't manage together. We spun an entire universe between us of beauty and darkness, of full moons and dark moons out in the open (an abandoned wheat farm around a grove of cottonwood trees, with coyotes howling and owls hooting all around us). Still, even now, my heart aches for him. For he had to leave too. He found a girl his own age who had no connections to the other worlds. After his time with me, he wanted the pressure off. I had to go "hunting" again and collected people as best I could.

On one fateful Beltane, I had to arrange (as a plan B) the ritual with a young man (my "wolf," see essay "Believe Me") who, for all intents and purposes, was more than a little bit dangerous, one step out of jail, completely amoral, but with a constitution that could accommodate a god spirit. There was another man (Plan A), one with whom I had hoped to have a relationship in the real world as well. I had asked him first to be my partner in the ritual, but he said he "couldn't go there with me." On the day of the ritual, though, he persuaded me to conduct the ritual with him instead of with my wolf. He changed his mind, he said. He was worried for my safety, he said. My "wolf" was a dangerous brute. I gave in to reason. I *let* him talk me out of my plan and then . . . he backed out. I was left with no one to perform my most sacred annual rite with. I sobbed and screamed at him, shredded by his betrayal. The Goddess's grief and rage also stormed in me. This man plunged me, and Her through me, into widowhood. He humiliated and starved the Goddess. His cowardice was unforgivable.

The next day, I painted the mirror over my altar. It was just a regular rectangular mirror, but when I was finished with it, it formed a gateway like a tunnel into my pain and into the Goddess's pain. I painted the middle surface with flat black paint, leaving only a small vertical oval for reflection. The rest was darkness. I painted the margins of the mirror, as a frame within the frame, with glossy red paint to look like torn flesh. It was the outer edges of an open wound, the tear in my heart and in the universe that would never stop bleeding. My plan A, who had betrayed me, came by for a visit, took one look at it, and nearly fell over backward. "Not good," he said, and left. This mirror became the focus of my altar, of my search, of my challenge to the universe to either heal me or kill me. And it set off a chain of events.

A couple of weeks later, I was driving on a country road on the way to Gavin's family farm (with his permission, I used it for private out-in-the-open rituals for decades), when a sink hole opened up and swallowed the front of my car. Gavin had to come out in the middle of the night with his 4-wheel drive to pull me out. I had to climb out of the window to get out. The car had fallen into the hole nose first and so far that the doors wouldn't open.

A few days after the Summer Solstice, a giant cottonwood tree fell over onto the house I was living in and destroyed it. When Gavin came home that night, he found a note from me in his house: "A tree fell through my house. My cats are in your basement. I took the Southern Comfort." Funny, now, in retrospect. Not so much then. Once in the next apartment I found, I fell down the back steps, cracking my tailbone. The pain was so intense I threw up for two days. The bruise that came up was as big as a luncheon plate.

The Goddess or the mirror or my destiny had clearly begun to shape my education. I did not destroy that malignant thing until many years later when I fled from Robin, my second husband, or to be more precise, from the demon that came to inhabit his body. By then, however, I was almost dead. But I was beginning to understand . . . .

Robin and I were united through a handfasting about a year after the tree destroyed my apartment. At Beltane. God and Goddess. But he was not the God. The relationship was compromised from the start. In every possible way, it drove me right into Hell (See essay "Promise Me"). To get free, I had to lose everything. I had to give up all that I owned to Robin or just give up. When I planned to leave, I wasn't sure if I would leave feet first or upright, so I prepared for both. Either way, I couldn't leave anything of my magickal paraphernalia behind. No matter which route I chose, I wouldn't be able to take my belongings, my household goods, with me. I had to dump all ballast overboard. In the end, there was nothing left that had mattered to me. I felt defenseless and unarmed. When I ran, I was essentially a refugee, taking only with I could carry, leaving behind an unbearable circumstance. Two of my five cats had to remain behind. The heartbreak comes back around still. My precious

Siamese came with me at least. They were tied to my soul, and without them, I would have died.

Before I left, I had to destroy two of the stone and gravel circles that I had created in the backyard, taking apart the Maiden and the Crone circles. The Mother circle had to stay. In the center of it, I had buried the shattered pieces of a ceramic money-bank (in the shape of a smiling sailor carrying a bundle on his back) when I consecrated it. I would not dig that up again. On top of it, I had put a bird bath, which I kept filled every day for years.

The little money-bank was from my childhood. It had sat on a shelf when my family lived in the motel. My mother would put money into it now and then, to save up for . . . for what? I have no idea. I didn't even know she had money in it. To me, it was just another knick-knack on a shelf with many, many knick-knacks. One day, she decided some of the money was missing. In retrospect, I am absolutely sure my alcoholic father had used it to buy provisions. Whenever he asked my mother for money for a bottle, there would be a row. But he never stepped forward to admit it. Therefore, I was punished for stealing the money to give to "my drug friends," of which, of course, I had none. No friends at all. My father, needless to say, never spoke up in my defense. He regularly threw me under the bus, so I wasn't surprised.

It was not the first time, nor the last time, I was charged with a crime I hadn't committed. The accusations ranged from wanting to abandon the family on Christmas Eve "to be with a man" (it was actually two weeks prior to Christmas, and the "man" was a gay boy!), to being an "attention seeking whore" when I said I needed to go to the hospital when I broke my arm skateboarding (it was, but I was made to wait all night while it swelled grotesquely), to organizing a gang to beat up my brother so that my family would let me go out with a boy that liked me (never happened!). The latter false charge was used to defame me before the whole family, and was the determining factor in my uncle's restricting my access to my inheritance. (See essay "Promise Me")

And no one stood up for me. Ever. Not my brother, not my father. Not that little ceramic sailor. I smashed it to smithereens and put the pieces in the ground so that the Goddess could feel my sorrow too, would somehow avenge me. My father stood as a ghost in the corner of the yard watching me till I sent him away. I was not going to dig up the shards when I left Robin. He didn't know what they were about anyway.

So, I left the Mother circle intact. But before I destroyed the Crone circle, I broke the mirror by putting it in the center, wrapped in a sheet, and bludgeoning it with a hammer. I undid the Maiden circle with a shovel and a rake. Then, into the space where it had been, I stirred the ashen remains of the Robin doll (See essay "Promise Me"). It was over. The home I had put so much effort into was no longer mine. I was ready to and did leave, upright, but only barely. To make my escape, I had had to destroy or disperse my entire magickal arsenal. And then, I stepped into a vacuum. I was displaced and, for years, did no spells, no protective magick, no evocations, no invocations. That reprieve, of course, would not last forever. The demons were not finished with me.

Back with my family (how I hated not having any other choice), slowly, very slowly at first, I began reestablishing my household, working toward getting a full-time job and buying the home I was living in. I put up a fence to the open field behind it so I could have a private and secure backyard. I took up an on-again-off-again (for eighteen years) relationship again, only to realize how terrible Mark really was, how condescending, how cruel. A helpless, hapless, hopeless failure. He had no career or profession. He had managed to screw up everything he tried, yet he was so sure of his superiority. Yet, my less than upper class upbringing was something he would never let me forget: "with a background like yours," "you wouldn't know any better," "it's a middle-class thing." He avoided taking me to places where he'd have to explain me to his friends, telling me I wouldn't fit in.

Mark's final trespass occurred when he put on a show of being willing to indulge my "belief system" in order to try to trick me into a pagan commitment ceremony, to be done at Ostara. He proposed that until such time, we should refrain from sexual activity until it was "sanctioned" by marriage. What he didn't tell me was that in the years we were separated, he had become impotent. That explained his "waiting to consummate our relationship till my divorce was final" – as if that mattered before when I was married to Gavin! He was going to keep that a secret, figuring that just the privilege of being with him would be enough for "someone like me." But on the intended day, one of my cats saved me. My male Siamese had a fit of pancreatitis, and I spent the night in the emergency vet. I had to apply for an emergency loan to pay for the visit. Mark just stood there, angry at having been thwarted. He could have helped pay the bill, and maybe if he had helped, I might have been persuaded . . . .

That night, I saw the black-eyed demon in his eyes, just for a moment, and the day afterward, I dreamed of that demon, dreamed of being eighteen years old again, back in the bathroom after Winston had raped me (See essay "Come to Me"), ready to end my life. It was so real. I found myself back there as if those moments still existed in time, and I had returned to them for a visit. The day after the dream, I wrote Mark a "fuck you!" letter of nearly thirty pages. I had no more doubt.

In the following year, I renewed my secondary teaching license and tried to move forward. I made one more attempt (perhaps the sixth time in our lives) to connect with my beloved artist Bjorn. But once again, well, I could say that our timing was off, but really what he did was reveal to me that I was never going to mean to him what he did to me, and I just couldn't bear it anymore. To spare myself any more grief in the future, I wrote him a monumentally long good bye letter too. He would not respond to it for a year. It took us a couple of years to be friends again, but whatever chance we might have had to be romantic partners again dissolved forever. So, by the time I began the one year contract teaching high school, all my remaining romantic hopes, all my ties to loves in my past were gone. Then, that year was one of the worst of my life. I was so not suited for it. Plus, the high school was in a in a horrifyingly conservative, rural community nearly an hour away. Still, I stuck it out. I had no choice.

It wasn't long, though, once that school year began, before I had to secretly take up my sword again. In that first semester, a demon that later we would call it the demon in the book in the box – the DBB (See essay "Say My Name") took possession of a student in my classroom. I have to say that there is very little as frightening as being a teacher and finding oneself at the mercy of a delinquent adolescent who was showing the potential to be a time bomb to one's career. In my vicinity, he was a raging, slobbering, lying, quaking, explosive vandal, but once removed and placed in another class, he was perfectly docile and well-behaved without incident for the rest of the year! I was lucky to have had several incidents observed by a colleague, or I my job would have been gone. No one would have believed me.

Before he was moved to another class, the little bastard put a note in a stack of papers I took home to grade. I didn't see it till I got home, but even before I did, I saw two images appear on the wall in my dining room, a classically demonic visage, complete with horns and a goatee, and a strange geometric symbol. When I finally found the note and opened it, I could feel the venom from the demented ramblings. I knew then the source of the symbols on my wall – and I dealt with them.

But I no longer felt safe at that school out in the middle of nowhere. On the rural, rumored-to-be haunted road, twice, I had a spirit manifest right in front of me. It looked like a real person at highway speed. I swerved, nearly losing control my SUV. The third time, I decided to just drive through it, glad in retrospect that it really wasn't an actual pedestrian. Just before I "hit" it, it dissolved with an audible laugh – and I knew.

In addition to the danger of the long drive on that iffy road to the school, my classroom was actually a temporary building in the far end of the parking lot. So, not only was the school in the boondocks, my classroom was in the north forty of the boondocks. One morning, when I went to unlock the classroom door, the demon actually peered at me from inside of the room, through the small rectangular pane of glass, just inches from my face, with the cold blue light in its eyes and a grimace from hell. Clearly, I had no choice. I had to set up protection. I could not do this on my own. After some years of no magick, I called in the elementals, and thus, ended up back on the radar. I was sporting a target again. There was no way I would have made it through that school year if I hadn't called up my guardians. Once I did, a small skirmish between them and the demon occurred, which overturned all the desks in my room and flung an entire shelf of dictionaries onto the floor over that first night, but afterward, the troubles remained minimal. That was also the time a young student, Terry, (See essay "Say My Name") set his sights on me, but he wasn't yet a proper vessel for the demon to use. He would catch up with me a few years later.

By this time, I was well into my forties. I was alone. I was writing poetry, yes, but I had no other joy. I also had no real freedom (long days at work made even longer by the near hour-long drive there and back, and grading, grading, grading at night). I also had no security with my family. At any moment, my place in the family could be revoked. I knew that. The house I was living in was finally mine, but only because I had to resort to extraordinary means. Before it became mine, it had belonged to my brother, and in his possession, it fell into foreclosure. After all I had been through, I was almost homeless. I could not allow that. I will never reveal what I did to rectify the situation, other than to say it was one of the most powerful spells I ever cast, the most ferocious appeals to entity I ever made.

The Goddess, I believe, heard my appeal for justice during those months. I knew that I could no longer allow myself to be at my family's mercy, dependent on them, without any way to establish my own sovereignty. I know She heard me. For, one by one, several significant factors toppled like dominoes, each one affecting the other, until I ended up able to establish myself for a while, with a new and more local fulltime job and a house that was my own. My brother quit the martial arts cult that had had him brainwashed for twenty-five years. I acquired two cats that eerily resembled the two I had had to leave with Robin, and they reconnected beautifully with my Siamese. I had a home, or at least a facsimile thereof, but there was no reason for it, no center, no heart.

Then that familiar and irresistible voice spoke to me again. Soon, I found myself compelled beyond any power to resist to go to the university to find the group of young pagans meeting there – and to meet Riley (See essay "Say My Name") for all that that and he meant and means to my life still. It was because of him that I resurrected the witch that I once was, that one more time, I allowed myself to relive as many of my magickal and occult experiences that I could. Seeing all of it through his eyes was enlightening, and I had a chance to re-evaluate them from a whole new perspective.

But my relationship with him was as fraught with agony as it was ecstasy. Riley, being gay, could only be my magickal partner for just so long, and that was it. There were several times in those first few years, I tried to give him back to the universe. I couldn't imagine a life without sex, without passion, without physical contact with another human being.

Understanding Evil: My Soul Contract

I raised up my usual audience in my circle again and again in order to declare my wish to set him free, until finally, an audible "No!" resounded all around me. That voice that speaks to me from beyond the Veil. The voice I cannot disobey. I am assuming now that I was set up to trade my sexual life for my actual life, for the role that Riley would play for me later. It was not a trade I would have made knowingly. As much as I love him, I am still not fully settled on it. A part of me has still not agreed to it.

At our first Beltane, which was actually a group ritual, we attracted the DBB directly into our lives, and it took nearly all our strength and a lot of our resources to finally dispose of it a year and a half later. (See essay "Say My Name") Our second Beltane was completely destroyed for a different reason. Riley let me believe we would at least be together, not sexually, but at last together, so I made no other plans. On the day itself, he informed me that he had a date with a man he'd met online. I felt the old agony of Goddess pain and betrayal nearly tear me in two. Another Beltane betrayal.

In the summer that followed, all three of my old Siamese died. I acquired two kittens, Silver and Trixie, because I could not bear the absence of my beloved cats. At the third Beltane, which was our first private and truly authentic ritual, while I thought he was embodying the God to be with the Goddess, in reality, he was making the commitment to me, not to the Goddess. The night was beautiful, but I didn't know at the time that it was somehow a little bit fraudulent. A betrayal, really, but there was a beauty to it still. We had in total all of one, but only one, year of Sabbats together, but then there were no more. We finally finished off the DBB. And we became essentially a couple, by all appearances, with regular activities and movie dates and cooking adventures.

Our fourth Beltane was overshadowed by the greatest trial of my life. Massive orthognathic surgery. That was the most prolonged, exhausting, physically debilitating struggle I'd ever known. Months and months of braces, a trip to the West Coast for the surgery, ten pieces of titanium to hold the bones of my face together after their rearrangement, three weeks for the preparation and recovery in an apartment hundreds of miles away from my cats, most of the trust fund money I had thought might have allowed me a good life, and the absolute terror of the entire ordeal. Riley saw me through every minute of the ordeal.

After the surgery, I was unable to sleep lying down for three months. My sciatica has never fully recovered from that. I had to be on liquid food for nearly four months. It was a daunting challenge. My face was swollen like a grotesque puffer fish. I had to hope and pray that my hearing would return, compromised by the swelling, for until it did, I was not able to drive. It took three months. I hoped that the bruising and distortion around my eyes would subside in order for me to be able to wear my contacts again. That also took three months. There was no guarantee on any of this. I had to wait and see.

So, a few days after my return from the West Coast, I cast a spell to help in my healing. I made my request of the universe from the perspective that I deserved to be well again, to have my beauty restored (which never happened), to be free of the weight (which I did lose but which has returned doubled), to be able to breathe (that, at least is true), and to live again (never fully again). I hoped the nerves in my jaw would regenerate fully, so that sensation in the lower part of my face and my gums would be restored (that also never happened). But I didn't yet know any of the outcomes.

It was the night of the Summer Solstice. I thought it was an appropriate time for such a spell, so I did it – in the house. But outside, that night, in my backyard, something toppled one of my ceramic birdbaths (never in the ten years I had them had that happened except for that night!). It didn't break, but it was completely inverted and on the ground. I felt something was very wrong. I could feel the reach of a counter spell thick in the backyard. *Oh, no.* The next day, my Silver cat began acting ill. The diagnosis: kidney failure. He was only three years old. I called to the Goddess with every molecule in my body. It was a pointless supplication. Deities don't grant requests. How very helpless I felt. Three months later, he was gone.

One time in those last few weeks of Silver's life, the black-eyed demon paid a visit. I often would just look at Silver across the room, trying to take in as much of his presence, his beauty as I could, to somehow store it in my heart for when he would no longer be there. One of those times, Silver's hazel eyes were not Silver's hazel eyes. They were the black-eyed demon's abysmal pits. The demon was looking at me through my dying cat, gloating, menacing. I went cold, the kind of cold that was all too familiar to me. My knees buckled, and I nearly fell over. Then the cat blinked, and the demon was gone.

That was the end. That was the ultimate betrayal. The demon, *that* demon, got into my house, into my Silver! That was a violation of my contract with the Goddess, at least from my perspective. So, I took the burnt remains of the spell I had done to try to save my cat, and placed them around the periphery of the circle and shouted to the Goddess that She and I were through. I would no longer call on Her. I would no longer serve Her either. After everything I had to endure in my life, this was the one that toppled the mechanism, voided the contract with Her. It felt as awful as the instant I realized that Mary/Jesus/God and all were of no use to me when the green-eyed demon floated into the mission in the Southwest. (See "Trust Me")

Despite all I tried to do to keep him with me, I had to let Silver go. He was suffering so much by then. Sitting at the vet, holding him for the last time, knowing I would never touch him again, was almost more than I could bear. I couldn't stand. I couldn't swallow. I held him as he died and sent part of my own soul with him. At any time, I may have several cats in my home, but only one at a time that's my familiar. Silver was the last familiar I would have in this life. He was truly my soulmate. Because I knew his best companion, Trixie, would be devastated by his absence, I had, in anticipation, brought two new kittens into my home, nearly identical litter mates that were born on Beltane! It took me a long time to bond with them, but they immediately bonded with Trixie, and she with them. But the loss of Silver left a black hole in the household.

Though I tried to take my sorrow to Her, the Goddess was never my protector, nor a source of comfort for me. That is not how it works, not how it ever worked. That was simply my wishful thinking. The two or three times I feel sure She intervened in my life, it was not a benign, maternal act. It was business. The Goddess was my teacher. We had a deal. I had asked for the means to learn about the demons. Well, I got what I asked for. I am only now fully taking stock of all I learned.

The death of the cat was the first event in a series of events that changed my destiny. My neighbor, a woman I really cared about, died of leukemia two weeks after Silver. So, I no longer had her to talk to. I was left to reassess my entire fate. The surgery I had undergone was horrific. But I had done it to save my life. The question then for me now was, "What life?" My face was never going to be my face anymore. Riley was showing signs of being restless.

The worst of it was that my everyday life was punctuated and regimented by my mother. In her late eighties, she was still living at home, but it was becoming difficult. Long before I met Riley, her diagnosis with diabetes changed her entire existence, which had up till then focused on her greatest joy – baking and food. Her fear of having to do insulin, her fear of death completely derailed her. She just sank. My brother, Rudyard, and I tried to offer to take her to the botanical gardens, to the aquarium, anywhere. We found out where we could borrow a wheel chair. But she wanted nothing.

Understanding Evil: My Soul Contract

Then, just months after I met Riley, she had a heart attack. I knew it was coming, or that something terrible was imminent. I saw the black-eyed demon. He appeared in my mother's garage when I went to visit her. Sure enough, exactly one day later, she had a heart attack that should have killed her! The demon had come to gloat about what was to come. A warning, yes, but also a sealing of my fate.

She survived her heart attack. I did not. My Saturdays, which I had always used for writing poetry, were from the day of her heart attack forfeit in order to take her shopping. She gave up driving. Her ability to manage her household by herself diminished little by little. I rearranged things in her house and took over several of her chores. I spoke to her every morning, stopped in every evening on my way home from work. Sundays, she invented "emergencies" for me to come deal with. So, other than my outings with Riley, this was my life. I could never plan anything, for if I did, she'd have a crisis. Her neighbor felt sorry for me, my being treated as a slave, and told me so often.

No matter what I had gone through with my surgery, my mother was as terrible, horrible, disgusting, embarrassing, mean, and manipulative as ever. There were days I would have rather torn the skin off my arms than talk to her, but I had no choice. Her cruel insanity was my prison, as she had always been. My brother did not participate in the daily care or the shopping. Toward the end of her stay at home, he did begin taking her to the dentist, the eye doctor. But he wouldn't put himself near her influence otherwise. He advised me to stay away too, but I did not see how that was possible. Her food was not going to deliver itself! Her mail was not going to walk itself to her door! Her bedding was not going to wash itself! Her trash was not going to remove itself! Sigh.

At least, my being nearly deaf and unable to drive the summer after my surgery was in a way a godsend. I had a reprieve from her (the work fell to my sister-in-law and my mother's neighbor), but the old pattern soon returned to me as soon as I was mobile again. I was desperate. I did not just go through the surgery in order to live, to live like this! Never, throughout my entire ordeal, did she show me any sympathy, not even one tiny acknowledgment of what had happened to me. She was only concerned about when I could come take her shopping again. She was still strong and vicious and showed no signs of giving up yet. Someone had to help me, or I would have to kill her myself!

Who? The Goddess was out of reach. Ah, but my dead father was not! I used all the necromancer powers (See essay "Believe Me") I had in me to call him back to this plane to come get her. I have to say he gave it a good try. On the 23rd anniversary of his death, he caused her to drop to the floor in her kitchen just after I left in the evening. Afterward, he stopped in at my brother's house to say hello to him too. My mother lay there for ten hours till she came to enough to remember the emergency help button on her wrist. At the hospital, no one expected her to make it. They put pint after pint of blood into her to raise her blood pressure.

My contention is that she, whatever was human about her, did die, and what animated her body for the next five years was the demon that had been in her all along. I think it was born into her. I think that happens. It's a theory. Yes, I am suggesting that her personality disorder is due to a demonic presence. I think there are many possibilities for mental illness and personality disorders that psychology doesn't recognize, but that I think are valid, nonetheless. For instance, it is *possible* that mental illness is due to person's accidentally picking up previously incarnated "passengers," (ghosts or spirits, in other words), and the coincidental chemical imbalances in the brain are the effect of the inhabitation or the cause, as in, that which attracts the new tenant. Chicken or the egg … but either way, a *possible* relationship. There are books about the phenomena, and they are credible.

However, I think it is *probable* that personality disorders are due to possession by demons, major or minor, because of some compatibility. At the person's core, something is wrong. Or there is no human soul at all, but something else, something maybe demonic. Neither vessel nor driver has empathy. I think some of these possessions can occur before or at birth. Tabula rasa is wishful thinking at best for all kinds of reasons.

So, my mother lived, but she could never go home again unless she went through rehab to regain her mobility. *That* she refused to do. It was too painful she said because of her arthritis. I can't imagine the monster that was my mother just saying she was fine with never walking again. I don't know what she thought that was going to accomplish. Either way, into the nursing home, she went. My tour of duty was over.

I remember going into her house at first with the intention to start the cleanup, but feeling absolutely terrified that she was yet going to come home, afraid to touch anything lest I jinx my liberation. I just sat on her couch, crying, quaking with fear. After a few weeks, I was finally convinced that time would not reverse itself. I went at it full force. Every item represented to me a chance I had been denied in my life. In three months, I emptied her house so it could be sold. I had to go through every item, piece by piece, all by myself. No one helped. No one kept me company. I was alone with her ghosts, her thoughtforms, her residual energies, and my unending bouts of PTSD.

I spent weekends and evenings in that place with her vibrations and her smells and her belongings, which somehow she thought were treasures. Until the end of her life, she thought all her stuff was in storage somewhere, as if it were our treasure to guard, but the truth is it was all gone. We didn't even sell it; we just gave it all away. I wanted nothing. My brother wanted nothing. By the time I was done, I was thoroughly poisoned by the energy her things emitted. Still, once it was all finished, my mother was as out of reach as the Goddess.

It was then that I grieved the loss of her, or more accurately grieved my original identification of home. It was the home (even though it was by no means the first or even the tenth residence) of my parents even long after my father's death because it still had my mother in it, still had the same paintings and photos on the wall, still had the same furniture in the living room, still had the same books on the shelf, still had her sewing machine and my father's butcher knives, and the smell of fifty years of her cologne, of fried onions and apple strudel, and furniture polish. It was gone. I no longer had a place I could go to, for good or for evil, to talk to someone – namely her – or just to be in a set of circumstances that was more familiar than anywhere else. The home of my childhood was finally gone. I had dismantled it.

It was one more loss. According to any number of definitions, I was living dead. All that was necessary to finish me off was Riley's departure. It came as well. Riley's job had ended; he couldn't go back to school until he paid back student loans; he hated the town. So he left. He joined the military and was gone. Just like that. I spent a few weeks in a stupor. But the universe wasn't done beating me up yet.

Shortly after he left, a hailstorm of all hailstorms destroyed my backyard, polluted my circle by flooding it. The waters brought in dog excrement from the neighbor's pit bulls and weed seeds from the field beyond my fence. Everything was desecrated. The hail absolutely shredded my roof. For a few weeks, tornadoes kept coming alarmingly close, and I twice had to capture my cats, put them in carriers and descend into the crawlspace with them. With the tornado siren blaring, the beep-beep-beep of the weather channel warnings screaming from the television, I chased my beloved companions around, hysterical with terror: "Oh, god, which ones do I grab first?" The stress was unbelievable. A month later, a small earthquake shook the area, cracking the concrete pads of my front and back patios, garage floor, and driveway. The only element that didn't take a shot at me was fire.

Understanding Evil: My Soul Contract

The final straw was the end of my job. Maybe this was fire – burning bridges! Changes at the college forced me to quit my tenured position. My department chair had retired. The department I had been part of for years was subsumed by another. The chair of that one and I were never going to get along. Most of my colleagues (including my sister-in-law) were not rehired, and my main cohort had moved out of state. It was all over. I had to go through legal proceedings to keep the rights to a grammar book I had put together, and then I quit. A tenured position. One that would have been secure for the rest of my life. Done.

The end of that summer, Riley helped me move to the Northwest to where he was stationed. I think if he hadn't done that, I would have been unable to go on. Of course, trying to get out of that awful town wasn't easy. Packing was a nightmare. I had too much stuff in my small place. I also could not create closure as I needed to, to say goodbyes as I needed to. For instance, I was unable to spend time with my best friend because her dog mysteriously broke its leg and needed, after the surgery (at a cost of $4,000), to be kept immobile for those weeks, so she couldn't leave her house, and this at the same time that her mother had to stay with her for a few months, so there was no privacy for us.

Also, the local entities had either become accustomed to me and didn't want to let me go, or they weren't done abusing me yet. Since I don't fly, I had to carefully plan the two-day drive out and back, to hunt for and purchase a house, and time it all with the sale of my house. The transition involved a bridge loan, reserving rooms at a hotel, getting everything arranged for being gone for ten days, including arranging a cat sitter. Well, exactly three days before I was to leave, Trixie, my then four-year-old cat, started showing signs of being ill. The diagnosis: kidney failure. Time was running out. There was nothing I could do but leave her at the cat hospital the eight days I was gone – at a cost of $4,000 (that number again!), which I only obtained by selling my mother's jewelry way too cheaply, but I had no choice. I talked to the vet hospital several times a day as I hunted for a home, each time afraid of what I would hear.

When I found a place in the Northwest to purchase, I made one last deal with the universe. I would give up wearing my pentacle in exchange for saving the cat. That meant no more elemental magick for me either, not as long as Trixie lives. (how desperately I long to wield my athame to cast a circle again . . . and yet . . . I know, I can never go back to that "place that is not a place, time that is not a time" – it's over) The afternoon I took it off, I was told by the veterinarian that Trixie had recovered kidney function. My bargain had been honored. Weeks later, I would give a pentacle to Bjorn. It was one half of a pair. One, my gargoyle (See essay "Believe Me") had worn, and as the gargoyle was always physically out of reach just as my artist always was, that is the pentacle I gave Bjorn. The other one, the one I had worn, I closed up in a box; I'll never wear it again.

The last roadblock to the move was the fully loaded truck's breaking down. The intended driver was my brother Rudyard, but the delay to get the truck repaired prevented it. It turned out to be Gavin, my first husband, who drove me out to the Northwest, ironically, after a quarter of a century, finally getting me out of town. The six years out here on the West Coast have been rough. Within the first two months, we were in a terrible roll-over car accident. I was the only one not wearing a seat belt (just for a few moments till I sorted out fitting it over my jacket collar) and flew around like a ping pong ball. The damage to my neck is permanent, and, because of arthritis, progressively degenerative. The accident derailed my life. I'm still stunned by the cruelty of it.

Yet, either because of or in spite of the accident, or either because of or in spite of my abjuration of associations with entities or deities, my perception changed. What I see now, when I look beyond the Veil, is not the usual darkness with its distant horizon and its sea of ghosts and ghouls (well, they're still there, but no longer significant). What I can see now is starlight, or better yet, the initiation of starlight. I am once again able to see what I could see before my trip to the desert Southwest, before I took on the practice of witchcraft, before I painted my mirror, before the demons came for me. It's not that I can't see the entities when I choose to, but it was as if I had forgotten starlight, and now, it has come back to me.

Mary left my life a long time ago. I am grateful that I found the comfort I needed in Her energy again in this life. That the church itself and, therefore, Christianity in general offered no defense against the demons was another matter. Later, the Goddess had to go too. She *did* provide the mechanisms by which I would learn about evil, and I am certain that She interceded on my behalf a rare few times when it suited Her to make sure I stayed on track. It was never just because I asked, and never out of love. Of course, I was never a fawning acolyte either. The price of my learning was heavy.

Just as my grandmother's demon took it upon itself to "rescue" or "avenge" me in precarious situations, the Goddess sometimes did the same. The trauma or betrayal would play itself out, but then later, the perpetrator would be utterly crushed and humiliated. I'm certain Mark's impotence will be permanent. The sick married church deacon who pursued me has to live with his son's being a murderer. The fellow graduate student who raped me was attacked and beaten by a mugger. Whenever someone hurt me specifically because I was a woman or if what happened posed a threat to my freedom, then divine intervention occurred. Then the punishment would be doled out appropriately because whatever unacceptable thing people did to me, they did to Her. Later, the ax would fall mercilessly. Well, most of the time anyway. There was no protection from my mother.

After being put in the nursing home, my mother still persisted for years. For that, I am furious with the universe, though her persistence did provide the diagnosis of her personality disorder as validation of her evil. I thought for certain she would yet outlive me, and the mandatory 6:30 PM daily phone call would be the leash to tether me to her forever. It was always her most effective method of invasive control. It is the one mind game that she could keep in operation even at a distance. But I couldn't *not* pick up when she called. While she was in the nursing home, I did so out of sympathy. For the rest of my life previous to her internment in the home, I did it because my ability to separate myself from her was too thoroughly broken. The brief exchanges at the end were entirely meaningless, except when she still tried to pit me and my brother against one another, or insisted I follow some bizarre piece of advice she offered. But I endured them because I didn't want her to suffer from utter isolation, wanted to give her some link to the outside world to something/someone that was familiar to her. Doing so probably meant more to me than her.

Mostly, unless her hearing impairment required a few repetitions, the more recent calls lasted no longer than one minute. However, because they were set for the exact time every day, my daily schedule had to be adjusted so that I was not in the middle of something and risked being interrupted or missing the call. If I didn't answer, she would call and call and call. If I turned off the phone, I would miss others' calls as well. If I had something planned, and would tell her not to call, she tried to negotiate for a later or earlier time. Despite all the power I had in other areas of my existence, in the arena, I felt like an insect pinned to the wall.

We played this evil game for decades. Before I left my second husband, the designated time for the call was also 6:30. After I left him and moved back to the town where she lived, the call was at 9:30 PM, usually the time I would be at movie or at a coffee shop. It was her contention that I should be at home by then, so she would call my home, then my cell, then my home, until I not only answered, but *was* at home. She was determined that I had to be home before then so she could go to sleep. More than once, when I got home after midnight, my phone would ring: "How can you keep me up so late!" I was in my mid-forties then! If I told her not to call on a particular night because I would be busy, she would extract an "admission" about what I was going to be doing and with whom, so she could pass judgement or make ludicrous assumptions or say she'll stay up, no matter how tired she it would make her just to know I got home. Finally, I had to get rid of my landline.

Every one of these "prisoner check in" conversations with her was like sticking my head into a meat grinder. She would ask the same question several different ways at different times, and god forbid, my answer deviated even slightly! She would have made an excellent Nazi interrogator! Still, I was never truly free to not answer my mother's call just in case there were still some vestige of salvageable humanity left in her. While I, for most of my life, engaged in the sparring (and it was) in order to circumvent extortion or to maintain a self-protective cover, in the last few years, I engaged in it out of pity, trapped by my own sympathy for her aloneness and disability (she was totally bedridden). The cognitive dissonance nearly shattered me every single time. Still, I could not say no.

My mother's last few years were miserable, arguably of her own design. She had no friends, did not keep up with family. She never in her life learned to have basic conversations, so she made no effort to acquaint herself with anyone at the nursing home. She refused television, radio, magazines, or decorations in her room. She did not participate in the nursing home's field trips. They couldn't put a roommate in with her because she was so hostile – that is, until they found a woman who was completely deaf and immune to her abuse. She lay in the bed wrapped up like a mummy except for visits to the toilet or shower or meal times when they lifted her with a contraption she called "the monster," put her into a wheelchair, and wheeled her into the dining room. Then it was back to bed. That was it. That was her life. So I felt sorry for her and answered the phone.

Until her death, there was no rescue from my mother. There will never be justice for me. But when Riley helped me to break a certain smoky quartz crystal (See essay "Say My Name"), my need to be loved by my mother broke along with it. The way I always felt I was begging for her affection stopped. The grief over never having been loved by her exploded right along with the crystal, but the psychological chains remained. Then, her physical capacities began failing. Finally, at the end of her life, she started forgetting the designated calling time, sleeping through it, imagining that she had already done it. It was a relief.

So, I was able to let go of her in seven stages. The first when Riley and I broke apart that crystal. The second during the reprieve after my surgery. The third when she went into the nursing home. The fourth when I sold her house. The fifth when I moved out to the Northwest. The sixth when at the end for about four months the calls tapered off. And lastly, the seventh when she died. Her influence on me had been so powerful, it defied my sense of self preservation. She lived a long, long time. Now, I feel like I am too soul-weary to enjoy my freedom from her. She broke me.

My brother finally sent me my mother's death certificate a few months after her demise (I did put a self-addressed, stamped envelope into the holiday card I sent him to facilitate that!). What a strange and sterile conclusion to a very messy relationship, a piece of paper. That's one way to look at it. But that's not where the closure lay. Something happened to me when I held it in my hand and read it. I had a vision. I saw her body being destroyed by the flame of the cremation. It was gruesome and unforgiving, and for a moment, I felt sad, at the waste of it all. But as I watched the cremation in mind's eye, I saw the demon that had been in her rise up from the cooking flesh, furious and defeated. It had a red, glowing face as it separated from the physical matter. I could hear it screeching. It was full of rage. Angry the body that housed it was no longer functioning. Mad that it found itself ousted and homeless. How very creepy – as so much of my life has been.

The vision reminded me of the time my father and I burned a particular one of my grandmother's dolls. (See essay "Believe Me") I remember how it screamed when we lit the gasoline, how something took form and departed from the trash barrel we used for the immolation and darted away down the alley. My father both heard and saw what I did. Seeing the demon leave my mother's body was verification/proof for me that what I've been saying all along is true. There was a demon in her. There was. There was. There was. Now it is free too. It will have to find another vessel to inhabit. But I am so glad that I was nowhere near for the moment of its eviction. Now, I can't say that I didn't get the chills a little bit when the vision came. Just a shiver and a bit of a stomach drop …but the resolution implied thereby has been as liberating as haunting. I am free.

All my guilt left me too, my self-recrimination that I left her when I moved and never returned for a visit. I was far away from her during the last years of her life. All my guilt for getting rid of her belongings, for lying about my own and my brother's activities, for being impatient with her, for telling everyone how terrible she was. It all just went away the instant I had the vision. There is nothing left.

Also it became clear that that thing never had it in for me personally. It didn't care enough to come after me. Neither did *she*. The possibility of her ghost coming back around as she always claimed her mother had was just horrifying to me. But there were no visits. She's gone. What is sad, though, is that my father seems to be gone too. Perhaps he stayed around all these years since his death to make sure she (and it) moved on, and that ended his purpose here. Until her departure, I could always reach into the ether and sense him there. No longer. The fight is truly over, and now I am facing a great emptiness from here on out.

What I learned throughout this whole process is that I believe in many beings, entities, deities, but it's not a good idea to have faith in any of them. They exist; they have power; they have their place in the larger scheme, yes. And, yes, I have been able to make deals with a few of them, but I am pretty sure the exchanges were never fair. Mostly, what one gets out of such a deal is what one creates oneself. I was terribly mistaken to assume any of the unearthly beings to have even one of what we normally consider human characteristics or emotions or motivations. Believing that one can appeal to any deity for mercy or assistance is foolhardy.

If the black-eyed demon hadn't peered at me from my dying cat's eyes... if the cat hadn't been dying... if my prayers hadn't been so useless... if I hadn't been so desecrated by the surgery (and the condition that demanded it)... if all the demons collectively hadn't done so much damage... if my mother hadn't been so irredeemable... if anyone would have ever loved me unconditionally or fought for me... if... then maybe I wouldn't have let the Goddess go out of my life. I don't know. But the cat died. There was no going back after that.

Understanding Evil: My Soul Contract

Post Script

It has been five years since I started this project. As I described in the preface, many strange things happened in my house every time I sat down to work on it. It has been difficult, sad, and sometimes spooky. Difficult in that the work exhausted me on a soul level, sad because of all that I had to recall, and spooky due to the nature of it all. I still worry about how the demonic evil and human evil are not always distinct in my stories. They sometimes weren't distinct in my life. It was hard to separate things. I hope also that my intention isn't lost on the reader. It is not to sensationalize the events, but to paint a picture of what a life (at first involuntary, and then remarkably reckless) in the occult might look like from the inside, and to comment on different facets of it.

Also, when I reached the point of these essays being finished, I simply could no longer work on them anymore because it had become too physically debilitating. Of course, as with every other revision, I remembered more details that I thought might be relevant. But, now, rather than go back in to weave in the additional material, I have decided on this post script as both an addendum and a final commentary. While I've decided to omit most of the details anyway, a few things still need saying.

During the years of my writing these essays, I have made it a point to watch as many of the paranormal shows on TV as I could manage. I've sat through literally hundreds of episodes, at last a dozen different series. I wanted to see what's out there, what kind of information someone could find in a search (since I am hoping to contribute). Occasionally, what I found seemed interesting. A few of the psychic mediums had some compelling bits of wisdom that were worth gleaning. But most of what I saw was not useful. Over and over, I watched muggles telling their personal stories in painfully slow, dragged-out, imprecise, repetitious (often with bad grammar) narratives to accompany cheesy reenactments. They recounted nothing that was new to me, and what's worse, is that either they or the narrator espoused cliché amateur theories to explain things. Most importantly, with a few rare exceptions, they did not deal with evil as I experienced it in my life.

For the shows with crews, sometimes, the investigators were respectful and helpful, but some were, as Riley and I came to call them, hardly literate "douche bags" who went into places, set up their equipment, antagonized the spirits, then acted shocked, scared, or startled when something responded. "Dude, did you hear that?" "Something just touched me, man!" What did they think would happen? I wanted to shout at the television: "You idiots!" I imagine someday, they will pay a great price for their ignorance and disrespect. In only a couple of the series did the experts try to do actual historical research or bring in authentic clairvoyants to use the information gleaned via the technology to try to solve the issues. Most of the time, the investigators were just greedy for or egotistical about what they could capture. Sometimes, they made the situations worse.

Anyone looking to these shows for answers wouldn't find them. The episodes generally followed standard plots with predictable endings. Many would end in smudging/cleansing of the house, and then everything would be fine – as if it were that simple! Some stories would end with the victims tossing two or three items into a bag and dashing out the door or even just running out barefoot and in pajamas and magickally having keys in the car ready for takeoff. Many involved some asshole male of the household who would not believe the rest of the family members, especially the children, and who just got more abusive or condescending as their trauma unfolded. Some were narratives about people moving into a place that still had the previous owner's belongings in it and just letting the things sit? Who *does* that? In my opinion, the people deserved what they got. The same goes for people buying antiques.

Also, every third story, it seemed, involved the consequences of using a Ouija board. Some blamed WICCA (which is truly not fair and simply shows Christian bias). One cited using tarot cards as opening a doorway. Just the presence of a pentacle could chaos! Not. As if just touching something magickal would result in a demonic invitation. Too many episodes either suggested all could be solved with a thorough smudging or involved an exorcism – the archangel Michael, the Lord's Prayer, and the 23rd Psalm – and a lot of screaming and flailing. Oh, and lots of holy water. Sigh. Eye roll. I don't believe an authentic exorcism can be accomplished in just one session or a few minutes of drama or by amateurs. Sometimes, it isn't even a demon, just a cranky ghost or disgruntled elemental that's causing trouble. Shadow people do not respond to any of the above. The Bible is erroneously presented as a cure-all. It isn't.

I remember when I decided to visit a local MUFON (Mutual UFO Network) presentation some years ago, long before my move to the Northwest. The public presentation seemed a little bit like an AA meeting, with people standing up saying, "My name is ____, and I saw a UFO," and then proceeding to tell how the event destroyed their lives, how they lost their friends and were turned out by their families. The presenters' only goal was to make sure no one recanted the stories. The story tellers were never to accept that what they had seen was Venus or a balloon or whatever. They should stick to their stories. UFOs were real!

Understanding Evil: My Soul Contract

Well, OK, I was already on board with that, not from personal experience, but from a "why not?" point of view. The thesis, the analogy, was that if someone on the way home from work drove past a red truck, would he/she let people say, "No, that wasn't a red truck; that was a white sports car"? Of course not. So why would someone let himself/herself be talked into agreeing that what he/she had really seen was just the planet Venus? Well . . . I'm not sure.

That was the big open public presentation, but those who were interested could come to a meeting of established members. So, I went. I took my mother along too, for she was fascinated by the topic, and I was at that time trying to get her interested in doing something, anything, social. The meeting was at the home of the director and consisted of a briefing of reports of local sightings and the documentation thereof, some plans for attendance at a big convention, and then, a lecture about what to do if we ran into an alien being, which, in summary, was "Pray to Jesus!" Really? That's the big plan? We never went back.

My immersion in the paranormal shows, however, has made me consider a number of things about my own behavior. For instance, I pondered how many portals I might have opened up in places I lived. Probably at least a few. I did hear from another tenant in a house-converted-to-apartments, which I left when an enormous cottonwood tree crashed through it, that the person who moved into my unit after repairs had been made complained of hearing screams and crashes, seeing shadows and things moving about, and . . . . oh, dear.

The home that I most recently left, where I had lived for over 10 years, surely carries residual impressions of what I did there. When I began packing up to move out, I took down more than 70 mirrors off my walls, all sizes and shapes. I put them up as invitations for ghosts, spirits, and other entities to come to me. They would anyway, so I just deliberately threw open the gates. I felt at home among the dead, and these mirrors created a vortex. Sometimes, in the dark, I would find myself literally wading through ghosts. I don't recommend anyone else doing this. Without exception, people who visited me were either a little bit or a lot uncomfortable. But for me, the phenomenon provided solace for my loneliness and promised me that the shell that was my body was just that, a temporary confinement. I can't imagine that when I left that all the ghosts simply went home even though I did suggest they do so.

Also, I considered the mundane aspects of my life. All of the standard fare in the paranormal shows had been present in my existence from pretty much day one. The list included (still includes) shadow figures, orbs, footsteps, weird mists, cold spots, knocking/tapping, objects moving by themselves (or disappearing and then reappearing), electrical problems, the atmosphere feeling heavy or threatening, feelings of being watched, negative energy, assorted smells that have no discernible source, pictures falling off walls, whispers, growls, nightmares, the sense that light is being sucked out of the room, gadgets turning on by themselves, doors opening and/or closing, and so on and so forth.

However, unlike the characters in the paranormal shows, my family never denied supernatural goings-on. It was a family reality. In fact, after the dust settled after the Old Hospital incident (See essay "Come to Me"), when strange annoying things happened, I was often asked to solve them. "Find out what is ringing that doorbell," or "Do something about the ghost in room 19," (at the small motel my family owned) or "Tell me what will happen to ____." Such events as kitchen cabinet doors opening on their own, something tapping on windows, the phone ringing even when it was unplugged, or objects suddenly falling over simply caused one of us to say in German the equivalent of "They're coming." We would laugh. Stuff like that happened so often, what else were we going to do? Sure, sometimes, things got creepy, but we were inured to the more mundane paranormal mischief. Therefore, unlike the interviewees in the shows, I was never unduly terrified, and never uncertain of what I experienced. Although I have to say, the constant acceleration of entropy in my physical environment is a bit annoying.

Given the chance to go back and start over, would I choose to not to have the occult so prominent in my life? No. I wouldn't trade away any of the extraordinary experiences I was able to have for anything, not even to avoid the painful ones. Would it have helped to have had some sort of religious grounding? No. I believe in the sovereignty of the soul and would not want to compromise it by submitting to a doctrine.

The advice I give anyone now, and really wish I had followed more stringently myself, is to be viable in the real world before any interaction with the occult. That means having a stable living condition, being educated, having an income, having reliable transportation, having friends, and NOT doing any drugs – legal or no. The idea is to not be vulnerable. Vulnerability in the real world can leave one open enough for human evil to take advantage. However, it more than doubles one's susceptibility in the occult world.

Financially, I might have made some headway had I been willing to charge for doing psychic or tarot readings. But I chose not to. It is my belief that performing such a service unfairly favors those with disposable funds and excludes those who might really be in need. I also believe that doing readings for money opens the practitioner up to all sorts of problems: clients who are mentally ill, entities that a client might bring along, clients' unrealistic expectations, assorted saboteurs, hostile Christians, etc. As a free agent, I could say no when I felt the need to say no. I didn't have a business or income to protect. I generally, also, did not read for muggles. That prevented a lot of misunderstandings right at the gate.

That is not say that I didn't myself go to various readers and pay them for their "trade." I did. Curiosity and all that ... I found some who were truly kind and gifted. But in some others, I recognized the signs of delusion and mental illness; some were deft manipulators on power trips; some were out-and-out fraudsters; some went on a sort of evangelical mission to "save" me from myself; and with rare exception, the advisors were not my educational or intellectual equals, which considerably limited any thorough exchange of ideas.

As for the demons, they are what they are. Some are really, really old, and some emerged more recently due to human conjuring or invocation. They show up when bidden and when *not* bidden. Practitioners of the occult are more likely to have dealings with demons, and these must be dealt with reasonably and proportionally. But honestly, I think most people get through life without ever having to deal with a demon directly. Evil perpetuated by fellow humans, however, whether instigated by demon or a defect in character or both, is ubiquitous. It is hard to say which is the more destructive. That may be the point to all of this.

Understanding Evil: My Soul Contract

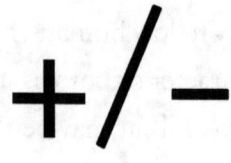

www.ingramcontent.com/pod-product-compliance
Lightning Source LLC
Chambersburg PA
CBHW071345290426
44108CB00014B/1445